THE POLITICS OF DIVIDED GOVERNMENT

THE
POLITICS OF
DIVIDED
GOVERNMENT

EDITED BY

GARY W. COX
University of California, San Diego

SAMUEL KERNELL
University of California, San Diego

WESTVIEW PRESS
Boulder • San Francisco • Oxford

Copyright © 1991 by Westview Press, Inc.

Published in 1991 in the United States of America by Westview Press, Inc., 5500 Central Avenue, Boulder, Colorado 80301-2847, and in the United Kingdom by Westview Press, 36 Lonsdale Road, Summertown, Oxford OX2 7EW

Library of Congress Cataloging-in-Publication Data
The politics of divided government / edited by Gary W. Cox, Samuel
  Kernell.
    p. cm.
  Includes bibliographical references and index.
  ISBN 0-8133-1145-4 (alk. paper). — ISBN 0-8133-1144-6 (pbk. :
alk. paper)
    1. Party affiliation—United States. 2. Political parties—United
States. 3. United States—Politics and government—1945- . I. Cox,
Gary W. II. Kernell, Samuel, 1945- .
JK2261.P67 1991
324.973—dc20
                                                                91-20269
                                                                    CIP

Printed and bound in the United States of America

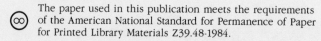

The paper used in this publication meets the requirements of the American National Standard for Permanence of Paper for Printed Library Materials Z39.48-1984.

10   9   8   7   6   5   4   3   2   1

To Our Parents

CONTENTS

☐1
INTRODUCTION: GOVERNING A DIVIDED ERA
Gary W. Cox and Samuel Kernell   1

PART ONE
FEDERAL CAUSES

☐2
DIVIDED GOVERNMENT: IS IT ALL IN THE CAMPAIGNS?
John R. Petrocik   13

☐3
THE REPUBLICAN PRESIDENTIAL ADVANTAGE
IN THE AGE OF PARTY DISUNITY
Martin P. Wattenberg   39

TABLES

FIGURES

ACKNOWLEDGMENTS

Editors of books such as this one invariably incur substantial debts. The bulk of the funds for this project was provided by Westview Press and the University of California, San Diego (UCSD), the latter money being funneled through the offices of Harold Ticho (vice chancellor for academic affairs), Michael Rothschild (dean of social sciences), Paul Drake (chairman of the Department of Political Science), and Samuel Kernell (coordinator of the American Political Institutions Project). Three members of the faculty—Gary Cox, Gary Jacobson, and Mat McCubbins—were also financial contributors. We owe a special debt of gratitude to Mat McCubbins and Gary Jacobson, who helped conceive and organize the project.

We must also thank Jane Weber at the American Political Institutions Project, UCSD, without whose organizational skills the whole project would have been lost in transit between the editors or in one or both of their offices; Jennifer Knerr, our editor at Westview Press, who has been uniformly efficient and helpful in shepherding the book through production; and, finally, the Republican and Democratic parties, without whose constant competition and differential success this volume would never have been conceived.

Gary W. Cox
Samuel Kernell

ABOUT THE CONTRIBUTORS

Gary W. Cox is professor of political science at the University of California, San Diego. In addition to writing numerous articles, he is the author of *The Efficient Secret,* a study of the development of political parties and political institutions in Victorian England, and coauthor of a forthcoming study of parties in the U.S. Congress, *Parties and Committees in the U.S. House.*

Morris P. Fiorina is professor of government at Harvard University and former chairman of the Board of Overseers of the National Election Study. In the area of electoral behavior he is author of *Retrospective Voting in American National Elections* and coauthor of *The Personal Vote: Constituency Service and Electoral Independence.* The latter won the 1988 Richard F. Fenno Prize for the best book on legislative studies.

Gary C. Jacobson is a professor of political science at the University of California, San Diego. His recent books include *The Electoral Origins of Divided Government* and the third edition of *The Politics of Congressional Elections.*

Samuel Kernell is professor of political science and coordinator of the American Political Institutions Project at the University of California, San Diego. He has authored and edited numerous books and articles, most recently *Going Public: New Strategies of Presidential Leadership* and *Parallel Politics: Economic Policymaking in Japan and the United States.*

Mathew D. McCubbins is a professor of political science at the University of California, San Diego. He is the coauthor of *The Logic of Delegation: Congressional Parties and the Appropriations Process* and a forthcoming book, *Parties and Committees in the U.S. House.*

John R. Petrocik is a professor of political science at the University of California, Los Angeles. His books include *The Changing American Voter* (with Norman H. Nie and Sydney Verba) and *Party Coalitions: Realignment and the Decline of the New Deal Party System.* Currently, he is writing a book on issue ownership of the political parties.

Charles H. Stewart III is the Cecil and Ida Green Career Development Associate Professor of Political Science at the Massachusetts Institute of Technology. He is the author of *Budget Reform Politics* and several articles on the history of Congress, budget reform, fiscal policy, and congressional elections. His current research concerns the modernization of the House after the Civil War and the consequences of divided government in the late nineteenth century.

Martin P. Wattenberg is professor of political science at the University of California, Irvine. He is the author of *The Decline of Political Parties, 1952–1988,* as well as *The Rise of Candidate-Centered Politics: Presidential Elections of the 1980s.* Professor Wattenberg currently is working on a project comparing U.S. and German electoral behavior.

1

INTRODUCTION: GOVERNING A DIVIDED ERA

Gary W. Cox and Samuel Kernell

With rampant inflation and widespread labor unrest following on the heels of the decontrol of the wartime economy, in the fall of 1946 political observers agreed that President Harry Truman's Democrats would do poorly in the upcoming congressional elections. Few, however, appreciated just how severe the backlash against this long-standing incumbent party would be or predicted that the Republicans would take control of Congress. Politicians and pundits alike were unprepared to deal with divided party control of Congress and the presidency. The election returns, however, brought both face to face with just that situation.

Collective consternation over the prospect of divided government was vented in a torrent of extraordinary corrective proposals, all seeking either to restore unity or to prevent this unfortunate constitutional anomaly from arising again in the future. Even more extraordinary, in retrospect, than the volume of proposals is the seriousness with which those proposals were received.

Democratic Senator J. William Fulbright was fast off the mark, so much so that his proposal shared headlines with the election results.

1

He called for President Truman to appoint a Republican secretary of state and then resign: With the vice presidency vacant, the new Republican appointee would go directly into the White House. Without some such drastic remedy, Fulbright argued, the nation faced an unstable international order like a "big helpless giant that is unable to make up its mind, unable to function" (Morris 1946, 19).

Congressional Republicans were understandably quite open to Fulbright's proposal. Surprisingly, so were many Democrats. Marshall Field, the prominent liberal Democratic publisher of the *Chicago Sun,* gave the idea a ringing editorial endorsement. It was picked up by the wire services and widely circulated by the nation's press ("Fulbright Invites" 1946, 3). President Truman initially dismissed Fulbright's proposal as unworthy of comment, but pursued by White House correspondents for a response, he eventually declared he was not about to alter the Constitution's prescription that he serve out his term.

Others with equally serious misgivings about divided government looked to the future. Senator Carl Hatch introduced a constitutional amendment to extend the terms of House members to four years and thereby eliminate midterm elections, which had produced the century's only other instances of divided government. With party voting prevalent in those days, proponents assumed that by aligning presidential and congressional elections, the House of Representatives and probably the Senate, too, would remain in the hands of the president's party.

Less drastic proposals simply called for extraconstitutional arrangements, such as having the president confer regularly with Republican congressional leaders. In these "summits," as they were then called, the politicians would hash out mutually acceptable policies to tide the country over until the next election, when the widely assumed Republican victory would return the political order to more familiar terrain. The president spurned these reforms as well.

The extent to which divided government was an aberration in 1946 is well documented in Table 1.1. There had been only three previous instances during the twentieth century, all at the midterm and each accompanied by turnover of party control of the White House in the next election. Contemporaries had no reason to doubt that the 1946 election would continue this pattern.

Table 1.1 also delineates the present era of divided party control, with Republicans holding the White House and Democrats encamped on Capitol Hill. Since their midterm victory in 1954, the Democrats have controlled the presidency in only three out of ten terms, and the Republicans have never captured both houses of Congress.

The prospect of divided party control no longer causes alarm. As it has become the norm, politicians and citizens alike appear to have

TABLE 1.1   Party Control of Congress and the Presidency, 1875–1992

Years	Presidency	House of Representatives	Senate
1875–1879	Republican	Democratic	Republican
1879–1881	Republican	Democratic	Democratic
1881–1883	Republican	Republican	Republican
1883–1885	Republican	Democratic	Republican
1885–1889	Democratic	Democratic	Republican
1889–1891	Republican	Republican	Republican
1891–1893	Republican	Democratic	Republican
1893–1895	Democratic	Democratic	Democratic
1895–1897	Democratic	Republican	Republican
1897–1911	Republican	Republican	Republican
1911–1913	Republican	Democratic	Republican
1913–1919	Democratic	Democratic	Democratic
1919–1921	Democratic	Republican	Republican
1921–1931	Republican	Republican	Republican
1931–1933	Republican	Democratic	Republican
1933–1946	Democratic	Democratic	Democratic
1947–1948	Democratic	Republican	Republican
1949–1952	Democratic	Democratic	Democratic
1953–1955	Republican	Republican	Republican
1955–1960	Republican	Democratic	Democratic
1961–1968	Democratic	Democratic	Democratic
1969–1976	Republican	Democratic	Democratic
1977–1980	Democratic	Democratic	Democratic
1981–1986	Republican	Democratic	Republican
1987–1992	Republican	Democratic	Democratic

made their accommodations. Republican presidents still campaign for their congressional compatriots, but their statements of how much better off the country would be if it were securely in their party's hands sound more wistful than serious. Growing Republican rumblings since 1990 in favor of a constitutional amendment to impose term limits on members of Congress appear downright quixotic. Meanwhile, Democrats have greater reason to hope every four years that they might manage to win the presidency, but they are busy fortifying Congress's prerogatives and limiting those of the president as though they are pessimistic about their chances.

Many voters split their ballots as if intent on preserving divided party control. Some students of elections have speculated that the U.S. public has, in fact, found virtue in this type of control. Desiring low taxes and a government willing to resist the claims of special interests, many voters, according to this argument, find conservative Republican presidential candidates appealing. At the same time, however, these voters want to maximize the federal dollars to which their communities are entitled. So, they elect Democratic representatives, who believe more earnestly in these government programs and therefore can more credibly campaign for the services they will provide for the district. The result is a string of conservative Republican presidents and liberal Democratic congresses.

THE SCRIPT OF DIVIDED GOVERNMENT

One of the central questions of this book concerns how the script of conservative presidents pitted against liberal congresses differs from the earlier one featuring unified Democratic party control, from which much of our current understanding of presidential-congressional relations is derived. When legislative and executive authority is unified, policymaking assumes the semblance of a cooperative enterprise. Presidents and their party colleagues in Congress differ among themselves in their constituencies and electoral calendar, but their electoral fortunes are linked by the favorable (and unfavorable) associations their performances in office imprint on their party's label. Whatever the ideological disputes among governing party members, they have a strategic interest in cooperating to produce an electorally attractive record of public policy. The incentive to cooperate renders the formal "checks" of the constitutional system, such as the veto, less relevant to these actors' performances than had been envisioned by the framers of the Constitution.

Under divided government, however, the formal authority assigned the branches becomes a vital asset as each party's politicians stave off encroachment by the other side. The opposition party in the legislature may find its electoral success, for example, lies in frustrating the president's performance. This, combined with the ideological distance represented by divided party control, is a recipe for conflict and impasse. It is reflected in the volume of Republican presidents' vetoes, in their efforts to centralize administration, and in the similarly unilateral methods Democratic congresses have employed to reduce Republican administrators' discretion in formulating and implementing policy.

Divided government will not always produce conflict and stalemate. On rare occasions, Democratic leaders have managed to muster two-thirds majorities in both chambers to override a veto. Far more commonly, overcoming partisan differences follows the traditional route of negotiation across the branches. But even here, divided government entails special strategic considerations that shape the policy agreements. With the president's leverage largely limited to the veto threat, his impact on legislation will be greater in preventing, rather than promoting, changes in current policy. Typically, this would appear to hamstring liberal Democratic presidents more than conservative Republican ones.

But even members of this latter group will encounter numerous instances where the asymmetry of the veto will limit their leadership. President Ronald Reagan's success in holding back taxes during his second term, coupled with his failure to cut entitlement programs and gain most of his proposed increases in the defense budget, illustrate the asymmetry provided by the veto. For the remainder of this introductory chapter, we shall concentrate on the institutional leverage available to each party for use in resisting the overtures of the other. In the conclusion, we shall return to the matter of how these features shape the bargaining that must occur between the Democratic Congress and the Republican White House if either side is to satisfy its policy goals.

Presidential vetoes of domestic spending legislation and disputes over the allocation of budget shares are divided government's most prominent features. Dwight Eisenhower's six years of presiding over Democratic congresses are not remembered as especially confrontational, yet during that time, he did find 130 bills to axe. And many of his most significant vetoes came near the end of his term, as the Democrats began resurrecting long-dormant New Deal programs in preparation for the 1960 presidential campaign. Presidents Richard Nixon and Reagan liberally employed this tactic, as well, with 43 and 78 vetoes, respectively. The moniker "The Great Vetoer" belongs, however, to Gerald Ford. In less than two and a half years in office, he exercised veto power 66 times. In the 1976 presidential campaign, Ford took his record to the country, promoting the virtues of divided government: By returning him to office, voters would keep in place the only barrier between the profligate Democratic Congress and the federal Treasury.

Despite the appearance of more conciliatory relations with the Democratic Congress than those of his recent predecessors, President George Bush has displayed similar vigor in wielding the veto. By the middle of his first term, he had vetoed 18 bills, most of them having to do with either domestic services and spending or trade provisions he viewed as intruding on his office's prerogatives. Although the Democratic leadership came within striking distance on several override attempts, the president's veto prevailed in each instance. This pattern is in keeping with the well-established record of failed overrides. For only 27 of the 284 Democratic bills that Republican presidents vetoed from 1955 through 1990—less than 10 percent—has the Democratic leadership managed to muster the two-thirds majorities in both chambers necessary to override.

Richard Nixon's strategy to stave off liberal Democratic programs also involved the innovative use of impoundment. Previous presidents had, at times, canceled the spending of appropriated funds. These instances, however, mostly concerned incidental funds, and their can-

cellation was justified by changing circumstances that made the expenditure unnecessary or imprudent. President Nixon differed from his
predecessors in both the amounts impounded and his reasons for taking
this action. In his hands, impoundment became a weapon for contending
with the Democratic Congress. From 1969 to 1973, he impounded funds
for over 100 programs, annually representing from 17 to 20 percent of
controllable expenditures, all in the cause of fighting inflation (Pfiffner
1979, 40–44). Individual Democratic congress members and interested
third parties responded with a flurry of law suits in the federal courts
challenging his impoundment authority. The issue was eventually resolved with the passage of the Budget and Impoundment Control Act
of 1974, which limited to sixty days the time funds could be impounded
without congressional approval. This legislation also created the Congressional Budget Office, which has proven to be a valuable congressional
resource in assessing taxation and spending estimates presented by the
president's Office of Management and Budget.

Beyond presidential vetoes and the near-continuous tug-of-war over
taxes and spending, divided government has also introduced another
realm of competition between Congress and the presidency, which,
though less public, is no less consequential for defining these institutions'
respective roles in making public policy. We refer here to competition
over control of the bureaucracy.

Newly elected "chief executives" talk and act as though they will
be firmly in charge of the personnel and policies of the federal
government. But such self-delusion is generally short-lived. Despite
appearances, Congress has long held the upper hand in managing the
bureaucracy. This control is reflected in a formidable body of historical
and judicial precedents that have accumulated over two centuries. With
a few exceptions, such as the single-chamber legislative veto that the
Supreme Court deemed unconstitutional, Congress can, by and large,
write whatever oversight and administrative guidance procedures it sees
fit. The courts have sanctioned its authority to insulate government
officers from presidential removal, to provide them with statutory responsibility and discretion beyond presidential guidance, and to mandate
regular reports to Congress. Under divided government, presidential
efforts to administer the bureaucracy confront Congress's extensive
prerogatives, thereby creating a battleground for political control.

Professional president-watchers have typically misunderstood this
confrontation. Noticing that Republican presidents tend to concentrate
more of their energies on administration than do their Democratic
counterparts, observers have erroneously interpreted this difference as
little more than a matter of style—a natural penchant of Republican
politicans, whose roots are in the military and business communities.

Republican presidents, this view continues, merely consolidate their Democratic predecessors' programmatic accomplishments. The politics of divided government suggests otherwise, of course. Political power is at stake, and attention to administration is a vital element of policy influence. Strengthening and rationalizing their administrative mechanisms are methods Republican presidents employ to resist Democratic congresses, which are similarly busy honing their own instruments of control over the bureaucracy.

Republican presidents have exercised great care in recruiting political executives who will remain loyal to them in the face of divided government's cross-pressures. President Eisenhower was the first to have White House staff members whose sole duty was to recruit appointees. After his reelection victory in 1972, President Nixon undertook a thorough and highly systematic review of appointees and a search for loyalists. Extending Nixon's innovations, the Reagan administration committed more time and effort in its early days to recruiting a team of loyalists in the bureaucracy than had any new administration before it. Bush's personnel effort was so thorough that only 156 of his 394 top policy-level positions had been filled by the anniversary of his first six months in office (Pfiffner 1990, 69).

In monitoring the bureaucracy's actions, Republican presidents have beefed up their formal mechanisms of control as well. Arguably, each Republican from Eisenhower forward has broadened the mandate of the Bureau of the Budget (rechristened the Office of Management and Budget, or OMB, under Nixon) beyond that of his Democratic predecessors. President Reagan issued an executive order requiring all regulatory policies to pass muster with OMB's cost-benefit analysts before being implemented.

Congress has not stood by idly watching these presidential advances. Through a variety of statutory and informal devices, it has sought responsiveness from Republican administrations. Since 1973, for example, Congress has exempted the budget requests and reports of a dozen or so agencies, including the post office, from OMB review. Nor can OMB any longer edit the annual reports submitted to Congress by the Department of Health and Human Services (Fisher 1985, 228–229).

Another congressional strategy to insulate agencies from presidential control has involved specifying the duties of subcabinet officers. An instance of this can be found in the 1988 revision of the Trade Reform Act, whereby responsibility for a "finding" that a trading partner has engaged in unfair practices was transferred from the president to the U.S. trade representative (USTR). The effect of this revision is evident in USTR Carla Hills's comment to reporters, "I consult with Congress on everything . . . particularly when Congress has an interest" (Elving 1990, 381).

Republican presidents and their staffs have also begun complaining loudly of a loss of executive discretion to conduct foreign policy. Congress's insistence that President Bush not take the nation into war with Iraq without its authorization was one of the most prominent instances of congressional involvement in foreign affairs. Especially galling to White House officials are legislative control provisions embedded in foreign policy legislation. Several of Bush's vetoes during the 101st Congress targeted what he viewed as unattractive precedents in extending that body's "micromanagement" of agency decisions. An early one involved a joint resolution directing the Pentagon to confer with the Commerce Department before finalizing agreements with Japan on the coproduction of the FSX fighter. And another veto concerned mandated sanctions against countries engaged in the manufacture or sale of chemical and biological weapons (Gerstenzang 1990, 12). A White House spokesman reiterated the familiar complaint: The sanction provisions were an "invasion of the President's prerogatives" to conduct foreign policy.

With 92 percent of military aid and 98 percent of economic aid in the 1989 budget fixed by Congress in the appropriations legislation, foreign aid also emerged as a major battleground on which institutional prerogatives are asserted and denied. Responding to administration complaints, Democratic Senator Patrick Leahy warned President Bush not to expect the relaxed oversight that comes with united party control: "It's not going to happen for him, for the reincarnation of JFK or Harry Truman" (Alston 1990, 294).

ON THE ESSAYS THAT FOLLOW

The script of divided government is only as significant as the prospects of this circumstance being realized. And although the essays in this volume are among the early efforts to systematically examine the implications of divided party control, its causes have already attracted substantial research. We begin, therefore, with consideration of the etiology of divided government.

Numerous possible causes of divided government have been proposed. As noted above, some view it as the intended result of voters following a kind of mini-max strategy—minimizing the costs of government while maximizing their share of its programs. The major pieces of evidence summoned in behalf of this view are the survey reports that show that respondents do not express alarm at the current balance of power between the political parties in Washington. Most, however, view divided government less as a product of design than as a reflection of some peculiarity or anomaly of either presidential or congressional elections. But which peculiarity is the question. The essays that lead off this volume each propose different, albeit not mutually exclusive, explanations for this modern development.

John Petrocik views the sources of Republican success as inherent in the advantages of that party's national coalition. He believes that the constituent parts of the Democratic New Deal coalition remain supportive as long as they are not asked to support the same candidate. Martin Wattenberg develops this theme a little differently by arguing that the Democratic party's nominating system is more likely to create internal fissures that make it more difficult for the activists to rally behind a common candidate and that give voters the impression of a party in disarray. Contentious Democratic gatherings are, of course, nothing new. But Wattenberg suggests that in an era of weaker party identifications, these disputes have become more influential in shaping citizens' images of the political parties and, hence, their votes.

Gary Jacobson examines the congressional side of the ledger, which contains numerous possible explanations for the Democratic party's success. These include malapportionment and the inherent advantage of incumbency. Weighing the evidence, Jacobson finds neither of these arguments very persuasive. Following the strategic rationale of split-ticket voting, at least in part, he concludes instead that Democrats dominate the legislative branch because they are more competitive in these contests, which revolve less around national policy than constituency representation and service.

If not a tragedy, the script of divided party control certainly appears to be that of melodrama. Each side finds frequent occasion to embarrass the other before the citizenry: Republican presidents wield the veto against legislation that appears to confirm their representation of a profligate Democratic Congress, and Congress looks for opportunities to send the president popular legislation that, for one reason or another, he will be obliged to veto. And when they do negotiate face to face, the scene is more akin to a game of "chicken" than a serious search for common ground.

Several of the essays that follow explore the consequences of divided party control in some detail. Samuel Kernell examines the principal avenues of leadership available to a president who finds himself cut off at Congress: concerted public relations, centralized administration, and the liberal use of veto threats. The attribute these strategies have in common, which commends them to Republican presidents, is that each can be enlisted unilaterally. Together, they compose a different kind of leadership than that of the virtuoso bargainer portrayed in the scholarly literature.

The next two essays—by Mathew McCubbins and by Gary Cox and McCubbins—deal with the budgetary consequences of divided governments. In Chapter 6, McCubbins tackles the spending side of the equation, explaining the enormous increase in federal spending during the Reagan years as the outcome of a bilateral bargaining game between the Republican president and Senate, on the one hand, and the Democratic House, on the other. Cox and McCubbins then look at the revenue side of the equation, using a similar technique. In both essays, the importance of reversion points and constitutionally mandated vetoes in structuring the bargaining process is highlighted.

Although the postwar competition between Republican presidents and Democratic congresses has been our chief concern, divided government in one form or another (see Table 1.1) is neither recent in origin in U.S. governance nor peculiar to our national institutions. Perhaps we can gain a better sense of why it has happened and what it portends for public policy by examining its effects in other settings.

Divided government was common in the nineteenth century, although the types of party control were more varied than today. Charles Stewart explores the causes and consequences of divided control in the third party system from roughly the end of the Civil War to the beginning of the twentieth century. His analysis suggests that there may be numerous alternative routes to this condition and that the distribution of party control across institutions has varying implications for policy.

Similarly, Morris Fiorina's survey of the incidence of division in state governments reveals a much greater variety of forms than have appeared in Washington. The forces producing divided government appear stronger in gubernatorial elections than in state legislative races. Not only do the former turn over more frequently than the latter, the minor party's candidates win a greater share of the races than would be true if outcomes were randomly distributed. Fiorina examines reasons for this phenomenon and explores its implications for voting theory and the meaning of divided party control in Washington.

PART ONE
FEDERAL CAUSES

2

DIVIDED GOVERNMENT:
IS IT ALL IN THE CAMPAIGNS?

John R. Petrocik

Divided government has been a distinguishing feature of U.S. national politics for most of the last half of this century. Between 1945 and 1990, the electorate selected a government in which the same party controlled the presidency and both houses of Congress only nine times in twenty-two election cycles. On ten occasions, there was complete division—requiring a Republican president to share power with a House *and* Senate controlled by the Democrats (the exception being Truman and the 80th Congress). The three remaining elections (those of 1980, 1982, and 1984) constructed a government in which one party (the Republicans) controlled the presidency and Senate while the Democrats held a majority in the House.

A quick look at the specifics that produce these marginals might lead to the conclusion that there is less here than meets the eye, that divided government is a grandiloquent restatement of a different well-known fact—that the Democratic party has trouble selecting a presidential candidate who can win. Republican presidents produced twelve of the thirteen instances of divided government between 1945 and 1990. Is divided government only another way of talking about congressional incumbency and Republican presidential success? Clearly, it is not. The U.S. voter's proclivity for splitting the ballot isn't confined to national elections. Following the 1988 election, thirty of forty-nine state governments were divided. (Unicameral Nebraska is omitted, of course.) Of the twenty-two Republican governors, seventeen faced legislatures in which one or both houses were controlled by Democrats; thirteen of twenty-seven Democratic governors faced legislatures in which one or both of the houses were controlled by the Republicans. Also, divided government is not a regional phenomenon. To be sure, southern Republican governors facing Democratic legislatures overcontribute. But the division persists even when the states of the old Confederacy and the border South are excluded. Among nonsouthern states, thirteen of nineteen Democratic governors faced legislatures in which the Republicans ran one or both houses, while ten of fifteen Republicans faced legislatures in which at least one house was controlled by the Democrats. As Morris Fiorina shows in Chapter 8 (Figure 6.2), this split has characterized state legislatures for the last several decades.

A less-known (or less–commented upon) feature of divided government at the state level is its considerable dependence on the outcome of gubernatorial elections, much as divided government at the national level has depended upon who wins the presidency. One party control is less entrenched in state legislatures, at least outside of the South, than in Congress, and partisan tides in state legislative races contribute to divided state governments. However, changes in the party of the governor are the more dynamic factor in creating divided governments at the state level. Consider the data. Between 1980 and 1990, there were sixty-nine instances of change in the incidence of divided government at the state level. In forty cases, divided government resulted from a change in the party controlling the governor's office; in only seventeen cases was a shift in legislative seats responsible for a change in the party division between the branches. The remaining twelve shifts involved simultaneous and contrary changes in the party of the governor and the legislative majority.

If divided government in Washington is a product of presidential Republicanism, is divided government in the states a result of something similar—a kind of gubernatorial Republicanism? The evidence is similar, and the logic that leads from the national data to presidential Republicanism would support similar conclusions with the state data. But the Republican party (GOP) has not dominated state houses as successfully as it has controlled the presidency, and state-level shifting is quite bipartisan. In brief, a first inspection of divided government in the states would not lead us to conclude that presidential Republicanism reflects (or *only* reflects) some kind of executive Republicanism in opposition to legislative democracy.

However, it might support some conjecture that executive elections and campaigns evoke more dynamic factors, and that is what this chapter explores as it offers a party/campaign explanation of divided government.[1] I will present a theory of issues in elections that describes how issues are linked to candidates, with what consequences, how members of Congress and presidents differ in this regard, and why legislative and executive elections in general—but, in this case, the elections of the president and Congress—may come out as they do. By examining the issue criteria used to decide between candidates, I attempt to explain why U.S. citizens can vote for executives of one party and legislators of another without feeling any apparent conflict. The evidence for this issue theory of divided government is partial. In this essay, which focuses on national elections, the evidence is limited to demonstrating two facts: how little voters conceive of representatives and senators in terms of issues and how these issues are related to the choice of a candidate for president. The foundation of the process is a particular theory of the way issues are injected into a campaign and how voters respond to them. The next part of the chapter sets out the general background of an issue explanation of divided government; the third part presents the issue theory; and the last part demonstrates the difference between legislative and executive elections, using the 1988 national election study survey.

AN ISSUE EXPLANATION OF DIVIDED GOVERNMENT

The extensive literature on incumbency provides the most common explanations for divided government. In most of these incumbency accounts, the critical variables are advantages that the officeholder enjoys over his or her challenger. Because a majority of incumbents are Democrats, there is a structural predisposition for divided government, given the relative success of the Republicans in presidential elections.[2]

However, although incumbency partially accounts for why party so commonly divides the Congress from the presidency, it is not a complete explanation for the comparatively greater success of the Democrats in Congress. It has little to say about why Democrats—not Republicans—become incumbents by winning at the outset. It also says little about open-seat outcomes. In addressing this gap, Gary Jacobson (1990a and Chapter 4 in this volume) has proposed an issue theory of Democratic congressional success that is keyed to the interaction between the tasks voters assign to different branches of government and their perceptions of the issue orientation of the parties.

According to Jacobson's theory, the institutional imperative of the presidency is to pursue the collective good of the national interest. Elected by the whole of the nation, presidents are supposed to provide goods that are national in scope. Foreign policy and military security, a healthy economy, and a stable social order are at the center of a president's job description. Members of Congress, by contrast, represent their districts, which leads them to focus their energies on providing benefits for these districts. The Democratic party, with an ideological and programmatic association with distributional politics (in Theodore Lowi's use of the term) is linked in the popular mind (and, one might argue, in fact) with a history of allocating noncollective benefits to defined groups—particularly those that are less advantaged and more in need of governmental assistance and protection—and is therefore better positioned to fulfill the congressional role than the Republicans are. This issue dimension in Jacobson's political explanation also explains why Democrats typically field stronger candidates: Democrats, rather than Republicans, might be expected to find the congressional role more attractive, given the correspondence between the ideology of the parties and the requirements of the position. Being a member of Congress is a more natural role for a Democrat; the best individuals among the Democrats should feel less strain and be more attracted to the distributional politics role played by members of Congress than would similar Republicans. On average, Jacobson asserts, this produces Democrats who are more skilled and experienced politicians—and better able to defeat their overmatched GOP opponents.

Campaigns and Issues and Divided Government

This chapter offers a slightly different issue account of congressional and presidential contests as a part of the explanation for divided government. Although it has similarities to Jacobson's issue explanation, it is fundamentally different.[3] Specifically, the issue explanation presented here links the difference in presidential and congressional election outcomes to the nature of the parties' constituencies and the different issue content of campaigns, not to institutional roles.

The link is provided by a theory of issue ownership that ties issues to parties and explains divided government by an empirical observation about differences in the conduct of congressional and presidential campaigns. On one side, the theory of issue ownership explains that the "futile" Republican struggle to increase their numbers in Congress, in general, and in the House, in particular, results from an almost insurmountable structural inability to make the issues that elect Republican presidents take hold in congressional races. On the other side, it assigns the Democratic party's frequently unsuccessful struggles in presidential races to an equal difficulty in making the issues that win congressional races the centerpieces of presidential contests. The theory does not assign any particular importance to public expectations about the tasks and responsibilities of members of Congress and presidents (or, generally, legislators and executives). Its critical variables are: (1) the public's perceptions of the issue competencies of Democrats and Republicans and (2) the ease with which the candidates can make these competencies and qualities the issues in the election.

At the center of the issue ownership theory of divided government is the assertion that Republicans have been inordinately successful at turning presidential elections into referenda on issues about which they are perceived as more trustworthy and competent than the Democrats. Their success partly reflects transient circumstances, but it also arises out of realignment-induced strains within the parties (but especially the Democrats) that have advantaged the Republicans. Divided government has become more common because these strains have become more severe. Republicans exploit these strains more easily at the presidential level than in elections conducted within homogeneous constituencies—such as congressional districts.

THE THEORY OF ISSUE OWNERSHIP

There are three elements to the theory of issue ownership. The first is the recognition that a party can "own" an issue—that there are some issues that help one party and hurt the other, almost without regard to the specific policies enunciated in connection with them. The second element is tied to the way in which candidates deal with issues, and the third is a model of the issue posture of voters. Each of these need some discussion before they are woven into an account of divided government.

"Owning" an Issue

In all political systems, parties are organized expressions of the social and economic interests of portions of the population. The competition among parties reflects attempts by groups to alter or protect some social or economic status quo. Parties may, as the old textbooks often asserted, promote the common good by advancing a position on a particular issue. But that is an incidental outcome of their main issue activity, which is promoting a vision of the common good that is constructed from the values and interests of their candidates, their leaders, and, particularly, their supporters. Parties may promote the common good, but it is often a common good that is unshared or even opposed by those outside the party. Issue concerns (to say nothing about policy prescriptions) are often specific to parties and identified with the particular groups from which they receive support. The issues become features of a party's policy agenda because the party's candidates and officials (who are disproportionately members of the groups demanding government action) respond to pressure from their constituents that the government do something about difficulties they (the constituents) are facing.

Although popular concern with generally recognized social problems (crime, traffic congestion, economic difficulties, and so on) is acknowledged by elites in both parties, all demands are not equal. The ones that receive particularly careful attention from a party are those associated with the groups that are part of the party's normal constituency. Examples abound. Democrats can be expected to be especially sensitive to a demand by blacks to reverse those Supreme Court decisions that make it more difficult to win discrimination suits because these blacks are a large share of Democratic voters and are strongly represented among Democratic party leaders. Similarly, Republican senators and representatives will be the most enthusiastic proponents of an amendment to protect the flag because the rural, small town, and more conservative citizens who cast many Republican votes will be among those most offended by Supreme Court decisions that provide First Amendment protection to those who burn the national flag. The groups that constitute a party's constituency are not the only source of policy proposals, but they are a major one. In particular, they are the principal source of the issue differences that separate parties and provide the electoral agenda.

This constituency-induced issue agenda establishes reputations for the parties with regard to issues. Such reputations have an agenda element, a solution element, and a credibility element. The agenda element reflects interparty differences in the frequency with which the parties urge attention to some matters at the expense of others. The groups that constitute a party's coalition provide unceasing (albeit uneven) pressures to deal with both the large aspects and small details of issues of particular interest. Even when both parties are willing to take some initiative on a given matter, the party that is usually supported by the group most concerned with the issue is likely to be the protagonist. And long after many voters are satisfied on (or weary of) a particular question, those from groups for whom the issue is of special concern continue to urge attention to the problem. The electoral pressure associated with such constituent demands is likely to make the issue a priority, even when there is intraparty division on it.

The solution element of the reputation arises out of the connection between defining something as a matter in need of attention and having a set of proposals for "fixing" the problem. Individuals who are un-concerned with a particular matter usually don't have a solution to its problematic features, partly because their inattention may keep them from perceiving that a problem exists. The concerned, by contrast, are likely to have many solutions. Parties have a similar character. Because of constituency differences, parties are likely to have a lot of things to say about some issues and relatively little about others. Moreover, if the link between a group and a party has existed for a sufficient length of time (such as the link between organized labor and the Democrats, for example), the party may—ceteris paribus—have a history of successful innovations on issues of particular interest to that group. Though it's possible that both parties will adopt supportive positions, the party of the most affected constituency will more often be particularly responsive, possibly more imaginative, and almost certainly more gen-erous in its proposals for government action. Such a posture may improve the efficacy of proposed solutions; it will certainly enhance a reputation for promoting serious solutions.

The credibility element of issue ownership is a complex product of the issue orientation of the parties and the limited issue knowledge of voters. After three decades of intensive research on voters and some disputes between classic (Campbell et al. 1960) and revisionist (Nie et al. 1979) models of the electorate, the modal voter seems well defined: He or she is frequently uncertain about what represents a serious problem and what does not; about which of the many problems being promoted for action deserve attention and which can be dealt with later; about how the problems should be dealt with; and about what position the candidates hold on them. But voters do harbor general impressions about the parties in terms of issues, and they are responsive to these perceptions (see Kiewiet 1983; Carmines and Stimson 1980). Further, voters are most interested in things going "well," and only a few are closed to several suggestions of what constitutes a good result or approach.[4] Although both Democrats and Republicans will address generally acknowledged problems (unemployment, crime, pollution, and the like), voters seem inclined to believe that one party will put more effort into resolving a problem when it has a history of voicing concern and proposing solutions to such matters. That party is more credible, sincere, and expert on the issue and particularly able to "handle" problems associated with it.

Consider a few examples. On racial and civil rights matters, the Democratic party frequently proposes policies and programs that promote the interests of blacks. Similar Republican initiatives are few and often overwhelmed by Democratic counter-proposals, which frequently put Republicans in the position of opposing the Democratic proposal. It's clear why this happens. Blacks are overwhelmingly Democratic in their voting, and virtually all black officeholders are found in Democratic ranks. The marginal difference between the parties in their racial composition assures that the Democrats and not the Republicans will be initiating proposals designed to assist blacks. Even if the Republicans are not opposed, they are likely to be less enthusiastic, resulting in a net perception of Republican opposition to blacks.

Social welfare issues are similarly affected. A history of Democratic commitment to expanding the government's responsibility for resolving social welfare needs has given Democrats effective ownership of these issues. The political debate surrounding George Bush's proposals for greater federal support for child care both during the 1988 campaign and in subsequent legislation illustrates Democratic control of social welfare issues. Bush's proposals were widely criticized by the Democrats as insufficient and were soon overwhelmed by a Democratic alternative that involved greater federal involvement and a larger commitment of public funds. Bush's rejection of the Democratic proposals as too costly and bureaucratic left the Republicans "opposing" child care. Republicans, of course, also have their own issues. Military security, crime, and taxation (to name a few) are issues on which the Republicans can usually outbid the Democrats.

Table 2.1 offers an abbreviated summary of the electorate's perception of the competence of each party to handle specific issues during 1988. Respondents were asked to indicate whether the Democrats or the Republicans would do a better job of handling a given issue, and clear differences in the electorate's perception of each party's abilities emerged. Social welfare issues such as Social Security and "fairness" are clear Democratic strengths. If voters can be persuaded that there are "fairness" or Social Security problems in need of attention, they are generally inclined to turn to the Democrats for solutions. Social issues such as promoting morality and fighting crime and foreign policy and defense questions are Republican strengths. When these topics are on the front burner, the Republicans are the "experts" to whom the electorate is inclined to turn. Other issues (economic ones, for example) have a more mixed ownership: Some are Democratic assets, some are owned by the GOP, and others are performance questions—where a recent record of success or failure provides a "lease" rather than a clear title. Spending, taxation, and inflation are traditional Republican issues.

TABLE 2.1   Voter Perception of Issue-Handling Competence of the Parties, 1988 (percentages)

	Problem Is Better Handled by:	
	Democrats	Republicans
Social welfare issues		
Developing policies that are fair to all U.S. citizens	45	31
Protecting Social Security	52	27
Promoting public education	48	33
Foreign policy/defense issues		
Reaching nuclear arms agreements	28	48
Dealing with the Soviet Union	21	58
Dealing with international terrorism	21	52
Maintaining military security	22	58
Economic issues		
Reducing the deficit	32	43
Solving farm problems	48	27
Dealing with foreign imports	34	40
Promoting growth and prosperity	33	43
Reducing unemployment	42	39
Holding down taxes	30	50
Controlling government spending	33	40
Controlling inflation	27	55
Social issues		
Promoting moral values	33	42
Solving the drug problem	27	36

Source: Data are drawn from various national surveys conducted by Market Opinion Research of Detroit, Michigan, during May and July 1988.

Unemployment was a Democratic strength until the economic turmoil of the Carter years and the prosperity of Reagan's terms (the 1982–1983 recession notwithstanding) moved the GOP ahead or into a tied position on unemployment issues.

The Candidate and Issue Ownership

The interconnection among issues, parties, and their constituencies provides an insight into why some issues and not others work their way into elections: The candidates emphasize issues on which their party has a reputation for commitment and interest, they express the coalition's normal position on these issues, and they ignore the proposals of the opposition (unless they deal with issues that the candidates' party owns). Both parties/candidates are trying to establish an advantageous interpretation of the issue "meaning" of the election and, implicitly, the criteria by which voters should make their decision. They do not, contrary to the Lincoln-Douglas great debate model, engage in point-for-point disputes over the details of issues. But the selection of issues is not unconstrained. Candidates must deal with existing and generally perceived problems. However, the problems facing government are, at any given time, both numerous and subject to different interpretations. As a result, candidates have considerable latitude in choosing which problems to emphasize and from what perspective they will deal with them. Not surprisingly, they attempt to turn the election to issues on which they have an advantage; that is, issues that their party "owns." By raising "their" party's issues, candidates hope to be perceived as more prepared and experienced than their opponents and more likely to craft a satisfactory solution. The more stable the party system (that is, the more predictable the group character and size of the party's base), the easier it is for candidates to select the issues upon which to focus their campaigns. The fluidity of the current electorate makes this a more difficult challenge than it once was, but the parties still have a stable set of issue themes from one election to another. Republican campaigns frequently have a place for government spending, high taxes, and inflation because they specialize in dealing with such matters. And Democrats rarely fail to find a place in their campaign ads and speeches for civil rights, economic deprivation, or more government services (education, child care, and so forth).

Voters and Issues Under Issue Ownership

The voters respond to this agenda setting in a way that can be best illustrated by the following seller/buyer analogies. Voters can be conceived of as buyers *and* (not or) consumers. In making purchasing decisions, the buyer puts together a list and then shops at the store that offers the optimal combination of goods and prices. In making voting decisions, the voter-as-buyer (following Downs 1957) canvasses the candidates and their promised policies and votes for the one whose proposals most nearly correspond to his or her own preferences. In principle, this is an original decision each time. The voter takes an inventory of the country's needs, reflects on personal preferences for how the needs should be addressed, and votes for the candidate who makes the most credible proposals on these problems. The candidate's role (again following Downs) is to attract voters by taking positions on issues that he or she believes correspond to the preferences of voters; they treat voters as buyers, and they assess the demands of the market and produce the desired goods.

Usually, of course, buyers don't work as hard as the preceding account implies. In the real world, purchasers don't decide de novo what product to buy every time they go shopping. Most of the time, they purchase the same brand as last time. Most purchasing activity is repeat business, with buyers continuing to make the same purchasing decisions until the need no longer arises, the product ceases to work satisfactorily, or a better product becomes available. The repeat business feature depends upon brand loyalties. Party identification and the concept of retrospective voting are familiar terms for the study of voting behavior described by this model. In any reasonably stable party system, recurring candidates, issues, and incumbent records make it reasonable for voters to consult their partisanships (which are linked to perceptions of the long-term behavior of the candidates and their party) and the prevailing state of things in deciding how to vote.

The problem with the buyer analogy is that it puts all the power in the hands of voters, suggesting that candidates are passive and only acted upon. Nothing could be further from the truth. As Anthony Downs (1957) understood, voter choices and candidate strategies are simultaneous, endogenous processes. Parties and candidates market themselves just as producers market their products. Voters are not just buyers, deciding which candidate meets their standards; they are also consumers who are having their standards and criteria influenced by the behavior of candidates.

Marketing emphasizes the role of the seller in creating the buyer's purchasing decision. Not only can buyers be directed to one brand over another, their sense of the type of good they should buy can be influenced by advertising that attempts to stimulate or create a demand. For example, merchants who persuade people that the casual clothes they sell are more desirable than formal wear will increase their market share at the expense of others who sell standard business attire. Candidates who make their party's issue agenda preeminent are similarly advantaged and by the same process. In the marketing model of campaigns, the candidates are sellers, and a significant component of the vote is determined by the candidates because many voters are so weakly involved with politics that they come to the election unsure of their preference. The candidate choice of these voters will be influenced (perhaps strongly so) by the ability of the candidates to define the criteria to be used in making the selection (Iyengar and Kinder 1987 have persuasive experimental data illustrating this effect). The marketing model does not expect to change the issue preferences of voters but to formulate the criteria by which voters make their choices among candidates. For the candidates, the challenge is to set the issue agenda: that is, to present the election as an occasion to deal with issues that they (because of their party) are better qualified to handle.[5] Most voters lack strong ideological convictions about political issues and are, on balance, more concerned with resolving generally acknowledged problems than they are with the specifics of the resolution (Fiorina 1981). As a result, many will vote for the candidate who is perceived as most likely to "handle" the issues that are helping to define the candidates. Of course, the most rigid partisans are immune to the tug of society's agreement about which party better handles a given issue. But most voters recognize the policy strengths of the parties (see Table 2.1) and respond to them. A social welfare or civil rights agenda benefits the Democrats; a concern with taxation and government spending, crime, or military security benefits Republicans. A Democratic agenda provokes Republican defections and a Democratic tide among independents; a GOP agenda causes Democratic defections and a Republican vote among independents.[6] How this works may be clarified by considering the 1988 presidential contest.

Bush in 1988: An Agenda of Republican Issues

In retrospect (although many would insist they foresaw it all), peace and prosperity may have been an irresistible platform for George Bush in 1988, but it did not seem so in the early spring of that year. Dukakis was ahead at the time. Bush changed these vote intentions, as the theory of issue ownership would predict, because he, not Dukakis, defined the issue criteria for the vote. Peace and prosperity *were* among the issues in the election calculus in 1988. But they were not the only issues that voters used to decide their ballots. Moreover, peace and prosperity were an asset to Bush only because voters were encouraged to use them to judge the candidates. As Table 2.2 shows, voters were positive about the economy in May 1988. Only 35 percent thought the country was experiencing bad economic times, and a 51 percent majority thought that the economy was doing well (the remaining 14 percent were unsure or saw good and bad elements to the economic situation). They were slightly less sure about how peaceful things were, with a 48 to 43 percent plurality more inclined to see conflict. Because most voters believed the country was enjoying peace and prosperity, Bush had a winning formula *if* he could only get voters to reward the Republicans for the good times they perceived. Unfortunately, in neither case was there much of a linkage between these perceptions and their vote intentions. Although a significant majority of those who thought times were bad and that the country wasn't really at peace were planning to vote for Dukakis, only a small majority of those who saw peace and prosperity intended to vote for Bush. But even that may overstate the

TABLE 2.2   Responses of Voters Regarding Peace and Prosperity and the Bush Vote, 1988 (percentages)

	Voter Opinion in:		Intention to Vote for Bush in:		Expected GOP Vote Based on Partisanship
	May	November	May	November	
Country is experiencing:					
Bad economic times	35	28	30	25	43
Good economic times	51	58	58	71	53
International climate is:					
One of foreign conflict	48	30	37	38	37
Peaceful	43	58	55	63	56

Source: Data are drawn from national surveys conducted by Market Opinion Research of Detroit, Michigan, in May and November 1988. The expected GOP vote is calculated from Petrocik (1989).

impact of the issues. If the vote intention is compared with expected vote (based on partisanship, see Petrocik 1989), Bush's vote among those who saw peace or prosperity was indistinguishable from the vote we might have expected given the partisanship of those who saw these as good times. It took a campaign that emphasized how good the times were to turn peace and prosperity into voting issues. (A good account of the strategy of the campaign can be found in Witcover and Germond 1989.)

Bush's emphasis on the success of the "Reagan-Bush" presidency as a promoter of peace and prosperity not only increased the proportion who saw a good economy (from 51 to 58 percent) and a peaceful world (from 43 to 58 percent), it also increased the relationship between these perceptions and the vote. For example, Bush's share of the vote among those who thought the economy was doing well increased from less than 60 percent to over 70 percent. Similarly, his fraction of the vote among those who believed that the country was at peace increased from 55 percent to 63 percent (see Table 2.2).

But, as the histories of the 1988 campaign have reported (and most of us still remember), peace and prosperity were not the only arrows in the Republican issue quiver. Foreign and defense policy, traditional morality, crime, and the economy were also issues on which vast majorities of voters believed Bush and the Republicans were more competent than the Democrats. The theory of issue ownership expected Bush to emphasize these matters because a majority of voters, from both Republican and Democratic groups, had essentially conservative preferences and believed that Bush and the Republicans could better handle such matters. Bush's behavior conformed quite closely to the

TABLE 2.3   Change in the Relationship Between the Vote and Attitudes and Issue Handling, May to November 1988

| | Foreign Policy/ Defense Issues | | Issue Attitudes | | | | | |
| | | | Social Issues | | Economic Issues | | Social Welfare | |
	May	Nov.	May	Nov.	May	Nov.	May	Nov.
Issue attitudes	44	55	26	30	30	45	34	29
Issue handling	73	74	71	83	75	84	70	75

Note: Table entries are coefficients multiplied by 100. The coefficients for the attitudes are zero-order correlations between the vote and the issue attitudes of the respondents. The coefficients are calculated on a subset of the electorate. Blacks, Jews, and Latinos are not included.

Source: Data are drawn from national surveys conducted by Market Opinion Research of Detroit, Michigan, in May and November 1988.

theory's expectation. He deemphasized or even ignored issues perceived to be Democratic strengths: Domestic social welfare and social spending issues such as child care, education, medical care, homelessness, and unemployment were not prominent in the GOP interpretation of what was at stake in 1988.[7] Between July and November, Bush's share of the vote among defense and foreign policy conservatives increased approximately 15 points (from 65 to 80 percent). There were similar changes associated with social issues. Voters became slightly more conservative on social issues, and Bush's share of the conservative vote on these issues increased. The increased correlations in Table 2.3 summarize the increased linkage between vote intention and attitudes and issue-handling perceptions.

Michael Dukakis, despite occasional attempts to make welfare attitudes germane to the vote decision, spent a considerable part of his campaign talking about Bush's Republican agenda (occasionally riding in U.S. Army tanks and meeting with police officers). The immediate result of his efforts to respond to Bush's attacks was to increase the salience of issues on which the U.S. electorate was more trusting of Bush and the Republicans. Why Dukakis behaved this way is a matter of pure conjecture. But the net effect is not: He further injured his own candidacy.

By making Republican strengths—a prosperous economy, defense and foreign policy, and certain social issues—major campaign themes, Bush increased their salience and made them more important criteria by which voters decided between him and Dukakis. A summary of the process is presented in Table 2.4, which has three different datums. The first is the frequency with which respondents in the 1988 American National Election Study (ANES) mentioned different types of problems

TABLE 2.4   The Effect of Perceptions About Important Problems on Presidential Voting, 1988 (percentages)

Type of Problem	Frequency[a]	Percent Voting for Bush[b]	Expected GOP Vote Based on Partisanship[c]
Republican issue			
Social issues/traditional values	44	58	50
Foreign relationships/foreign policy	19	61	52
Military security and defense	12	58	53
Big government/taxes/spending	47	56	51
Democratic issue			
Civil rights and race relations	2	43	35
Social welfare	64	44	44
Class or other group relationships	1	46	51
Environment[d]	16	55	51
Performance issue			
Economy	22	52	47
Government functioning	3	52	49
Unassigned issues			
Farmers and agriculture	2	26	42

[a]The first column is the percent who mention the issue at least once across the three mentions of important national problems that are coded.
[b]The second column is the percent who report voting for Bush.
[c]The third column is the Republican vote expected by virtue of the partisanship of the respondents (see Petrocik 1989).
[d]This was a neutralized issue in 1988. Bush's attack on the Dukakis record in connection with the cleanup of Boston harbor effectively took that issue out of the Democratic arsenal.

Source: 1988 American National Election Study.

as those which the country and the next administration would have to face. The table also presents the reported vote of those mentioning the different problems and, as a baseline for judging the former, their expected vote. Several things are noteworthy. First, Republican issues were substantially more common than Democratic issues. If only the incidence of mentions is considered, Republican problems were mentioned an average of 1.3 times; Democratic mentions averaged about .85. More important for the theory, Bush won a majority of the vote among those who mentioned Republican issues, and Dukakis carried those who mentioned Democratic issues. Not everybody who mentioned a Republican problem voted for Bush, just as every mention of a Democratic issue didn't produce a Dukakis vote. Committed Democrats who voted for Dukakis could mention the deficit, taxes, and government spending as a problem for the government; similarly, loyal Republicans could mention a social welfare problem as a matter needing attention. In general, however, such cross-party mentioning was overshadowed by issues that are the province of a given party, as the theory predicts (data not shown), and these party-linked issues reinforced partisans and tugged at the independents and undecideds. The general issue ownership pattern is clear. Republican issues were more common than Democratic issues, and majorities voted for the candidate of the party that was generally perceived as better able to handle those issues. From the point of view of issue ownership, Bush won the election because more voters were concerned about Republican issues, as opposed to Democratic issues.

ISSUE OWNERSHIP AND DIVIDED GOVERNMENT

A major reason for divided government in Washington is the different issue agendas of presidential and congressional elections. Presidential candidates are often personifications of the policy disputes and symbols dividing them from their opponents. They are more visible to voters, more is known about them, and voters have less freedom to project issue positions (or ignore them altogether) because presidential candidates are frequently forced to take a position and have that position subjected to wide and extended comment. For high-visibility presidential candidates, inertial partisan predispositions and personal traits can be overwhelmed by highly visible policy issues on which many or most voters will be focused.

Congressional elections, in contrast, are almost never contests that require voters to choose a candidate based on his or her stance on important issues. Challengers frequently attempt to craft an election agenda that will produce huge defection rates from the incumbent, but they are rarely successful. Inertial partisanship and a reputation for serving the district or being a good representative are the major factors in legislative elections. Incumbents are rarely threatened because, as so many have demonstrated (and Fiorina 1989a has nicely summarized), members of Congress behave in ways that preclude them from being judged by the policy and programmatic criteria applied to presidents, who serve as the standard-bearers of their parties. Senators and representatives are substantially policy-neutral figures, rather like secretaries of state, county clerks, and city attorneys, with little connection to the debates that are centerpieces of the society's policy decisions and its understanding of what the parties represent programmatically. Members of Congress do so many things—often almost anonymously and without any connection to major policies—that they can be evaluated by criteria that have nothing to do with the issues that define top-of-the-ticket presidential races.

In short, incumbents are rarely defeated because: (1) Most come from districts with a party balance predisposed to select candidates from their party, and (2) they behave in ways that keep them from being evaluated in terms of the policy and programamtic criteria that lead many voters to set aside their partisanship in a presidential election. In 1988, Democratic congressional candidates were largely unaffected by the Republican win because they avoided being characterized by the issues that defeated Dukakis. Michael Dukakis may have been "soft" on crime, but a Democratic incumbent could, for example, point to his or her record as a tough prosecutor; if Dukakis's support for a defense that would keep America strong was questionable, some Democratic congressional candidates could stress their own tours of duty in Vietnam or service in Korea and World War II and their many votes for new weapons.

Similarly, almost all Republican incumbents survived in 1990, and only a few Republican open seats were lost (the net decline was 9 seats) despite a popular tide that was opposed to Bush. Bush may have seemed unconcerned about the plight of the elderly and the needy, but Republican members of Congress could point to all the Social Security problems they had resolved and their votes in favor of Social Security cost-of-living adjustments. Bush's tax proposal may have promoted higher taxes, fewer social services, and tax breaks for the wealthy, but most Republicans voted against it and denounced it in the campaigns (at the suggestion of National Republican Congressional Committee [NRCC] Chairman Ed Rollins, whose first interest was the number of Republicans in the House).

Individual congressional candidates aren't completely immune to the issue agendas at the top of the ticket or, in off years, the prevailing sense of what their party is up to, but they can distance themselves from these agendas. The distancing is not always as successful as the candidates might like; in 1988, for example, the 53 percent of the total vote won by Democratic congressional candidates was below their percentage in the 1986 off year, when Republican issue themes were quite weak. But the distancing is sufficient to obscure the relationship between themselves and the policies and programs that are the subject of debate between the presidential candidates or (in off years) the parties. The net effect of this divergence in on years is a congressional vote that is only marginally affected by the presidential vote. In off years, it blunts all but the largest electoral tides and leaves most incumbents safe in their well-constructed districts.

TABLE 2.5   Issue Agendas in the Nation and in Elections, 1988 (percentages)

Type of Issue	Perceived as a National Problem	Cited as a Factor in Evaluating: Bush/ Dukakis	House Candidates	Recalled as a Factor in House Campaigns
Republican issue				
Social issues/traditional values	44	21	5	7
Foreign relationships/foreign policy	19	8	2	0
Military security and defense	12	11	1	1
Big government/taxes/spending	47	10	2	5
Democratic issue				
Civil rights and race relations	2	3	2	0
Social welfare	64	28	10	7
Class or other group relationships	1	9	5	0
Environment	16	2	3	3
Performance issue				
Economy/government functioning	24	17	12	6
Unassigned issues				
Farmers and agriculture	2	1	4	2
Nothing/no issues/like-dislike nothing	4	16	42	71

Source: 1988 American National Election Study.

CANDIDATES AND ISSUES:
MEMBERS OF CONGRESS VERSUS PRESIDENTS

Any difficulty that voters experience in linking issues to congressional candidates doesn't arise out of an inability to see problems in need of solution. Consider Table 2.5, which permits a comparison among citizens' responses to questions about the most important problems facing the country in 1988, the issues they perceived in their House campaigns, what they liked and disliked about their House candidates, and what they liked and disliked about Bush and Dukakis. Several things are clear. First, only 4 percent were unable to suggest at least one problem facing the country in 1988. However inattentive citizens may be to politics and government, very few are so encapsulated by their private lives that they are unable to formulate some ideas about society's needs. And though they are less able to link these problems to the candidate choices they make in elections (see Wattenberg 1986 for the most forceful statement of this thesis), the inability is much more severe in congressional than in presidential elections. In 1988, voters had ideas about Bush and Dukakis that paralleled their agenda of problems facing the country (compare column two with column one in Table 2.5). The fit may not have been close: For example, many of the 64 percent who saw a social welfare problem in need of attention did not express any thoughts about the candidates along the lines of this problem (only 28 percent mentioned social welfare problems as a reason for liking or disliking the candidates). But, of course, we shouldn't have expected them to make such a connection. If Bush's issue strategy succeeded, we would expect to find Democratic issues less prominent than Republican issues. If the Republican campaign marketed Bush better than the Democratic campaign marketed Dukakis, Republican issues should be relatively more prominent in the voters' observations about the candidates. The point is different: An overwhelming proportion of the citizenry (84 percent) were able to say something about Bush and Dukakis in terms of problems that they saw facing the country.

Congressional candidates, on the other hand, ran races that produced few memorable issues (see column three of Table 2.5). The issues that were mentioned rank in frequency in roughly the same order as they occur as problems or presidential candidate evaluations, but they occur far less often. Over 40 percent had nothing at all to say about the candidates, and a majority of all the responses referred to specific candidate qualities. A more telling indicator of the modest issue content of the campaigns is found in the last column, which reports the respondents' memories of the issues that characterized the congressional campaign in their districts. As the table indicates, just under three-quarters were unable to recall *any* issues being discussed in the election, and the items that *were* mentioned had a very low frequency compared to their incidence as problems generally.

The consequence of these differences is illustrated in Table 2.6, which examines the House vote in terms of the items mentioned in Table 2.5. An issue ownership explanation of divided government has quite specific expectations about how the issue agenda of an election is linked to voting choices. Its first prediction is that the election outcome will reflect the issue agenda. A Republican agenda should produce an overall GOP victory; a Democratic agenda should yield a Democratic win. As Table 2.5 makes clear, the congressional elections in 1988 had a very low issue content, with neither party particularly favored (although Democratic issues were more frequently mentioned). In general, issues should not have mattered much; factors such as incumbency, candidate quality differentials, and straight partisanship should have been more important; and the 1988 election should have produced a Congress that was divided much like the 1986 Congress—and it did.

Because congressional elections rarely reflect major conflicts over issues, most of them simply reproduce the preexisting partisan division. But that does not mean that congressional voting is unresponsive to

TABLE 2.6   The Effect of Perceptions About Problems on House Voting, 1988 (percentages)

| Type of Problem | Normal Vote[a] | Percent Voting GOP When Problem Mentioned Was Connected with: | |
		The Candidates[b]	Issues in the Campaign[b]
Republican issue			
Social issues/traditional values	50	73	49
Foreign relationships/foreign policy	52	57	
Military security and defense	53	69	} 78[c]
Big government/taxes/spending	51	73	57
Democratic issue			
Civil rights and race relations	35	28	—
Social welfare	44	22	21
Class or other group relationships	51	22	—
Environment	51	36	33
Performance issue			
Economy/government functioning	48	52	42
Unassigned issues			
Farmers and agriculture	42	44	45

[a]The first column is the Republican vote expected by virtue of the partisanship of the respondents. The normal vote is calculated from Petrocik (1989).

[b]The second and third columns are the percent who report voting for the Republican House candidate when they mention the indicated issues as a characteristic of the candidates (the second column) or as an issue in the election. Differences in the total Republican vote reflect missing data.

[c]Very few respondents mentioned foreign policy or defense issues as topics in their congressional elections. The few who did are combined to produce enough cases to support some analysis.

issue ownership. As Table 2.6 indicates, congressional vote choices did match the issue agenda. Voters who recalled that Republican issues were important in their congressional election or who offered Republican-owned issues as reasons for liking or disliking the congressional candidates voted more heavily for the Republicans than one would have expected from their partisanship alone. Similarly, those who remembered Democratic issues in their congressional election or who evaluated the candidates in terms of Democratic issues voted more Democratic than partisanship alone would have predicted. In short, voters behaved as issue ownership theory expected them to, but issues were such marginal features of congressional campaigns that their net effect was quite small.

Indeed, information about the candidates in general was largely absent. In 1988, only 46 percent of the ANES sample were able to

TABLE 2.7 The Effect of Information Levels on Voting for Incumbents, Controlling for Incumbency (percentages)

Voter Information Level	Vote for Democratic Incumbent		Vote for Republican Incumbent	
	Reported	Expected	Reported	Expected
No information	85	56	79	55
Nonissue information	63	51	75	56
Issue information	61	52	68	58
Republican issue	54	52	70	59
Democratic issue	76	60	50	55

Note: Table entries are the percentages voting for the incumbent and the proportion who were expected to vote for the incumbent by virtue of their partisanship. For more on the expected vote, see Petrocik (1989).

provide any impression of the candidates running for Congress, and many of these (18 percent) could provide information only about one of the candidates (usually the one representing their party). Only 28 percent of the sample could offer information about both candidates. Looked at negatively, at least 54 percent of the voters were uninformed about their congressional candidates, and, if we are to be more demanding, perhaps as many as 72 percent could be said to have been substantially unaware of the character and issue positions of their congressional candidates.

The effect of this low awareness of congressional candidates is apparent in Table 2.7, which compares the observed vote for the incumbent with the expected vote. Incumbents had a substantial advantage, exceeding their base party vote by significant margins. But how substantial that surplus was depended on the voters. Voters who had information about the candidates provided less (by one-half to one-third) of an incumbent bonus than voters who had no information about the candidates.

More striking still is the meagerness of the incumbent bonus when the issue agenda of the voters was at variance with the party of the incumbent. Consider the rows in Table 2.7 that focus on the kind of issue mentioned by the respondents. Voters from districts with Democratic incumbents supported the incumbent about 16 percentage points more heavily than expected *if* their issue perceptions of the campaign or the candidates involved issues owned by the Democrats. The incumbent bonus is almost absent if they recalled Republican issues: The Democratic incumbent got slightly more than a bare party vote. Voters in districts with Republican incumbents behaved as a mirror image: Those who reported Republican-owned issues as candidate-likes or campaign topics voted 11 percentage points more Republican than expected; those who reported Democratic-owned issues voted 5 percentage points *less* Republican than their partisanship would have led us to expect.

Clearly, the linkage between the voters' choices and their issue agendas at the congressional level follows the pattern observed for presidential voting. The process of congressional and presidential voting is similar; the variables are the same. The difference between them is that the former are rarely characterized by a significant number of voters who see the election as a choice about policies, programs, or, in some large sense, the direction of the country. Divided government is, in part, a product of this difference between congressional and presidential elections. A presidential election is presented as—and perceived to be—a choice about policy. Voters, to a significant degree, select their president with this task in mind. But they select their senators and representatives according to more idiosyncratic considerations and in an environment where choice is more structurally constrained.

CONCLUSION

Congressional elections are not intrinsically more or less partisan than presidential elections. Or, to the extent that they are, it is not as helpful to focus on the partisan distinction as on the differential importance of issues in both presidential and congressional contests. Following the logic of issue ownership, I would assert that presidential elections are basically partisan affairs in which partisanship is reinforced and undermined (although most votes are reinforced) by the issues that provide the substantive discussion between the candidates. The weakly partisan and nonpartisan are swayed by the issue agenda. In some elections, partisanship is eroded by the issue agenda; in others, it is completely undermined. When the agenda of one party completely dominates (examples would include 1964, 1968, 1972, 1980, and 1984), it will provoke high defection rates and a win by a large margin.

Like the presidential race, congressional elections are also largely partisan affairs, but the intrusive element is not issues. Rather, the intruding elements are the quite stable structural features of U.S. politics. Among these, we would have to include: an electorate that is more Democratic than Republican, districts that are drawn to favor their Democratic incumbents, the relative homogeneity of a congressional district, "better" Democratic candidates for some of the reasons mentioned by Jacobson (1990a), and such endogenous features as the incumbents' greater ability to raise campaign funds and weak challenges that reflect the reputed hopelessness of any challenge. All of these stable features suppress the ability of challengers to make a case against the incumbent, his or her party, and what both represent program-matically. The highly charged issues that are the stuff of presidential contests are usually absent, and voters do not see the same things at stake. In this milieu, the not-very-salient member of Congress acquires personal qualities and a familiarity to the district's opinionmakers that limit the challenger's ability to define him or her in abstract issue terms. Incumbents get defined, first and foremost, by whether they are "good" and "effective" representatives. The standard is so vague that few disappoint the voters or the opinionmakers so thoroughly that they are defeated.[8]

Generally speaking, it may not be possible to define congressional races in programmatic terms to quite the same degree as presidential races (although those less able to shed issue disputes—for example, senators—are less protected by their incumbency). And because congres-sional elections do not reflect the problems and issues of the moment, we can expect divided government to mark U.S. politics with some frequency. Divided government will occur as long as the inertial structural advantages noted above isolate the "issueless" legislators (predominantly Democratic) from all but the most massive political tides *and* as long as Republicans are successful at defining presidential elections around agendas on which they are advantaged.

Can we expect the GOP to remain successful with their issues? We can certainly expect them to continue with their issue agenda as along as it is successful. In recent presidential elections, the Republicans have focused on a set of issues that follow cleavages within the Democratic party, as well as those that separate Democrats from Republicans. Such issues have been exceptionally good campaign themes because they reinforce the partisanship of Republicans and drive a wedge between Democratic candidates and some of their traditional voting groups (some of which are becoming more Republican; see Petrocik 1991).[9]

Campaigns reflect prevailing social, political, and economic events and trends. If these events and trends play to Democratic issue strengths, divided government will take a rest as Democrats assume the presidency. But if they do not—or until other changes erode the structural advantages Democrats have in electing their own to Congress (some noted above) or until other changes or special events make it possible to conduct a cycle or two of congressional elections around themes that mark presidential contests—divided government is likely to be a prominent feature of national politics in the United States.[10]

NOTES

Some of the data used in this analysis were supplied by the Interuniversity Consortium for Political and Social Research. Other data (noted at each table) were supplied by Market Opinion Research (MOR) of Detroit, Michigan. Neither the Consortium nor MOR bears any responsibility for the analysis presented here.

1. To be sure, there are important differences between the state and national political systems, and the use of data on the former to corroborate patterns in the latter may be suspect. However, at a minimum, the similar data indicate that something systematic may be common to both settings. Because the data for national elections are more available and richer, this chapter concentrates on them. It is worth keeping in mind, however, that the president-congress manifestation of divided government may only be a better-known manifestation of a generic process. That possibility will be discussed later.

2. The advantages are several, including a greater ability to finance their campaigns, the freedom to use their offices to assist constituents in ways that reap rewards on election day, and (there is less agreement on this) an ability to construct districts that provide an electoral base that is immune to any probable electoral tide. Generally speaking, students of congressional elections have rejected the notion that gerrymanders played much of a role in the emergence of greater incumbency advantage during the middle to late 1960s (Erikson 1972; Ferejohn 1977; Jacobson 1990a). I have never found their data or analysis persuasive. A good gerrymander is bipartisan, increasing the margin of safety for all incumbents but just making sure that an excess of safe incumbents are from the party controlling the redistricting. The all-too-typical approach to testing for gerrymanding effects—regressing margin changes on a measure of whether a district was significantly changed—is too crude to measure something so subtle.

The traditional hallmarks of a gerrymander—a consistent discrepancy between the vote share and the seat share, even after adjusting for demographic differences between party supporters and shapes that approximate "Gerry's salamander"—show that the fine art of partisan redistricting has retained its vitality into the 1990s. The fact that congressional margins and the Democratic "lock" on the House of Representatives became pronounced in the middle to late 1960s shouldn't occasion too much surprise. These events followed the Supreme Court reapportionment decisions of the early and mid-1960s. That so many of the legislatures that did the redistricting were filled to capacity with Democrats following the Goldwater debacle was the coincidence that initiated a Democratic advantage, which carried through subsequent apportionment cycles in 1970 and 1980. Finally, though many have emphasized the number of districts that went for one party for Congress and another for president, we have overlooked the high proportion that match. The 1988 election is a good observatory because of the relative closeness of the presidential race. Bush won, but by a smaller margin than recent Republicans, and the vote corresponded to partisanship more closely than in any election since 1976. In 1988, with the South excluded because of the strong Democratic tradition that is resisting the region's emerging Republicanism, only about 26 percent of the House districts voted differently for the president and for the House. These 75 districts (along with the 72 southern and border South districts that produced, for the most part, Democratic Congress members as they voted for George Bush) are the stuff of divided government. However, the similarity of the voting in these districts is a reflection of the fact that most members of Congress are secure because they represent districts in which their partisans are numerous.

3. Another account for divided government has emphasized a conscious choice by voters to put the parties in a position where each can check the other—the Republicans in the presidency and the Democrats in the House. In this new interpretation of checks and balances, the voters have consciously added a political dimension to the constitutional mechanism for limiting government power. Needless to say, when this idea is proposed to voters, it appeals to them, and substantial majorities accept it as a desirable feature of divided government. However, there is *no* evidence that voters consciously seek such an outcome, and the theory has nothing to say about elections (1960, 1968, and 1976) after which all branches of government were controlled by the Democrats. It also misses the fact that the overwhelming majority of voters—most of the time—vote for candidates from the same party for House and president. The investment and information economics thinking behind these accounts provides some interesting positive theory results, but the choice mechanisms it presents are without empirical warrant. Further, the aggregate data that have been studied (Erikson 1988; Alesina and Rosenthal 1989) do not provide any results that are inconsistent with a modified surge-and-decline hypothesis.

4. Fiorina (1981) provided the compelling contemporary analysis of this phenomenon as retrospective voting, but V. O. Key, in his earlier classics on issues and voting (1961, 1966), also understood how the electorate's limited commitment of time and energy to politics didn't foreclose popular control of the government.

5. I am greatly indebted to Ian Budge and Dennis Farlie (1983), who were the first to use this idea systematically and consciously in studying elections. I have substantially modified their formulation to accord with my understanding of party systems and how I have found campaigns to be conducted in the United States. However, there is no way to minimize the importance of their conceptualization to my thinking on this matter. Related themes underpin David Repass's (1971) reconceptualization of issues and D. Roderick Kiewiet's (1983) longitudinal study of policy and program voting. See also Barbara Salmore and Stephen Salmore (1989, 115–143).

6. In highly divided societies, with several parties that depend on one or a few groups, the effect of issue selection is largely limited to reinforcement. For the best discussion of this kind of asymmetrical party competition, see Giovanni Sartori's book on party systems (1976).

7. This observation is based upon extensive discussions of campaign strategy with several high-level strategists within the Bush campaign.

38   JOHN R. PETROCIK

8. The distance between legislators and the events of the world of government and politics is occasionally quite striking. Examples abounded in the 1990 election cycle. In California, voters supported strict term limits for legislators and drastically reduced their staffs and personal benefits while simultaneously reelecting virtually every one of them. In Massachusetts, the voters essentially "purged" statewide Democratic officeholders while reelecting almost all Democratic state legislators. Fiorina discusses this in more detail in Chapter 8.

9. Perceptions of a party's issue competence probably change very slowly, when they change at all. Most change is likely to be confined to a reinforcement of the general perception. That is, a party's advantage is likely to grow in response to campaigning on the issue. However, there are instances of abrupt shifts in a party's issue competence. The first year of Reagan's presidency saw the Republicans given high marks for their ability to deal with unemployment, normally a Democratic strength. By 1982, the perception of the greater ability of Democrats on this issue had reasserted itself, although their lead over the Republicans was much smaller than it had been earlier (during the 1970s, for example).

10. The pattern of outcomes of legislative and gubernatorial elections at the state level lacks the Republican/executive and Democratic/legislature bias of the national elections. The state-level races would be an ideal observatory to assess the various explanations of divided government. My very preliminary examination leads me to believe that the predictions of issue ownership match these outcomes quite closely.

3

THE REPUBLICAN PRESIDENTIAL ADVANTAGE IN THE AGE OF PARTY DISUNITY

Martin P. Wattenberg

At the heart of the phenomenon of divided government is the decline of U.S. political parties. Divided government would not be possible without a substantial degree of split-ticket voting, and ticket splitting has only become prevalent in the recent period of weakened partisanship.

Mountains of survey evidence attest to U.S. citizens' declining concern with partisanship and the role of political parties in their government. The belief is now pervasive that one should vote for the man, not the party. For example, in a 1986 national survey, Larry Sabato found 92 percent of the public agreed with the following statement: "I always vote for the person who I think is best, regardless of what party they belong to." On the other side of the coin, only 14 percent of respondents in his survey agreed with the statement that "I always support the candidates of just one party" (Sabato 1988, 133).

Such attitudes should not be interpreted as indicating negative attitudes toward the parties, but rather neutrality or a lack of relevance (Wattenberg 1990). During both the 1950s and the 1980s, only about

3 to 5 percent of the public expressed more dislikes than likes toward each party in response to open-ended survey questions. However, the proportion that had nothing to say at all (either good or bad) about both parties increased from 10 percent in 1952 to an average of 32 percent during the 1980s.

Similarly, a comparison of the presidential elections from 1980 to 1988 and those from 1952 to 1960 shows a clear drop in party identification and a corresponding increase in split-ticket voting. Whereas an average of 75 percent of the public identified with one of the two major parties from 1952 to 1960, an average of just 64 percent did so from 1980 to 1988. As a result, the percentage splitting their tickets between president and House doubled from an average of 14 percent in the 1952 to 1960 period to 28 percent for the 1980s.

This greater level of split-ticket voting has clearly increased the probability of having a president of one party and a Congress of the other. It is important to remember, however, that party decline has not made divided government inevitable or even probable. In fact, if people were to vote totally without regard to partisanship, the presidency and the House would be divided between the parties exactly half of the time—substantially less than has been the case in recent years.

Party decline has therefore merely opened the door to the possibility of divided government, allowing other factors to guide outcomes for presidential and congressional elections in opposite directions. Incumbency, for example, would not be as important a factor in maintaining Democratic control of the House if political parties were as strong as they used to be. Nor would it be possible for the party with the most identifiers in the electorate to regularly lose presidential elections in a strong party system.

Other chapters of this book will deal with Democratic congressional advantages in the era of weakened partisanship. The aim of this chapter is to outline the Republican presidential advantage in recent years. The major thesis is that as the role of partisanship in shaping political attitudes has greatly diminished, unified party support has become more crucial than ever to a presidential election victory. Indeed, one of the key features of the candidate-centered age is the increasingly difficult task of unifying a political party in November when the various factions within it have been competing for so long. Internal animosities stirred up by the reformed nomination process are more likely to continue to haunt the nominee in November. These animosities hurt a candidate not only with his own party's voters but with independents and the opposition party, as well. After all, if members of the candidate's own party find fault with their nominee, why should those outside the party view him favorably?

TABLE 3.1   Party Identification and Ideology, 1988 (percentages)

	Democrats	Independents	Republicans
Liberal	24	16	8
Moderate	23	26	17
Conservative	19	28	55
Haven't thought about it	35	31	21
	101[a]	101[a]	101[a]

[a]Due to rounding, the percentages add up to 101 rather than 100 percent.

Source: 1988 American National Election Study.

This process benefits the Republicans on two accounts. First, since the Goldwater wing took over the Republican party (GOP) in 1964, the GOP has been more ideologically cohesive and thus easier to unite. Table 3.1 shows that in 1988, conservatives outnumbered liberals among Republican identifiers by a margin of nearly 7 to 1. Thus, there has been little incentive for Republican presidential contenders in recent years to fight over policy issues. In contrast, among Democratic identifiers, liberals and conservatives are almost equally divided, with only a small margin of advantage for the liberals. The existence of markedly different constituencies has given Democratic presidential candidates much more to fight about in the primaries compared to the Republicans in recent years.

Second, the Republicans suffer less from the potential divisiveness of primary campaigns due to their greater use of winner-take-all delegation selection rules. In 1988, the Republicans selected roughly three-fifths of their delegates in this fashion, compared to only about one-fifth of the Democratic delegates.[1] The winner-take-all method offers little incentive for losing candidates to continue divisive nomination campaigns for very long. In contrast, the strict adherence to proportional representation in most Democratic primaries fosters "Timex" candidates, that is, candidates who "take a licking and keep on ticking." For example, both George Bush and Michael Dukakis won important 1988 Super Tuesday victories in Texas and Florida. As a result, Bush won virtually every delegate from these two states, but Dukakis ended up with only a few more than fellow Democrat Jesse Jackson did. Robert Dole thus soon had to drop out of the Republican race, but in the Democratic camp, Jackson (like Gary Hart in 1984 and Ted Kennedy in 1980, to name two other examples) had every incentive to continue the battle. And, of course, the longer losing campaigns for the nomination go on, the more likely they are to splinter the party. A party that is divided in the spring and early summer—as the Democrats have been so regularly in recent elections—can no longer be easily reunited in the fall.

THE HISTORY OF PARTY DISUNITY

Partisan splits have figured prominently in electoral outcomes at various times throughout U.S. history. For example, the William Howard Taft-Theodore Roosevelt split within the Republican party in 1912 opened the way for Woodrow Wilson to win the presidency in that year. Surely the most divisive contest of all was the Democrats' 103-ballot marathon in 1924, which left the party so torn apart that it was not able to mount much of a challenge to Calvin Coolidge even with the Republicans' Teapot Dome scandal still fresh in the electorate's mind.

Yet, taking the number of presidential ballots at the conventions as a measure of party unity, we can see that unity was by no means a sure predictor of election outcomes in the pretelevision era. From Reconstruction through World War II, there were twelve cases in which one party took more ballots than the other to choose its nominee. Of these twelve campaigns, just seven were won by the party that was the first to reach its decision.

Party disunity also did not fatally damage the campaigns of Harry Truman in 1948, Dwight Eisenhower in 1952, and John Kennedy in 1960. Truman was faced by splinter party candidates Strom Thurmond on the right and Henry Wallace on the left, both of whom represented Democratic factions he had alienated. Eisenhower had to resort to credentials challenges at the convention to pry the Republican nomination away from Taft. And Kennedy barely managed to squeeze together a majority of delegates, whereas Richard Nixon ran unopposed on the Republican side. In all three cases, however, the candidate whose party exhibited the most divisiveness at the convention went on to win anyway.

In contrast, the candidate with the most united party won every presidential election from 1964 to 1988. One paradoxical effect of dealignment has been that party unity has taken on greater importance as it has become more difficult to achieve. Therefore, I believe that one of the most appropriate labels for party politics in the years since Kennedy's death is the "era of party disunity." The remainder of this chapter provides evidence for the thesis that a successful presidential campaign now depends on wrapping up the nomination faster and with less lingering bitterness than the opposition does—a turn of events that has clearly advantaged the Republicans.

STATE-LEVEL DATA
ON DIVISIVE PRESIDENTIAL PRIMARIES

Numerous studies have shown that a divisive state primary adversely affects a nominee's chances of winning the state in the fall. Party activists who invest their efforts in losing campaigns for the nomination are often reluctant to continue their campaign involvement during the general election. For example, Emmett Buell's (1986) study of New Hampshire primary activists in 1984 found that about half of the supporters of Walter Mondale's Democratic rivals virtually sat out the November campaign. Thus, just when Mondale needed all the support he could get from his party, he found it difficult to overcome the divisions of the spring's campaign. This phenomenon seems to be primarily due to personal loyalty to the losing candidates, rather than to ideological differences. As Walter Stone (1984) found in his study of 1980 Iowa activists, nomination preferences in both parties significantly affected participation, independent of the effects of ideology, past levels of political activity, and attachment to the party organization.

Throughout history, divisive state primaries have seriously hurt a party's chances of winning those same states in November (Lengle 1980). In the most comprehensive study to date, Patrick Kenney and Tom Rise (1987) used the percentage of the primary vote received by both nominees in each state from 1912 to 1984 to assess the relative effect of divisive primaries. They found that for every percent that one nominee does better than the other in a given state, an additional .07 percent of the vote is gained over what would otherwise be expected in November. The effect is analogous to becoming a favorite son candidate; having done well in the state during the primaries, a nominee naturally begins the general election campaign in that state with the image of a winner—both well known and well liked. In contrast, when a candidate makes a poor showing in a state primary, he starts the general election campaign there with a serious handicap.

To illustrate this effect, Table 3.2 presents exit poll data from selected 1988 primaries in which voters were asked, "Regardless of how you voted today is your opinion of (George Bush/Michael Dukakis) favorable or unfavorable?" For both candidates, the correlation between primary votes and favorability ratings is over .90. Despite the fact that Bush averaged a much higher percentage of the vote than Dukakis, the two equations predicting positive ratings from the vote are nearly identical. The constant is slightly over 40 percent in both cases, and for every point gained in the primary vote, the nominee gains .57 percent in popularity.

TABLE 3.2   Primary Vote Total and Favorability Ratings, 1988

	Bush[a]		Dukakis[b]	
State	Percent Favorable Among Own Partisans	Percent of Primary Vote	Percent Favorable Among Own Partisans	Percent of Primary Vote
Alabama	82	65	44	8
Arkansas	63	47	53	19
Florida	73	62	67	41
Georgia	71	54	54	16
Illinois	70	55	60	16
Louisiana	75	58	50	15
Massachusetts	74	59	72	59
Mississippi	80	66	42	8
Missouri	67	42	50	12
New York	—	—	72	51
North Carolina	70	45	60	20
Oklahoma	62	37	50	17
Tennessee	75	60	44	3
Texas	77	64	64	33
Virginia	73	53	60	22
Wisconsin	—	82	73	48

[a]Bush favorability = 40.9 + .57 (VOTE), R = .90, t stat = 7.33, std err = .08.
[b]Dukakis favorability = 43.3 + .57 (VOTE), R = .93, t stat = 9.88, std err = .06.

Source: Data from *New York Times*/CBS exit polls, as reported in *Public Opinion,* May/June 1988, pp. 24–25. Table reprinted by permission of the publishers from *The Rise of Candidate-Centered Politics: Presidential Elections of the 1980s* by Martin P. Wattenberg, Cambridge, Mass.: Harvard University Press, Copyright © 1991 by the President and Fellows of Harvard College.

Thus, in primaries where a candidate shows poorly at the ballot box, his approval rating suffers markedly. In states such as Mississippi, Alabama, and Tennessee, for example, Dukakis's single-digit finish left him with meager favorability ratings of under 50 percent among Democrats. Similarly, in states where Dole gave Bush a strong challenge (Missouri, Oklahoma, and Arkansas), positive ratings for Bush were notably less than elsewhere in the South. Although primaries are contested by like-minded politicians who should be widely approved of by party members, the zero-sum nature of the electoral process often works to the contrary.

Should one party have a long set of divisive contests and the other none at all, as occurred in 1984, the impact is particularly marked. Overall, Mondale received about 38 percent of the Democratic primary vote, versus Ronald Reagan's 98 percent of the Republican vote. Extrapolating from Kenney and Rice's equation, this translates into an additional 4.2 percent (.07 [98 − 38]) of the vote for Reagan in a typical 1984

TABLE 3.3 Margins over Closest Opponent in Nominations and General Elections (popular votes)

Candidate	Nomination Margin (percent)	General Election Margin (percent)
Bush (1988)	+48.5	+7.8
Reagan (1980)	+37.5	+9.7
Carter (1976)	+23.5	+2.1
Carter (1980)	+14.1	−9.7
Dukakis (1988)	+13.2	−7.8
Ford (1976)	+7.4	−2.1
Mondale (1984)	+1.7	−18.2
Goldwater (1964)[a]	+1.0	−22.5
McGovern (1972)	−0.5	−23.2

[a]Based on contested primaries between Goldwater and Rockefeller in New Hampshire, Oregon, and California only.

Source: Data from *Presidential Elections Since 1789* (Washington, D.C.: Congressional Quarterly Press). Table reprinted by permission of the publishers from *The Rise of Candidate-Centered Politics: Presidential Elections of the 1980s* by Martin P. Wattenberg, Cambridge, Mass.: Harvard University Press, Copyright © 1991 by the President and Fellows of Harvard College.

primary state. In 1988, Bush received 68 percent of the total Republican primary vote, compared to Dukakis's 42 percent of the Democratic vote, thereby giving Bush a predicted edge of 1.8 percent in the average primary state over what would normally be expected in November.

NATIONWIDE DATA FOR THE DISUNITY HYPOTHESIS

Several studies have attempted to assess the effect of divisive presidential primaries at the state level, but there has been little examination of this phenomenon using national data. With the passage of time since the first successful candidate-centered insurgency by Barry Goldwater, one can now compare data from a dozen national campaigns. Between 1964 and 1988, the candidate with the least encumbered path to the nomination proved to be the victor in November. As shown in Table 3.3, the greater the margin a nominee accumulated over his closest rival in the primaries, the better he did in the general election. Candidates who ran virtually even with their closest challenger throughout the primaries, such as Goldwater, George McGovern, and Mondale, ended up on the losing side of landslide elections. In contrast, Carter in 1976 and Reagan in 1980—both of whom far outdistanced their primary rivals—unseated incumbent presidents who faced relatively close nomination contests. Of course, incumbent presidents who were scarcely challenged in the primaries fared best of all.

During the nomination campaign, there are four key points at which party divisiveness can arise: (1) early primaries, (2) late primaries, (3) the convention, and (4) the vice presidential selection. In the era of party disunity, the candidate who locks up his party's nomination the quickest and is therefore able to bypass the problems of the later stages establishes a great advantage for the fall campaign. In other words, the more partisan dissension a nominee accumulates during these four stages, the less chance he has of actually winning the presidency.

The first stage of party divisiveness occurs in the early primary contests in states like New Hampshire and Illinois. Even a brief series of early challenges, such as Bush and John Anderson mounted against Reagan, can leave a lasting imprint on party unity. Of course, such contests have now become inevitable in races without an incumbent. Even established front-runners, like Reagan in 1980 or Mondale in 1984, faced challenges from half a dozen opponents who hoped they could overcome the uphill odds. The best a party can expect in this situation is to have the nomination decided quickly, with as little bitterness as possible.

A second stage of divisiveness in the nomination process hence occurs if the contests continue through the later primaries, such as California. What *Newsweek* once labeled "caucus fatigue" or "post-primary depression" comes into play at this point. As the article facetiously but insightfully noted in April 1984, this can be defined as "a rare form of exhaustion, usually temporary, known to afflict presidential candidates. Common symptoms include listlessness after victory, a pattern of tactical blunders often blamed on one's staff, a propensity for negative campaigning, and a crippling inability to say anything inspiring about America's future" ("The Democrats" 1984, 30). As the number of candidates is winnowed down to two or three, the press has a greater ability to focus on their particular weaknesses and criticisms of each other. The longer and more wide-open the campaign becomes, the more candidates must develop new issues and reasons for people *not* to vote for their opponents. Intraparty criticism is hardly new in U.S. politics. J. Morgan Kousser's analysis of the rise of primaries in the South around the turn of the century, for instance, showed how it became necessary for candidates "to lambaste their opponents publicly" and to "fabricate issues" in order to attract attention (Kousser 1974, 80).

The continual backbiting in the nomination process has been greatly exacerbated in recent years by the custom of regular televised debates between candidates prior to each major primary date. When debates were first introduced at the dawn of the television era, one might say that they showed the characteristics of a kinder, gentler America (to use George Bush's famous phrase). For example, when Adlai Stevenson and Estes Kefauver debated prior to the 1956 Florida primary, the *New York Times* reported, "The nationally televised 'debate' found the two chief contenders for the Democratic Presidential nomination taking virtually identical positions on almost every issue discussed" (Baker 1956, 1). Similarly, when Kennedy debated Hubert Humphrey on West Virginia television in 1960, the United Press International (UPI) story led with the following introduction: "Sens. Kennedy and Humphrey staged a debate with kid gloves tonight and found little to disagree about except whether Humphrey has a chance to win the Democratic Presidential nomination" ("Humphrey Denies" 1960, 1). Rather than tearing each other down, the two candidates focused on the merits of Democratic party proposals. Indeed, the Republican national chairman demanded equal time, arguing that the "debate" had enabled the Democrats to advertise their positions. In his view, the joint appearance had "all the sharpness of a duel with bananas," and "a pillow fight between two small boys would have been more controversial" ("GOP Attacks" 1960, 2).

By the 1980s, party leaders were delighted to see the other party's candidates debating on television. As presidential primaries proliferated and their results became decisive, the incentive for openly criticizing one's opponents increased dramatically. That the kid gloves of the early television era had been dropped was evident in the *New York Times's* description of the 1984 Atlanta debate, which was "marked by sharp clashes," with Walter Mondale using "every device from wisecracks to condemnation." Other candidates were variously described as having "attacked," "ridiculed," "ganged up on," "jabbed," and "accused" their opponents (Raines 1984, A1 and B9).

With so much riding on their public performances, candidates now feel compelled to differentiate themselves as much as possible—even if they have few policy differences. Nelson Polsby pointed out that Henry Jackson and Morris Udall, for example, were perceived as polar opposites on domestic policy during the 1976 Democratic campaign despite the great similarity in their congressional voting records (Polsby 1983, 149 and 256). Therefore, the public comes to see more conflict within the party than really exists and is led to doubt whether the party label means anything. In this sense, it is clear that primaries do more than merely display the existing disunity.

Recognizing the dangers of such internal conflicts, Democratic National Chairman Paul Kirk set up a committee of party elders in 1988 to monitor the campaign and to "publicly bring political pressure to bear on any candidate who refuses to be civil" ("Cut Out" 1987, 29).

Yet, though the Democratic campaign of 1988 contained nothing as extreme as Gary Hart's 1984 charges that Walter Mondale was the unelectable candidate of the past, Dukakis hardly emerged unscathed from his thirty-nine debate appearances. It was Albert Gore in the New York debate who first introduced the issue of the furlough of Willie Horton—an issue that George Bush would later pick up on. And Jesse Jackson often stated that whereas he wanted to reverse Reaganomics, Dukakis wanted only to "manage" it. He further criticized Dukakis for not preparing a federal budget, for being as "bland" as Bush, and, at one point, he even accused him of being to the right of Reagan on Mozambique (Drogin and Rosenstiel 1988, 14).

If these sorts of criticisms continue week after week, the enthusiasm for the front-runner inevitably fades. As Lee Atwater said, every Tuesday a candidate is "facing two challenges: (a) people saying that this guy is not capable of leading the country, and (b) people saying that not only is he not capable of leading the country, he's not capable of leading this party" (Runkel 1989, 104). The phenomenon of "negative momentum," therefore, often occurs as a candidate nears the point of clinching the nomination (Bartels 1988, 287). Gerald Ford, for instance, not only still faced opposition at the end of the 1976 primary season but was soundly defeated by Reagan over the last three weeks in Arkansas, Idaho, Nevada, Montana, and, of course, California. As a result, he limped into the Republican convention with barely enough delegates to win.

Negative momentum at the end of the primary season often leads to a major floor fight at the convention itself. Even a convention fight that seems little more than a last gasp, such as Reagan's in 1976 or Kennedy's in 1980, can cause much damage to party unity. Despite the decline of the convention as a decisionmaking body, more media coverage is nevertheless focused on it than on any other event in the nomination process (Shafer 1988). It is, therefore, especially harmful for a nominee to be challenged from within at this highly visible stage, which constitutes our third indicator of nomination divisiveness.

Indeed, the data on convention television exposure in Table 3.4 further support the party disunity hypothesis, according to which the more a party exposes its differences on television at the convention, the less likely it is to unite and attract independent voters. The networks will devote additional coverage if there is a showdown at the convention, and viewers will be more likely to tune in to watch the fireworks. Yet, what is good for drawing television attention to the convention is clearly bad for the party's chances in November. The 1960 election apparently marked the end of the era in which parties could survive nomination battles with relatively little effect. As Table 3.4 demonstrates, from 1964

TABLE 3.4   Convention Television Exposure, 1956–1988

Year	Democratic Convention			Republican Convention		
	Ratings ×	Hours =	Exposure	Ratings ×	Hours =	Exposure
1956	24.3	104	2527	29.4[a]	65	1911
1960	29.3	79	2315	12.3[a]	73	898
1964	27.9	69	1925	20.4	103	2101
1968	28.8	81	2333	26.6	71	1889
1972	18.3[b]	92	1684	29.6	45	1332
1976	22.5	69	1553	25.2	73	1840
1980	24.8	56	1389	20.5	57	1169
1984	23.2	33	766	19.1	30	573
1988	20.6	31	639	18.7	35	655

[a]The first session was held in the afternoon, thereby decreasing the ratings.
[b]Includes ratings for the last session, which went until 4:00 A.M. (Eastern Daylight Time).

Source: Data from Byron E. Shafer, *Bifurcated Politics* (Cambridge, Mass.: Harvard University Press, 1988), p. 274; updated by the author for 1988. Table reprinted by permission of the publishers from *The Rise of Candidate-Centered Politics: Presidential Elections of the 1980s* by Martin P. Wattenberg, Cambridge, Mass.: Harvard University Press, Copyright © 1991 by the President and Fellows of Harvard College.

to 1984, the party that received the most television convention exposure (as defined by ratings multiplied by hours) consistently lost.

In 1988, this pattern was broken because both dull conventions received little attention. The combined television ratings in 1988 were the lowest ever, with the highest rating any network garnered being an 8.7 for NBC on the night of Jackson's impassioned speech to the Democratic convention. By comparison, the following week CBS obtained a rating of 15.1 for its coverage of the Miss Teen USA Pageant.

The fact that both parties managed to virtually eradicate any conflict from their conventions in 1988 shows how each has learned its lesson from past defeats. It is both a sad commentary and a bad omen for the future of nominating conventions to note that accepted wisdom now holds that a carefully scripted convention is the soundest electoral strategy. Thus, to use Walter Bagehot's terms, the national nominating convention has changed from an efficient institution to a dignified one. The convention is no longer where the nomination is made, any more than the British monarchy is where governing decisions are made in Britain; each plays a role only in legitimating choices made by more modern political institutions.

Although this sort of dignified status might be fitting for the British monarchy, it does not suit the U.S. party convention very well. The convention is the best chance the parties have every four years to show the U.S. public what they stand for and to demonstrate their role in the governmental process. Eliminating conflict and decisionmaking from the conventions has made the public more likely to neglect the parties and view them with indifference. With party organizations less institutionally relevant, they are less salient in the public mind, and, therefore, the party symbol no longer serves the unifying function it once did.

In fact, the only significant event still likely to occur at future conventions is the choice of a running mate. The nominee's effort (if necessary) to assuage the dominant opposition faction via the selection of a vice president is the fourth and final stage at which the nomination process can lead to a divided party. The strongest possible statement of reconciliation is for the new nominee to select the runner-up for the nomination as the vice presidential candidate (as Reagan chose Bush in 1980). Alternatively, selecting someone who represents the ideological point of view of the runner-up (as Ford did in choosing Dole in 1976) will also help mollify any division within the party. In contrast, as Polsby and Aaron Wildavsky write, "A refusal to heal the wounds and placate dissidents is nothing less than a declaration of internal war. It can only lead to increased conflict within the party (1988, 155–156). Barry Goldwater's choice of William Miller in 1964 is one such example.

Even a widely popular choice is sometimes insufficient to heal the wounds of the primary season. Mondale's choice of Geraldine Ferraro as his running mate, for instance, won much praise at the convention, but it did little to help draw Hart supporters back into the fold. Many of them apparently saw Ferraro's selection as just another example of Mondale's pandering to special interest groups.

And in 1988, the search for a Democratic vice presidential candidate clearly illustrated how this stage can prove to be a political minefield for a new nominee. The second place Democratic finisher, Jesse Jackson, not only said he would take the position but also insisted he had earned "serious consideration." When he was passed over for a southern conservative, the major story of the convention became whether the rift between Dukakis and Jackson could be healed. Dukakis aide John Corrigan expressed his camp's frustration with Jackson stealing the show when he told the Harvard campaign managers conference, "Our 15 minutes of being famous was being consumed by somebody else. And that inevitably did its damage" (Runkel 1989, 230).

In sum, by adding together the number of indicators marked in Table 3.5, a rough index of "nomination fighting" from 1964 to 1988 can be constructed, ranging from 0 to 4. The greater the index figure, the more likely that the nominee's party identifiers had a divided opinion about him. Of course, some candidates are inherently more divisive

TABLE 3.5   Index of Nomination Fighting, 1964–1988

Candidate	Early Primary Contests	Late Primary Contests	Convention Battle	VP Does Not Heal Wounds	Total
Barry Goldwater (1964)	X	X	X	X	4
Lyndon Johnson (1964)					0
Richard Nixon (1968)			X	X	2
Hubert Humphrey (1968)	X	X	X	X	4
Richard Nixon (1972)					0
George McGovern (1972)	X	X	X	X	4
Gerald Ford (1976)	X	X	X		3
Jimmy Carter (1976)	X	X			2
Ronald Reagan (1980)	X				1
Jimmy Carter (1980)	X	X	X		3
Ronald Reagan (1984)					0
Walter Mondale (1984)	X	X		X	3
George Bush (1988)	X				1
Michael Dukakis (1988)	X	X		X	3

Source: Reprinted by permission of the publishers from *The Rise of Candidate-Centered Politics: Presidential Elections of the 1980s* by Martin P. Wattenberg, Cambridge, Mass.: Harvard University Press, Copyright © 1991 by the President and Fellows of Harvard College.

than others because of their background or stands on various issues. To attempt to control for this factor, attitudes toward the candidate held by members of the opposing party can be used as a baseline for comparison.

Ideally, nominees would like to have their own parties united about their candidacies and the opposition divided toward them. In such a case, they can count on votes from most of their own parties' identifiers and a good number of independents and members of the opposition party, as well. Figure 3.1 displays how close each candidate in the 1964–1984 period came to this ideal situation. Positive entries mean that the candidate's own partisans were more unified in their evaluation of him than were the opposition party's identifiers. The unit of measurement is the standard deviation on the count of likes minus dislikes concerning the candidate.

As can readily be seen, the greater the battle for the nomination, the more a nominee's party ended up divided about him in comparison to the opposition. The relationship is as close to being perfect as one is ever bound to find in social science. The only case that was somewhat out of line was that of Gerald Ford in 1976. Yet, as with all the other years, the pattern of standard deviations in 1976 was nevertheless quite consistent with the actual election results. Because Ford and Carter

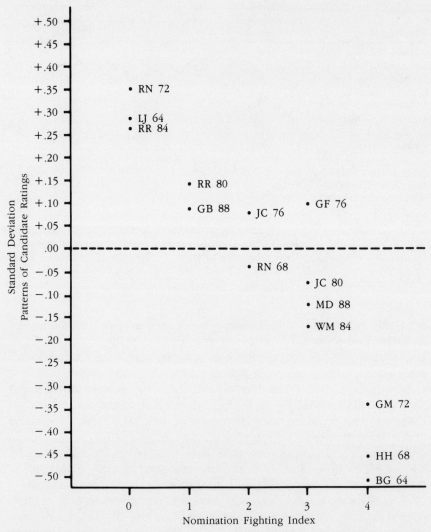

FIGURE 3.1   Party Unity by Index of Nomination Fighting. Positive entries on party unity mean that the candidate's own partisans were more unified in their evaluation of him than were the opposition party's identifiers, as measured by the standard deviations.

Source: 1964–1988 SRC/CPS American National Election Studies. Figure reprinted by permission of the publishers from *The Rise of Candidate-Centered Politics: Presidential Elections of the 1980s* by Martin P. Wattenberg, Cambridge, Mass.: Harvard University Press, Copyright © 1991 by the President and Fellows of Harvard College.

had virtually identical levels of party unity, one could have predicted a close race, with the majority candidate winning by a narrow margin.

To play the devil's advocate, one might argue that both variables displayed in Figure 3.1 are little more than surrogate measures of candidate popularity. It might be that popular candidates are simply not strongly opposed for their party's leadership. Similarly, a candidate with many electoral assets should find it easier to maintain party unity.

I would argue, however, that the causality between candidate popularity and party unity runs in both directions. A candidate with clear vulnerabilities will naturally encounter greater opposition for the nomination. In turn, the amount of internal opposition plays a key role in determining the degree to which vulnerabilities are exacerbated. For instance, Ted Kennedy's decision to run in 1980 stemmed, in large part, from Carter's unpopularity, and his challenge further weakened Carter's chances of reelection. Yet, Kennedy could well have chosen to end his campaign in April rather than fighting on to the convention in spite of hopeless odds. Thus, the key to the argument is that candidate decisions such as Kennedy's make an independent impact on party unity, which, in turn, greatly affects a nominee's chance for victory in November.

Interestingly, Humphrey in 1968 and Reagan in 1980 had nearly identical percentages of positive comments on the likes/dislikes questions (Wattenberg 1990, 144). The Democrats' primary and convention battles in 1968, however, were so divisive that Humphrey was able to hold on to only 68 percent of the Democratic vote in the general election—in spite of his respectable level of overall popularity. An even more striking example of the importance of party unity can be found in the data from 1984. In this case, the percentage of positive comments regarding Reagan was surprisingly similar to that for Mondale—51 versus 48 percent. Yet, the distribution of partisan opinion was more favorable for Reagan and is therefore crucial to understanding how he won a landslide victory.

Mondale probably lost what little chance he had to defeat Reagan in 1984 in the New Hampshire primary (of February 28), where his plans for quickly locking up the nomination were derailed by Gary Hart. During January and February of that year, Democrats were somewhat more unified than Republicans in their evaluations of Mondale. As Table 3.6 shows, this difference all but evaporated in March as the battle with Hart got under way. The timing of this change in the distribution of attitudes is no mere coincidence. Had Mondale been as successful as Reagan in unifying his party during the nomination campaign year, he might have been able to give him a close race—

TABLE 3.6   Standard Deviations of Candidate Feeling Thermometer Ratings by Party, 1984 (0–100 degrees)

Month	Mondale			Reagan		
	Repub-licans	Demo-crats	Differ-ence	Demo-crats	Repub-licans	Differ-ence
January	22.4	19.5	+2.9	28.0	21.8	+6.2
February	22.0	19.2	+2.8	28.8	17.2	+11.6
March	20.1	19.6	+0.5	26.0	18.2	+7.8
April	22.5	22.4	+0.1	30.1	18.7	+11.4
May	21.1	23.3	−2.2	28.6	20.6	+8.0
June	22.3	21.9	+0.4	28.7	22.3	+6.4
July	22.2	21.8	+0.4	30.1	18.7	+11.4
August	22.8	22.8	0.0	29.6	18.5	+11.1
September	23.4	25.9	−2.5	30.8	17.3	+13.5
October	20.9	23.9	−3.0	29.2	15.0	+14.2
November	22.7	24.2	−1.5	29.6	19.0	+10.6

Source: Data from CPS Rolling Cross-Section Survey. Table reprinted by permission of the publishers from *The Rise of Candidate-Centered Politics: Presidential Elections of the 1980s* by Martin P. Wattenberg, Cambridge, Mass.: Harvard University Press, Copyright © 1991 by the President and Fellows of Harvard College.

the economic boom notwithstanding. By sweeping the primaries and then adding Hart to the ticket, his chances in November would surely have been improved.

CONCLUSION

In the recent era of party disunity, the ideal path to victory has been a series of unbroken early primary wins, concessions from all major contenders before the convention, and a harmonious convention that awards the second slot on the ticket to the leading opposition faction. Reagan's path to the nomination in 1980 and Bush's in 1988 followed this course. It is a course that puts the nominee in a good position to gain close to unanimous support from his own party and to attract a substantial proportion of independents and identifiers with the opposition party.

Although the electorate's focus has clearly been on the candidate and not the party, it has been the harmony of the party that has been the key to presidential victories since 1964. Clearly, this has benefited the more cohesive Republicans. Their road to presidential victory might best be described as "sit back and watch the other party tear itself apart," rather than "divide and conquer." Thus, their conquest has been an incomplete one—leaving them as the minority party nationwide and in the nation's most representative political body, the House of Representatives. The result has been regularly divided government and continuing policy paralysis.

NOTES

1. Elaine Ciulla Kamarck (1990, 177) provides a good overview of how the differences in party rules have evolved over recent years and how they have disadvantaged the Democrats.

4

The Persistence of Democratic House Majorities

Gary C. Jacobson

Divided partisan control of the federal government has become the normal condition of U.S. politics. Between 1968 and 1988, Republicans won five of six presidential elections, twice by landslides. They took an average of 55 percent of the popular vote and won 78 percent of total electoral votes cast for major party presidential candidates. Yet, Republicans have not won control of the House of Representatives since 1952, and they have not won more than 192 seats—44 percent of the total—since 1956. Despite George Bush's 7.1-million-vote margin over Michael Dukakis in 1988, the Democrats actually increased their House majority by a couple of seats, holding 260 to the Republicans' 175. And the Republicans were also unable to recapture their Senate majority, won in 1980 and lost again in 1986. Thus, Bush entered the White House with less partisan support in Congress than any newly elected (or reelected) president in history.

Why has Republican success at the top of the ticket not extended downward to other political offices? Why, in particular, have Republicans failed to win more seats in the House? The mystery is deepened by the other things the Republican party has had going for it. The Democrats' advantage in party identification, which stood at 20 points in 1972, has shrunk to insignificance.[1] National Republican campaign committees continue to be better organized and far more generously financed than their Democratic counterparts (Herrnson 1988; Jacobson 1989a). Partly as a result, Republican House candidates have usually enjoyed better-financed campaigns than those of Democrats during the era of Republican presidential hegemony. Through the 1988 election, Republicans could also boast of steady growth in the economy (after 1982) and dramatic improvements in the international sphere as evidence of their party's ability to govern. Yet, these advantages failed to pay off in House seats, and the net loss of only 9 seats under grimmer circumstances in 1990 left them precisely where they had been after 1982 (with 167 seats, 38.4 percent of the total).

Proposed explanations for the Republicans' inability to make headway in the House fall into two broad categories: structural explanations and political explanations. Republican leaders naturally prefer structural explanations. Democrats continue to control the House, they argue, because they have rigged the game. Democratic majorities are protected by gerrymandered districts, abuse of the frank and other perquisites of office, and biased campaign finance laws. "The left wing in the House," according to Minority Whip Newt Gingrich, "is engaged in a conspiracy to avoid fair elections" (Cook 1989, 1060).

A more restrained version of this view derives from the scholarly literature on the incumbency advantage. The well-documented increase in the electoral margins enjoyed by House incumbents, most notably during the 1960s, was expected to insulate House members from swings in national sentiments (Mayhew 1974a). With wider margins of safety, House incumbents would be able to ride out contrary electoral tides that earlier would have delivered their seats to the other party. This outcome, according to some investigators, is precisely what has happened, with Republican challengers emerging as the chief victims (Ansolabehere, Brady, and Fiorina 1988; Fiorina 1989a).

An alternative view is that the federal government is divided between the parties because voters—perhaps consciously, perhaps not—choose to have it that way. Several quite distinct variants of this argument have been proffered, but all share the view that divided government is the result of political choices rather than structural features of congressional election politics. That is, divided control reflects, rather than thwarts, the popular will.

In this chapter, I shall argue that all of the structural explanations are wrong or, at best, woefully inadequate and that most, if not all, of the political explanations are at least partially right. The Democrats' continued dominance of the House (as well as of other lower offices) despite a string of Republican presidential victories is a consequence of electoral politics: of candidates, issues, electoral coalitions, and voters' reactions to them. To oversimplify, Republicans have made little progress in the House because they have fielded inferior candidates on the wrong side of issues that are important to voters in House elections and because voters find it difficult to assign credit or blame when control of the government is divided between the parties.

STRUCTURAL EXPLANATIONS FOR THE DEMOCRATIC HOUSE MAJORITY

Incumbency

Though differing on the details, numerous studies have documented a sharp increase in the value of House incumbency, measured in votes, during the 1960s (Erikson 1972; Cover and Mayhew 1981; Alford and Brady 1988; Gelman and King 1990; Jacobson 1990a). Regression analysis indicates that an incumbent's expected share of the two party vote grew from 59.2 percent to 67.6 percent over the postwar period ($R^2 = .83$); incumbency was worth approximately 2 extra percentage points in the vote prior to the 1960s; it is now worth 5 to 10 points more (depending on how one measures it; typically, it is compared to what the vote is in a district when no incumbent is running). Perhaps it was simply the Democrats' good luck to be the majority party when the value of incumbency rose, nullifying the effects of growing Republican strength in the electorate. Or perhaps the "conspiracy" sniffed out by Gingrich lies behind the change. In either case, the enlarged incumbency advantage is sufficient to explain why Democrats retain firm control of the House.

As plausible as it may seem, however, the incumbency explanation runs into insurmountable difficulties. First, the wider margin of victory enjoyed by the average House incumbent has not affected the translation of vote swings into seat swings nearly enough to account for the Republicans' inability to take the House. And, more critically, the Republicans' failure to achieve net gains through open seats makes it clear that Democratic incumbency cannot be the only barrier to Republican advances.

The Swing Ratio

David Mayhew (1974b) and other scholars who first noticed the growth in House incumbents' vote margins understandably concluded that the change would serve to insulate House incumbents from partisan swings in popular sentiment. They believed it would diminish the "swing ratio" (the share of seats a party adds for a unit increase in its share of the vote) and that the party favored by a given national vote swing would have less to show for it (in additional House seats) than before. Steven Ansolabehere, David Brady, and Morris Fiorina (1988; see also Fiorina 1989a) took this argument a step farther, concluding that not only had the swing ratio fallen dramatically but the change had deprived Republicans of House majorities no fewer than five times since 1966 (in 1966, 1968, 1972, 1980, and 1984). They presented the strongest evidence in the scholarly literature that Republican grievances are fully justified.

Ansolabehere, Brady, and Fiorina's conclusion derived, however, from the peculiar way they measured the House vote. When the problem is corrected, the Republican majorities disappear.[2] (For a detailed critique, see Jacobson 1990a.) The corrected models confirm that the swing ratio has, indeed, diminished in recent decades—by about 25 percent— but also reveal that other changes in the seats/votes relationships have limited the impact of this decline. In most instances, the distribution of House seats produced by elections since 1966 would have been little different had the old swing regime remained in place. Democratic dominance would have continued. In no election would Republicans have been predicted to win a majority (though they would have come closer in 1966, 1968, and 1984), and the Democrats would have won a few more seats in 1974 and 1982 (Jacobson 1990a). Based on this evidence, the enhanced incumbency advantage in house elections has had an observable but surprisingly modest effect on congressional representation.

Ansolabehere, Brady, and Fiorina rightly noted that "the vanishing marginals literature is primarily about incumbents and the changes taking place in incumbent contested elections" (1988, 14). They then proceeded to estimate separate swing ratios for incumbents' and open seats. They found that the swing ratio for incumbents' seats fell by more than 50 percent after the mid-1960s. But they did not carry the argument far enough—the focus should not have been merely on seats held by incumbents but on seats held by incumbents of the party facing contrary national tides. Swings of voter sentiment to a party's incumbents cannot give it additional seats; only swings to its challengers

TABLE 4.1   Vote Swing to House Candidates of the Party Gaining Votes, 1946–1990[a] (percentages)

Year	Mean Swing to:	
	Incumbents	Challengers
1946–1964	4.0	3.8
1966–1990	4.7	2.0
Democrats	5.1	3.2
Republicans	4.6	1.4

[a]Includes only those contests with major party competition in the previous and current elections.

(and to its candidates contesting open seats held by the other party) have this potential. With this in mind, observe the data in Table 4.1.

For the 1946–1964 period, average swings were balanced between incumbents and challengers. In five of the ten elections, the average challenger of the party gaining votes enjoyed a larger vote increase than the party's average incumbent. Since 1966, however, incumbents have absorbed a greatly disproportionate share of the aggregate swing. And Republican challengers have done notably worse than Democratic challengers on this score. Only in 1974, 1982, and 1990—all "Democratic" years—was the swing to challengers larger than the swing to incumbents.[3] In the eight elections in which national tides favored their party, Republican incumbents added an average of 4.6 percentage points to their vote, while Republican challengers added only 1.4 percentage points; if 1966 is omitted, the mean swing to Republican challengers in these years is a paltry 0.9 percentage points.

Models estimating changes in the swing ratio for seats contested by challengers of the party favored by national trends produce no evidence that the swing regime in force in 1946–1964 would have increased turnover or expelled more incumbents had it been maintained subsequently. If anything, the parameters from the earlier period underestimate seat changes for the later period in these contests (Jacobson 1990a). Thus, the responsiveness of seat swings to vote swings *to challengers* has changed little, if at all, with the rise of incumbents' vote margins. As a group, incumbents are no more insulated from contrary shifts in district sentiment than they were prior to the mid-1960s. If House members are now harder to defeat, it is not because contrary vote swings have a diminished impact on seat swings but rather because contrary vote swings have themselves diminished. And if Republicans have been unable to advance in the House, it is not because their challengers' votes have failed to translate into seats; it

TABLE 4.2   Open Seats Changing Party Control[a]

	Seats Held by:			
	Democrats		Republicans	
	1968–1990			
Seats won by:				
Democrats	248	(77.7%)	80	(32.3%)
Republicans	71	(22.3%)	168	(67.7%)
Total	319		248	
	1980–1990			
Seats won by:				
Democrats	99	(76.2%)	29	(25.4%)
Republicans	31	(23.8%)	85	(74.6%)
Total	130		114	

[a]Includes general and special elections for open seats.

is because their challengers have not won enough votes. The reasons for this are political, not structural—or so I shall argue below.

Open Seats

Incumbents don't last forever. Fewer than 10 percent of both Democrats and Republicans elected in 1990 had served in the House prior to 1968. That is, more than 90 percent of the incumbents of both parties who were in the House when the incumbency advantage underwent its sharpest increase subsequently died in office, quit, or were defeated.

Even if incumbency has made it more difficult for a party to reap the benefits of a favorable trend in any single election year, a party on the rise should still be able to accumulate seats over a series of elections as the other party's incumbents exit and their seats are thrown open. Consequently, if Democratic incumbency has been the main barrier to Republican progress in the House, we should observe cumulative Republican gains through victories in Democratic districts no longer defended by incumbents.

But, in fact, what we observe is something quite different. Table 4.2 lists the number and percentage of open seats that Democrats and Republicans were able to take from one another from 1968 through 1990 and from 1980 through 1990. Over the full period, Republicans have taken 22.3 percent of Democratic open seats while losing 32.3 percent of their own; the difference is statistically significant (at $p<.05$). Of course, the Democratic majority had more open seats to defend. But even in strictly numerical terms, Republicans have lost more open seats to Democrats (80) than they have taken from them (71) since 1968. The parties have broken precisely even in the number of new seats created by redistricting in which neither or both parties fielded incumbent candidates (31 each). Even when analysis is confined to the Reagan and Bush elections, Republicans have gained nothing through open seats; their net gain of 2 seats (shown in the lower part of Table 4.2) is more than offset by a net deficit of 5 seats in newly created districts. Clearly, Democratic incumbency cannot explain the Republicans' failure to add to their House delegation if they cannot add to it even when incumbency is not a factor.

Gerrymandering

Republican officials might excuse their party's failure to advance through open seats by mentioning another favorite allegation, namely, that Democratically controlled state governments have drawn House districts that discriminate against Republican candidates. Flagrant gerrymandering, so this claim goes, protects Democrats (incumbent and otherwise) from the electorate's wrath. In reality, however, Republican difficulties have little to do with gerrymandering. The equations in Tables 4.3 and 4.4 offer no support whatever for the claim that Republicans have suffered systematically when districts have been redrawn. They show that when incumbency, national tides, and (in the second equation in each table) the Democratic vote in the previous election are taken into account, the Democrats' probability of victory was unrelated to whether or not the district lines were redrawn for either the 1968–1990 or the 1982–1990 period. Indeed, the redistricting coefficients are negative, suggesting that Democrats did slightly *worse* after redistricting, though the coefficients are statistically indistinguishable from zero (they are much less than twice their standard errors).

These equations do not prove the absence of partisan gerrymanders, of course; they merely indicate that partisan effects, if any, have balanced out. Republican officials are fond of pointing to California, where Democrats drew up a plan that, with the help of the strong national swing to their party in 1982, enlarged a 22 to 21 Democratic majority in the state's House delegation to 27 to 18 (after a 2-seat gain from the 1980 census). But this was offset by Republican efforts elsewhere, notably in Indiana, where the Republican state legislature drew district lines intended to turn a 6 to 5 Democratic advantage to a 4 to 6 or even a 3 to 7 disadvantage (Indiana lost a district after 1980).

The Indiana gerrymander was a striking—and highly instructive— failure (Democrats currently hold an 8 to 2 majority in the Indiana House delegation). Gerrymandering works only to the degree that

TABLE 4.3 The Effects of Redistricting on the Outcomes of House Elections, 1968–1990 (probit estimates)

Variable	Equation 1	Equation 2
Intercept	.145[a]	−2.608[b]
	(.058)	(.186)
National shift in the two party Democratic vote (%)	.101[b]	.131[b]
	(.010)	(.012)
Vote won by Democratic candidate in last election (%)		.053[b]
		(.003)
Democratic incumbent	1.807[b]	1.190[b]
	(.075)	(.098)
Republican incumbent	−1.845[b]	−1.208[b]
	(.075)	(.097)
District was redrawn	−.073	−.053
	(.068)	(.083)
Log likelihood	−1,107	−813
Number of cases	5,219	4,410

The dependent variable is 1 if a Democrat won the seat, 0 otherwise; "Democratic incumbent" is 1 if the Democrat is an incumbent, 0 otherwise; "Republican incumbent" is 1 if the Republican is an incumbent, 0 otherwise; "District was redrawn" takes the value of 1 if district lines were redrawn since the last election, 0 otherwise; standard errors are in parentheses.

[a]$p < .01$, one-tailed test.
[b]$p < .001$, one-tailed test.

electorates are reliably partisan—which they no longer are. Consider that no fewer than 19 of the 27 California House districts held by Democrats produced pluralities for Ronald Reagan in 1984 and that, statewide, Reagan was, by congressional standards, a "marginal" winner, with 58 percent of the vote. In 1986, Republican Governor George Deukmejian won 20 of the 27 districts. With the right matchup, all but a handful of California's notoriously "Democratic" House districts were perfectly capable of opting for the Republican.

Campaign Finance

Republican leaders have recently concluded that the campaign finance system is anticompetitive and biased against their own candidates. But in a large majority of elections since 1972 (when accurate campaign finance data first became available), Republican House candidates have been more generously financed than similarly situated Democrats. In nine of ten elections between 1972 and 1990, the average Republican incumbent spent more than the average Democratic incumbent. Among candidates for open seats, Democrats spent more than Republicans in

TABLE 4.4 The Effects of Redistricting on the Outcomes of House Elections, 1982–1990 (probit estimates)

Variable	Equation 1	Equation 2
Intercept	−.093	−2.983[a]
	(.100)	(.318)
National shift in the two party Democratic vote (%)	.103[a]	.127[a]
	(.020)	(.023)
Vote won by Democratic candidate in last election (%)		.057[a]
		(.006)
Democratic incumbent	2.212[a]	1.496[a]
	(.136)	(.183)
Republican incumbent	−1.653[a]	−.936[a]
	(.119)	(.166)
District was redrawn	−.063	−.174
	(.125)	(.150)
Log likelihood	−395	−273
Number of cases	2,175	1,811

The dependent variable is 1 if a Democrat won the seat, 0 otherwise; "Democratic incumbent" is 1 if the Democrat is an incumbent, 0 otherwise; "Republican incumbent" is 1 if the Republican is an incumbent, 0 otherwise; "District was redrawn" takes the value of 1 if district lines were redrawn since the last election, 0 otherwise; standard errors are in parentheses.

[a]$p < .001$, one-tailed test.

elections from 1972 through 1978 and in 1990, but Republicans spent more from 1980 through 1988. And the average Republican challenger outspent the average Democratic challenger in every year but 1974 (for obvious reasons), 1986, 1988, and 1990 (Jacobson 1990a).

It is, of course, the experience of these latter three elections that converted Republicans into eager reformers. The 1988 election is especially conspicuous when compared to the other years in which the Republicans took the White House. The average Republican challenger spent 56 percent more than the average Democratic challenger in 1980, 45 percent more in 1984, but 31 percent less in 1988. Political action committees (PACs) were especially disdainful of Republican challengers in 1988; even corporate PACs, normally the Republicans' best friends, gave only 3 percent of their funds to Republican challengers, in contrast, for example, to the 20 percent they contributed to such challengers in 1980. No wonder Republican party officials, who once defended PACs as democracy in action, now propose to ban most of them outright (Alston and Craney 1989).

In attacking PACs, however, Republicans mistake effect for cause. Corporate and other probusiness PACs did not undergo a conversion to liberalism after 1980; rather, their choices simply reflect a dearth of

Republican challengers whose prospects were encouraging enough to be worth an investment—a dearth that requires a political explanation.

POLITICAL EXPLANATIONS
FOR THE DEMOCRATIC HOUSE MAJORITY

None of the structural explanations for divided government survives analysis. Republican frustration is understandable, but the blame is misplaced. The Republicans' problem is not that incumbency and gerrymandering have deprived them of a rightful share of House seats but that their candidates have not won enough votes; Republican challengers in particular have continued to fare poorly at the ballot box. Nor does the campaign finance system discriminate against Republicans; instead, the party has suffered a shortage of challengers with the attributes, issues, and electoral prospects that attract contributors. In reality, Democratic dominance of the House derives from the politics, not the structure, of congressional elections.

The conjunction of three circumstances is required to defeat a House incumbent: There must be a good candidate, a good reason for voters to desert the incumbent, and enough money to acquaint voters with the challenger and his or her strengths (Jacobson 1991b; Iyengar and Kinder 1987). All are necessary, none is sufficient by itself, and all are related. Good candidates attract money, and the promise of money attracts good candidates. But both depend on the prospect of winning, which depends, in turn, on the availability of issues and arguments that might erode the incumbent's support. Without exploitable issues, even experienced, well-financed challengers can expect to make little headway. And even vulnerable incumbents win easy reelection if they avoid a challenger with the skill and resources to exploit their vulnerabilities.

Despite their dominance of presidential elections, Republicans continue to find it difficult to recruit talented challengers and to arm them with telling issues. Both long-term and election-specific conditions have hampered their search for effective candidates and issues, and, as always, the difficulties are mutually reinforcing.

The Quality of Republican Challengers

Gauged by the standard of experience, the quality of Republican candidates has actually declined during the period of Republican presidential hegemony. This has made it harder for their party to add to its House contingent because experience translates into additional votes and victories for House challengers. I have presented the full evidence for this claim elsewhere (Jacobson 1989b and 1990a), but two findings are relevant here. First, experienced challengers—those who have previously held elective public office—win significantly more votes and have a significantly higher probability of defeating the incumbent than do inexperienced challengers (taking the district's electoral history and national trends into account). Second, experience is equally valuable to Republican and Democratic challengers.

Assuming that career politicians follow rational career strategies, a party's ability to field experienced challengers is endogenous: The better a party's prospects, the more likely its career politicians are to pursue higher office (Jacobson and Kernell 1983; Jacobson 1989). Certainly, this has been true of Democrats. But it has not been true of Republicans in recent decades (Jacobson 1990a). Figure 4.1 traces the incidence of experienced Democratic and Republican challengers in House elections from 1966 to 1990.

The strategic calculation of experienced Democratic challengers is readily apparent; note, for example, the peaks for 1974 and 1982, the two most promising Democratic years in the period under review. Potential Republican challengers were much less sensitive to their party's prospects, especially during the Reagan-Bush years. Since 1966, the Republican party has consistently fielded a smaller proportion of experienced challengers than has the Democratic party, regardless of electoral prospects. The data reveal a decline over time in the quality of Republican challengers, and the downward trend is substantial and significant.

The average quality of Republican challengers has declined during the period of Republican presidential dominance (though experienced Republican challengers have been significantly more common in presidential election years). Because the quality of the challenger is just as important to Republican as to Democratic chances of defeating an incumbent, this decline stands as one proximate explanation for the party's failure to make inroads into the Democratic House majority in recent elections.

Republican challenges were especially feeble in 1988. Measured by experience, the quality of Republican challengers reached a postwar low; moreover, the average Republican challenger spent less money in real terms than in any election since 1974 (Jacobson 1990a). Over the entire period of Republican presidential ascendancy, only in 1974 did Republicans mount weaker challenges than in 1988. Under the circumstances, it is easy to understand why Bush's victory failed to increase Republican representation in the House. But it is not so easy to understand why the Republican party has fielded fewer and fewer experienced challengers while garnering a string of presidential successes. At least

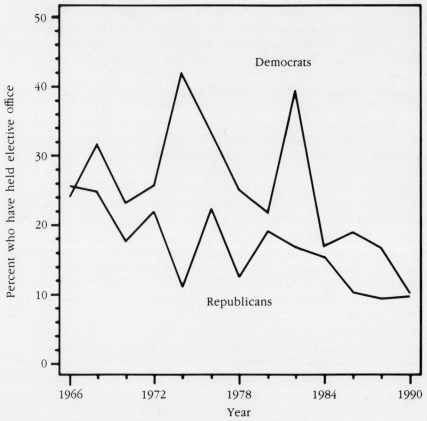

FIGURE 4.1 Experienced House Challengers, 1966–1990

part of this answer, I think, lies in particular features of congressional election politics that reflect important differences between what voters look for in representatives and what they look for in presidents.

What Do Voters Want?

Voters are, by definition, ultimately responsible for the disjuncture between presidential and congressional election results. The simplest political explanation for divided government is that Democrats control Congress and Republicans control the White House because voters want it that way. In one version of this argument, Morris Fiorina proposed that "some small but important portion of the electorate is engaging in a kind of sophisticated ticket splitting that permits them to register a preference for a middle course between two parties, neither of which they fully trust to govern" because of their ideological extremity (Fiorina 1988, 442).

The spatial logic of Fiorina's argument is convincing, but the initial empirical evidence for it is tenuous, and its strictest formulation requires an uncommon level of strategic sophistication on the part of the pivotal voters. Fiorina (1990) also outlines an interpretation of ticket splitting that holds that voters divide control because they do not trust politicians of either party; setting the parties at institutional loggerheads lets them foil each other's self-serving schemes. If this were true, we would expect those voters most distrustful of government to split their tickets most often in national elections. However, evidence from the 1988 American National Election Study (ANES) indicates that this is not the case. On all the familiar "trust in government" and "efficacy" questions,[4] trusting voters were more likely to split their tickets than were the disaffected (though the difference achieves statistical significance for only one of the six questions).

I prefer yet another variant of this approach, one rather less demanding of voters than deliberate ideological balancing—it doesn't require any conscious calculation at all—and less driven by disenchanted cynicism. Its logic arises from different expectations people have of presidents and members of Congress, as well as of Republicans and Democrats, and it emerges from the voters' own self-contradictory policy preferences. A full statement of the argument may be found in Jacobson (1990a, Chapter 6). Its basic point is that voters face a standard collective goods dilemma that is resolved, not necessarily consciously, by voting for Republican presidents and Democratic congresses.

Majorities plainly and quite understandably desire some broad collective goods: low tax rates, a balanced budget, low inflation, a less-meddlesome government, adequate national defense. Aside from defense, all of these goods presumably contribute to economic efficiency, itself a quintessential collective good, and hence to another—economic growth. But just as understandably, majorities prefer to avoid paying the costs of achieving these goods: cuts in government programs and benefits, higher unemployment, greater exposure to market forces, greater environmental risk. These costs are more narrowly focused, and they outweigh the benefits of the broader collective goods to those who get stuck with them. People rationally prefer a job to lower inflation, a larger Social Security check or even a local sewage treatment facility to an imperceptibly smaller deficit or tax bill. No one has an incentive to sacrifice income or personal or local benefits to greater economic efficiency, nor even to risk such a sacrifice if the risk is appreciable.

In the past decade or so, the parties have taken positions that allow voters to express both sets of preferences at the polls: They can vote

for Republican presidential candidates committed to the diffuse collective goods of low taxes, economic efficiency, and a strong national
defense, and for congressional Democrats who promise to minimize
the price they have to pay for these goods in terms of foregone benefits
and protections.

The basis of this sort of ticket splitting is evident in the way the
public views the strengths of the two parties. During the 1980s,
Republicans were judged to be better than Democrats at ensuring
prosperity, handling inflation, reducing the deficit (at least until 1988),
maintaining a strong defense, and, between 1984 and 1988, keeping
the nation out of war. Democrats were thought to be better at handling
unemployment, protecting Social Security benefits, dealing with farm
problems, handling the problem of toxic wastes, improving education,
and helping the poor and the middle class. Democrats were also
considered more likely to create a fair budget and tax system, and they
were perceived as more attentive to groups stuck with the bill for the
collective benefits of greater economic efficiency and growth: women,
union members, farmers, blacks, and "people like you." Republicans
were thought to be more solicitous only of "big business" and "the
rich" (Jacobson 1990a).

Perceived differences between the parties coincide with differences
in what people expect of presidents and members of Congress, which,
in turn, reflect differences in the political incentives created by their
respective institutional positions. Presidents are supposed to pursue
broad national interests; uniquely among elected officials, they can
profit politically by conferring diffuse collective benefits at the expense
of concentrated particular interests. Members of Congress, in contrast,
survive by looking out for the particular because this is what voters
want from them.

This combination of partisan and institutional expectations strength-
ens Republican presidential candidates, especially when they are given
superior marks for personal competence, which presumably enhances
their ability to deliver desired collective goods. It also helps congressional Democrats because people want representatives who will protect
them from damaging policies, regardless of the policies' broader benefits.

By this argument, then, it is not so much that voters balance Democrats
in one branch against Republicans in the other to get a government
closer to their centrist views but that majorities prefer a president
committed to a set of diffuse collective goods and congressional
representatives committed to minimizing the local or personal costs
of achieving them. This requires neither egregious cynicism nor even
conscious calculation on the part of voters. Offered two presidential
candidates, voters choose the one they think more likely to keep taxes

low and defense strong and to govern competently. Offered two House candidates, voters choose the one they think more likely to deliver local benefits and to protect their favorite programs. Voters need not even recognize that the decisions are interdependent.

My argument is that decisions are framed rather differently in presidential and House elections, with the presidency contested on Republican turf and the House, on Democratic turf. Voters simply use different standards for judging presidential and congressional candidates. The literature on voting behavior is broadly consistent with this claim. Presidential candidates are evaluated according to their positions on major national issues involving peace and prosperity and their competence in dealing with national problems (Popkin et al. 1976; Kiewiet and Rivers 1985), and congressional candidates are evaluated on their personal character and experience and on their devotion to district services and local needs (Jacobson 1991b).

Voting Decisions in 1988

The 1988 American National Election Study provides a further opportunity to test this notion by comparing the components that shaped presidential and House voting.[5] In one set of questions, respondents were asked what they thought was "the most important single problem the country faces" and which, if either, party "would be most likely to get the government to do a better job in dealing with [the] problem." They were also asked what they thought was "the single most important issue" in the House campaign and which, if either, candidate they tended to prefer because of the issue.[6] Responses were coded by type of problem or issue, with the same coding scheme applied to the answers to both questions.

Responses to both sets of questions were strongly linked to vote choice; 94 percent of the respondents who thought one of the parties would do a better job on the "most important problem" voted for the presidential candidate of that party, and 97 percent of the respondents preferring a House candidate on the "most important issue" voted for that candidate. Although few voters held conflicting partisan positions on these two questions (22, 2 percent of the sample of voters), 64 percent of them split their tickets in the expected direction. Only 1 of the 93 voters (composing 10 percent of the sample) whose positions on two questions were consistent cast a split ballot. In between were voters who favored either a party or House candidate on one question but did not differentiate the parties (or candidates) on the other (45 percent of the sample); 24 percent of them split their tickets, with 95

TABLE 4.5   The "Most Important Problem" and "Most Important Issue," 1988 (percentages)

	Perceive Party Difference on Problem	Better Party:		National Problem	District Issue
		Democratic	Republican		
Democrats much better on:					
Environment	27.2	88.9	11.1	5.6	10.3
Domestic policy	55.3	76.8	23.2	19.7	30.9
Economy	58.1	60.7	39.3	9.0	15.1
Subtotal				34.3	56.3
Republicans better on:					
Crime	39.6	44.4	55.1	19.3	15.5
Functions of government	43.8	42.9	57.1	1.4	10.1
Subtotal				20.7	25.6
Republicans much better on:					
Defense/foreign affairs	59.6	32.4	67.6	9.8	3.5
Budget deficit	47.3	32.3	67.7	34.2	8.3
Abortion	85.7	25.0	75.0	1.2	6.3
Subtotal				45.2	18.1

Source: 1988 American National Election Study.

percent voting in accord with their party or candidate preference on the relevant question.

Table 4.5 presents the distribution of responses to the two questions. The first four columns are taken from the question on the most important national problem. The first column lists the proportion of respondents mentioning a problem in each category who thought one of the parties would do a better job. The second and third columns give the partisan breakdown of their responses; note that the categories are ranked from most pro-Democratic to most pro-Republican. The fourth column lists the percentage of problems mentioned that fell into each general category, and the fifth column gives the same breakdown for House election issues.

Table 4.5 reveals notable differences between what voters regard as the most important national problems and what they consider to be the most important issues in House elections. Moreover, things mentioned more frequently as national problems clearly play to the Republicans' strength, and things mentioned more frequently as district issues play to the Democrats' strength. For example, more than a third of the respondents thought that the budget deficit was the most important national problem, and of those who thought one of the parties would do a better job on it (47.3 percent), more than two-thirds favored the

Republicans. But only 8.3 percent said the deficit was the most important issue in the House campaign. So, although it helped Bush, this issue was of little benefit to Republican House candidates.

Similarly, the Republicans' advantage in foreign and defense matters did not help the party's House candidates much because it was so rarely considered the most important issue. On the other hand, the Democrats' advantage on domestic problems (mainly education, unemployment, housing, and other social welfare issues) and the environment availed them far more in House elections than in the presidential election in 1988.

Models of voting in the 1988 presidential and House elections also reveal differences in how issues shape the choice in the two kinds of elections. The questions in Table 4.6 model the vote as a function of party identification and responses to four questions concerning party superiority (on handling the most important issue, keeping us out of war, and doing what the respondent wanted done on taxes and Social Security), three issue-proximity measures (which, if either, party is closer to the respondent on each issue), and two assessments of Ronald Reagan's performance as president. Incumbency status is included, for obvious reasons, as a control variable in the equation for House voting. (A description of the variable may be found in the appendix.)

Although all eight issue variables are mildly collinear with one another (that is, their effects overlap), each had a separable impact on the probability that the respondent would vote for the Democratic candidate, Michael Dukakis, with six of the eight coefficients achieving statistical significance and the remaining two displaying the expected sign (positive on the party variables, negative on approval of Reagan's performance), with coefficients larger than their standard errors. Respondents' views of which party is better able to handle the most important issue had the largest effect on the presidential vote; we can calculate from its coefficient (.844) that voters who, on other grounds, would have a .5 probability of voting for the Democratic candidate, would have a .8 probability of voting for Dukakis if they thought the Democrats would handle the most important problem better but only a .2 probability of voting for Dukakis if they thought the Republicans would handle it better.

Among House voters, in contrast, only proximity on the medical insurance scale and general approval of Reagan's performance were significantly related to the vote. Social Security was the only remaining variable whose coefficient approaches statistical significance at the conventional $p<.05$ level. The largest coefficient on any of the issue variables (medical insurance, .223) indicates that a .5 probability of voting for the Democratic candidate would increase to .59 if the

74

TABLE 4.6   Determinants of the Vote for President and House, 1988 (probit estimates)

Variable	President	House
Intercept	.144	.347[a]
	(.079)	(.094)
Party identification	.586[a]	.633[a]
	(.068)	(.071)
Democratic incumbent		.629[a]
		(.115)
Republican incumbent		−1.180[a]
		(.139)
Party better on:		
Most important issue	.844[a]	.126
	(.110)	(.092)
Keeping out of war	.261[b]	−.102
	(.112)	(.100)
Taxes	.124	.090
	(.091)	(.075)
Social Security	.188	.189
	(.120)	(.112)
Party closer on:		
Spending/services scale	.234[a]	.084
	(.088)	(.080)
Medical insurance scale	.186[b]	.223[c]
	(.091)	(.078)
Defense spending scale	.201[b]	.019
	(.086)	(.077)
Cooperation with Russia scale	.206[b]	.096
	(.099)	(.084)
Approve Reagan's performance	−.479[a]	−.206[c]
	(.080)	(.077)
Reagan's policies improved economy	−.264[a]	.049
	(.087)	(.082)
Log likelihood	−300	−409
Number of cases	1,192	1,050

Note: For a description of the variables and coding, see the appendix.
Standard errors are in parentheses.

[a]p < .001, two-tailed test.
[b]p < .05, two-tailed test.
[c]p < .01, two-tailed test.

respondent's views on medical insurance were closer to the Democrats' and decrease to .41 if they were closer to the Republicans'. In House races, the usual factors of incumbency, name familiarity, and candidate evaluations dominated the decision (equation not shown; see also Jacobson 1991b), but those issues that did influence the choice arose from domestic welfare matters such as medical care and Social Security. The parties' reputations on matters concerning defense and foreign affairs do not appear to have influenced House voting at all.

Voters, then, employed different criteria for choosing a president and a representative in 1988. The criteria that shaped their presidential choice favored the Republican candidate, George Bush; the criteria that governed their House choice favored the Democrats.

Differences between what voters want and expect from presidents and representatives point to part of the explanation for the Republicans' curious inability to field more of the high-quality congressional challengers we would expect to represent an ascendant party. The view of government that has served Republican presidential candidates so well clashes with the realities of what it takes to win and hold seats in Congress. For the most part, congressional careers are built on delivering particularized benefits to constituents, not on dismantling, in the name of efficiency and economy, programs that create the benefits. Members are elected to minimize the local cost of producing national collective goods, not to pursue visions of the national interest regardless of local consequences. Thus, any Republican seriously embracing the minimalist conception of government underlying the Reagan revolution is unlikely to view a career in Congress as attractive or satisfying. If government is the problem, not the solution, why pursue a career in politics that can only succeed if you become part of the problem? Those Republicans most strongly attracted to the party's conservative ideology are, by that very fact, ill suited to the politics of congressional elections.

The view of government held by most Democrats is, in contrast, far more positive. Their conception of the federal government's role justifies assistance to all sorts of groups for all sorts of purposes. To Democrats, government remains an honorable calling, and the activities sustaining a congressional career continue to be socially valuable. Democrats thus have far less trouble fielding attractive, experienced challengers who are comfortable with the demands of contemporary electoral politics.

Strategic Politics Under Divided Government

What voters seem to want from representatives leaves Republican House candidates at a general disadvantage on some of the very same dimensions that benefit Republican presidential candidates; it also discourages talented Republican politicians from pursuing careers in Congress. A Party unable to mobilize talented challengers with effective issues can hardly be expected to take over the House. Still, it could be argued that short-term conditions specific to the most recent set of elections were nonetheless sufficiently promising to have attracted ambitious Republican challengers. Economic growth, presidential politics, international developments, and Republican gains among party identifiers certainly ought to have been conducive to Republican success in elections from 1984 through 1988. But on closer investigation, conditions may, in fact, have offered Republican challengers little leverage against congressional Democrats, reinforcing the reluctance of ambitious, experienced Republicans to run.

Under divided government, the very success of the Republican administration deprives Republican congressional challengers of arguments to use against Democratic incumbents. Divided control of the federal government splits responsibility for success or failure, as well. If the public mood is positive, if peace and prosperity reign, incumbents of both parties can claim a share of the credit. A campaign for reelection (or to elect a sitting vice president) that promotes themes of affirmation and continuity gives congressional challengers from the president's party little rhetorical ammunition. How do you make a case for throwing out the rascals in Congress when you're telling voters, "Don't worry, be happy?"

The historical pattern of electoral swings since the New Deal realignment bears out this intuition. Table 4.7 shows how partisan representation in the House has changed under three levels of presidential success. The difference in House seats is measured from the previous presidential election, not from the immediately preceding midterm, because I am concerned with changes over the course of the entire administration; the relative contribution of the midterm and presidential elections to the total is beside this point. Elections held in circumstances of divided party control (when at least one house of Congress is controlled by the other party at the time of the election) are marked with an asterisk.

Failed presidencies—those followed by a switch in party control of the White House—invariably cost the president's party a substantial number of House seats, and this happens regardless of whether or not the president's party also controls the House. When a party has relinquished the presidency in the postwar era, it has won, on average, 46 fewer House seats than it won in the previous presidential election year. When a party has retained the presidency but with a smaller share of the vote than before, it has also lost House seats—with the notable exception of the Democrats in 1948.

TABLE 4.7   House Seat Swings Between Presidential Elections, 1932–1988

Presidential Success	House Seat Swing to or from President's Party[a]
President's party relinquished White House	
1932[b]	−150
1952	−50
1960[b]	−28
1968	−52
1976[b]	−50
1980	−49
President's party retained White House with reduced vote	
1940	−66
1944	−24
1948[b]	20
1988[b]	−7
President reelected with increased vote	
1936	20
1956[b]	−20
1964	33
1972[b]	0
1984[b]	−10

[a]The seat swing is measured from presidential election year to presidential election year; see the text.
[b]Elections held in circumstances of divided party control.

The most successful presidencies have produced additional House seats for the president's party under unified government but not when control is split between the parties. The landslide reelections of Franklin D. Roosevelt in 1936 and Lyndon Johnson in 1964 raised Democratic House majorities above the levels reached in the previous presidential elections. The Republican landslides of 1956, 1972, and 1984, however, left the Republicans with the same number or fewer House seats than they had won when the Republican president was first elected.

Of the five elections held under circumstances of divided party control in which the president's party retained the White House, only that in 1948 left the president's party stronger in the House than it had been four years earlier. The 1948 election was also the only one of this set that was held amidst widespread public discontent and that did not feature a highly personalized, "feel-good" presidential campaign. Truman sought, with evident success, to saddle the Republican Congress with blame for inflation and economic difficulties (strikes, dislocations produced by the transition to a peacetime economy), as well as for threatening popular New Deal programs, and congressional Democrats were the beneficiaries.

In historical perspective, then, the Republicans' inability to match or exceed the 192 House seats they won in 1980 in any of the subsequent four elections is not so surprising. The recession of 1982 hurt, as midterm recessions always do. But the years of prosperity that followed the recession, though contributing strongly to victories by Reagan in 1984 and Bush in 1988, did not leave Republican congressional challengers with persuasive arguments that could be used to unseat Democratic incumbents.

I do not wish to make too much of these data. The available observations do not distinguish clearly between outcomes deriving from divided control and simple partisan differences (for example, all of the highly successful presidencies occurring under divided control were Republican; those occurring under unified control were Democratic). The point remains, however, that the logic of retrospective voting (Fiorina 1981), applied in circumstances of divided control, does not offer much encouragement to congressional Republicans when Republican administrations produce good times, but it continues to promise punishment when these administrations fail to do so. And if prospective Republican challengers could find no way to make the public angry at House Democrats during the Reagan-Bush years, sitting tight was a rational strategy. The dearth of vigorous Republican challenges in recent elections may thus reflect strategic decisions predicated on a shortage of exploitable issues, as well as the more generic impediment raised by the party's ideology of government.

Party Coalitions

The different expectations voters have of presidents and representatives turn some Democratic presidential liabilities into congressional assets. Democratic presidential candidates in recent years have suffered from the perception that their party is subservient to a host of unfashionable "special interests," including organized labor, racial minorities, feminists, teachers, homosexuals, and other liberal activists (Miller, Hildreth, and Wlezien 1988). They have also suffered from the taint of "liberalism," portrayed as an inclination to tax and spend, as an excessive tolerance of social deviance, and as a doubtful commitment to law and order at home and to U.S. interests abroad. All these perceptions left serious doubts about a Democratic president's ability to deliver the kinds of collective goods people desire from the chief executive.

Moreover, Democratic presidential candidates face a daunting task in trying to build a national coalition out of mutually antagonistic groups: blacks, Hispanics, Jews, working-class whites, feminists, southern traditionalists, and affluent college-educated liberals. And they are handicapped in this endeavor by a nominating process that rewards candidates who can mobilize factions at the expense of those who attempt to build coalitions (Polsby 1983).

Congressional Democrats, on the other hand, are free to assemble local coalitions that may or may not include groups important to the party nationally. They can run as staunch friends of organized labor, civil rights activists, feminists, or the environmental movement when this adds votes, and they can avoid such alliances when it does not. A wide range of ideological stances is available to them; southern Democrats, for example, can present themselves credibly as military hawks regardless of their party's national image. A fragmented, decentralized electoral process allows congressional Democrats to turn a severe national problem—diversity and discord—to local advantage. Moreover, Democrats suffer little damage from the charge that they are too solicitous of special interests because members of Congress are *expected* to serve special interests—those of their constituents. The same image that hurts presidential Democrats may, in this way, actually help congressional Democrats.

Conversely, the benefit Republican presidential candidates derive from perceptions that their party is better at promoting economic efficiency and growth, as well as other diffuse national goods, may not extend to Republican congressional candidates at all if they can be portrayed as caring more about national issues than local needs.

CONCLUSION: AN OSSIFIED CONGRESS?

The high reelection rate of House incumbents in the four most recent elections, perpetuating the Democrats' seemingly unassailable majority, has been portrayed by some observers as a failure of democracy. They contend that the overwhelming advantages of incumbency, financial and otherwise, deprive voters of meaningful choices; the dearth of closely fought contests makes voting pointless in a large majority of districts. The low turnover of seats in 1988, according to the president of Common Cause, Fred Wertheimer, "simply reflects the fact that we don't have elections in the House of Representatives any more" (Rovner 1988, 3362). Moreover, he said, "if you don't have real elections, you don't have accountability. Democracy starts with elections, and if you have a rigged system, you don't have a representative government" (Rovner 1988, 3365). Thus, changes in public preferences expressed in presidential voting and in polling on party identification are echoed only faintly, if at all, in congressional elections. And divided party control of the federal government is seen as an artifact of a structure rigged to prevent Republicans from winning their rightful share of congressional seats.

The evidence, however, points to a rather different conclusion. The roots of divided government are political, not structural. The Democrats' continuing control of Congress expresses, rather than thwarts, the popular will. Electoral swings have been modest in recent elections because national conditions and issues have not been conducive to change. Anticipating little help from the political climate, neither party has mounted more than a handful of strong challenges.[7] It is scarcely surprising, then, that inexperienced Republican challengers who lack adequate funds and profitable issues should fail to defeat Democratic incumbents, regardless of what happens in the presidential election.

Obviously, it would be a mistake to infer from recent House elections that incumbents—Democrats or Republicans—have become immune to national tides if, in fact, no national tides were running or if they avoided challengers capable of exploiting them. We only learn the true measure of an incumbent's strength when it is tested under adverse conditions by a vigorous challenge. The end-of-competition view is remarkably myopic; adequately financed challengers wielding potent issues swept a total of 49 incumbents out of office in 1980 and 1982. There is no reason to believe that such swings would not happen again under similar conditions. Indeed, the example of 1980, in which 27 incumbent Democrats were defeated (including 8 who had served more than 9 terms) shows how fragile political support may be for even ostensibly entrenched incumbents in an era of fickle electorates.

There is, however, good reason to believe that the effect of both national and local issues is less automatic and more contingent today than it was in earlier decades. The increasingly fragmented, candidate-centered style of electoral politics that has emerged during the postwar period has not made issues irrelevant, nor has it insulated incumbent members of Congress from national tides (Jacobson 1987 and 1990a). It has, however, made the impact of issues more dependent on how candidates exploit them. Incumbents clearly find it easier now to escape the consequences of bad times or other threatening circumstances if they can manage to avoid challengers with the skills and resources to tag them with a share of the blame and present an acceptable alternative. Hence, for example, the anti-incumbent and anti-Republican mood of the electorate in 1990 did not produce large-scale changes in House representation because so few credible challengers were in the field when the mood took hold (see Figure 4.1 and Jacobson [1991a]).

Voters are not willing to throw rascals out without knowing something about the rascals they would, at the same time, be throwing in. This means that unless its strategic politicians anticipate emerging oppor-

TABLE 4.8   Public Opinion on Divided Control of the Federal Government, 1981 and 1989 (percentages)

Do you think it is better for the country to have a president who comes from the same political party that controls Congress, or do you think it is better to have a president from one political party and Congress controlled by another?

	November 1981	September 1989
Same party	47	35
Different parties	34	45
Don't know	19	20

Source: New York Times/CBS News Poll surveys of specified date.

tunities and act accordingly, the party favored by national conditions will not benefit as much as it would have when the party cues were more decisive (Jacobson 1990a). It also means that a party suffering a shortage of attractive challengers will derive smaller benefit from favorable secular trends.

Will divided government continue in its current form? The politics that generate it make persistence likely. Democratic congresses and Republican presidencies reinforce one another. Voters need not consciously divide control of government between the two parties for divided control to influence their voting decisions. Democratic majorities in Congress make a Republican presidential candidate's promise (however ephemeral) of "no new taxes" more appealing; at the same time, people may feel more comfortable voting for a Republican president knowing that the Democrats in Congress will keep him from gutting their favorite programs. Conversely, it becomes more difficult to persuade voters to boot Democrats out of Congress when there is a Republican in the White House to control their collective excesses. Finally, familiarity has only increased public acceptance of divided government, as Table 4.8 demonstrates.

Credit for good times is shared, so incumbent Democrats are not threatened by successful Republican administrations. Indeed, the only serious threat to congressional Democrats in the past four decades has come from failed Democratic administrations (Jacobson 1990a). More than a grain of truth resides in Robert Erikson's (1989) delightfully ironic demonstration that losing the presidency is a rational strategy for congressional Democrats. In this light, the most plausible scenario for ending divided government is for a Democrat to win the presidency. All it takes is for a Republican administration to stumble badly and for the Democrats to nominate an acceptable alternative; neither is guaranteed, but neither is unimaginable. Indeed, if the analysis in this essay is on target, a Democratic presidency is also the only scenario offering Republicans much hope of making substantial gains, let alone winning majorities, in the House during the remainder of this century.

APPENDIX

The variables for the probit equations in Table 4.6 were constructed from the following 1988 ANES questions (the variable number is in parentheses):

- Presidential vote: 1 if for Dukakis, 0 if for Bush (763)
- House vote: 1 if Democratic, 0 if Republican (768)
- Party better on most important issue: 1 if Democrats, -1 if Republicans, 0 if neither (819)
- Party better at keeping out of war: 1 if Democrats, -1 if Republicans, 0 if neither (253)
- Taxes: 1 if Democrats closer to respondent's position, -1 if Republicans closer, 0 if neither is closer; from combination of responses to questions on which party is more likely to raise taxes (354) and whether respondent is willing to pay more taxes to reduce deficit (249)
- Social Security: 1 if Democrats closer to respondent's position, -1 if Republicans closer, 0 if neither is closer; from a combination of responses to questions on whether respondent wanted spending on Social Security increased or decreased (348) and which party he or she thought more likely to cut it (353)
- Proximity variables: 1 if Democrats closer to respondent's position, -1 if Republicans closer, 0 if neither is closer; from placements of respondent, Democratic party, and Republican party on 7-point scales:

  Spending versus services (302, 307, 308)
  Medical insurance (318, 321, 322)
  Defense spending (310, 315, 316)
  Cooperation with Russia (368, 373, 374)

- Approve Reagan's performance: 1 if approve, -1 if disapprove, 0 if neither (1042)
- Reagan's policies improved economy: 1 if policies made the economy better, -1 if worse, 0 if neither (1032)

NOTES

This essay was completed while I was a fellow at the Center for Advanced Study in the Behavioral Sciences, Stanford, and I am grateful for the support of the center and its fine staff and for financial support provided by the National Science Foundation ENS-8700864. I am also obliged to Gary Cox and Samuel Kernell for helpful comments. Some of the data used here were made available by the Inter-University Consortium for Political and Social Research. The data for the American National Election Study, 1988: Pre- and Post-Election Survey were originally collected by Warren E. Miller and the National Election Studies. Neither the collector of the original data nor the consortium bears any responsibility for the analyses or interpretations presented here.

1. The cumulative results of seven *New York Times*/CBS News Polls conducted during 1989 (N = 8,179) found 46 percent of the respondents calling themselves Democrats and 44 percent calling themselves Republicans (*San Diego Union,* January 21, 1990, p. A-10).

2. The swing ratio is commonly estimated by regressing the percentage of seats on the percentage of votes won by a party over a series of elections; the regression coefficient measures the swing ratio. Most studies have measured a party's vote as the share of total votes cast nationwide for major party candidates (Tufte 1973; Ferejohn and Calvert 1984; Jacobson 1987). Ansolabehere, Brady, and Fiorina measure it as a party's mean district vote share and include uncontested seats in their analysis, assigning the winners 100 percent of the vote. The partisan distribution of uncontested seats changes substantially over time, however, and the distortion introduced by measuring the independent variable this way is the source of the projected Republican "majorities." See Jacobson (1990a, 83–89).

3. In 1990, for the first time in the postwar era, the mean swing favored challengers of *both* parties, though the mean swing to Democratic challengers was greater (3.7 percentage points) than that to Republican challengers (2.0 percentage points). See Jacobson (1991a).

4. The questions are: (No. 955) "How much of the time do you think you can trust the government in Washington to do what is right—just about always, most of the time, or only some of the time?"; (No. 956) "Do you think that people in government waste a lot of the money we pay in taxes, waste some of it, or don't waste very much of it?"; (No. 957) "Would you say the government is pretty much run by a few big interests looking out for themselves or that it is run for the benefit of all the people?"; (No. 958) "Do you think that quite a few of the people running the government are crooked, not very many are, or do you think hardly any of them are crooked?"; (No. 959) "How much do you feel that having elections makes the government pay attention to what the people think—a good deal, some, or not much?"; (No. 960) "Over the years, how much attention do you feel the government pays to what people think when it decides what to do—a good deal, some, or not much?" (W. Miller et al. 1989).

5. As usual, ANES respondents overreport voting for House incumbents, so the analysis in this section cannot be as definitive as I would like.

6. These are questions 817, 819, 702, and 704, respectively, in the 1988 ANES Codebook (W. Miller et al. 1989).

7. The 1990 election is something of a special case. A strong anti-incumbent trend and a milder anti-Republican trend developed just before this election, but their electoral effects were muted by the general absence of credible challengers of either party because the events of the fall could not be anticipated at the time when final decisions about candidacy were being made. See Jacobson (1991a).

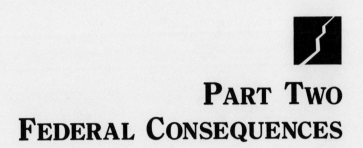

PART TWO
FEDERAL CONSEQUENCES

5

FACING AN OPPOSITION CONGRESS: THE PRESIDENT'S STRATEGIC CIRCUMSTANCE

Samuel Kernell

Our understanding of presidential leadership has primarily been acquired by studying the successes of presidents who presided over unified governments. It is here, after all, where one finds the most dramatic instances of success, even, at moments, mastery. The president proposes clear departures from the status quo; they are enacted substantially intact by Congress and faithfully implemented by the bureaucracy. Even the lesser success stories that fill the lore of presidential leadership are skewed toward settings of unified party control. Whether measured by passage of the administration's legislative program, the unfettered pursuit of foreign policy, or simply by managing to complete one's tenure free from scandal, the president's prospects of success improve directly with his party's control of Congress. We look to Franklin Roosevelt and Lyndon Johnson for lessons of presidential leadership, not to Dwight Eisenhower or even, despite his recent admirers, to Harry Truman and certainly not to Richard Nixon.

Yet, this is an era of divided government. With the exception of a single Democratic term—barely won and easily lost—divided government has fixed Washington's political relations for the past quarter of a century in ways quite at odds with those of unified party control. Of course, much more is involved than simply the numbers of representatives and senators disposed to carp at the president's performance and policies. The institutional control that comes with majority status elevates the opposition party's policy preferences to a level on a par with or above those of the president and his party. Divided government vests with each party a veto over the other's pursuit of policy in legislation and administration. It requires us to rethink presidential leadership. How does the switch from stable unified party control to stable divided party control alter the ways in which presidents strive for leadership?

To answer this question, I begin by reviewing what the prevailing wisdom on the presidency has to say about implications of party control of the legislature. Grounded in pluralist conceptions of the office and U.S. politics generally, this literature offers surprisingly little guidance. Party control of Congress is largely ignored, which should not be too surprising given that most of the still influential scholarship on the presidency occurred during the 1950s and 1960s, when instances of divided party control were still regarded as aberrations. This means that to assess the consequences of divided control on the presidency, I shall need to lay out explicitly the effects of competing political parties on presidential-congressional relations in both of these settings.

Under divided government, presidents must employ methods that do not require the active cooperation of Congress. Accordingly, appeals to the public for support for the president and his policies and centralized administration of the executive branch are foremost trends in presidential leadership. Nowhere is the distinction between unified and divided party control more apparent than in the value of the veto in these two settings. It is simply the one fundamental and concrete authority available to a president dealing with an opposition Congress. And yet, it has little relevance in terms of helping a president under unified party control solve his problem of finding a common ground on which the party can unify. By carefully examining the formal properties of the veto, we can better appreciate the structure of modern relations between the president and Congress.

PLURALIST THEORY OF THE PRESIDENCY

The social pluralism of the nation and the institutional pluralism of the governmental system mean that virtually every public policy that will be adopted has accumulated a history rich in exchange and compromise. Among politicians, hardly any political relations exist that are not similarly founded on reciprocity and bargaining. "The politician," wrote Robert A. Dahl and Charles E. Lindblom in 1953, is an individual "whose career depends upon the successful negotiation of bargains— it is the skill that distinguishes the master-politician from the political failure" (1953, 333). Bargaining as the necessary, ubiquitous activity of politicians implies two things about the political community: First, the actors who jointly control the outcome of a policy decision hold differing preferences, and second, these differences are reconcilable through mutual adjustment.[1]

Let us begin with the latter, about which pluralist theory has more to say. Some have argued that a general consensus over goals and means makes compromise of policy differences easier in the United States than in most other democracies (Lipset 1963). However similar their predictions, such cultural statements are unnecessary to the pluralist argument. The constitutional system guarantees one side will rarely prevail outright over the other. Therefore, compromise will be the norm, if only because it is the sole method available to politicians to achieve their goals.

The Constitution's separation of powers, its checks and balances, and its federalism have spawned a multitude of forms of mutual adjustment. Their variety is well represented in America's political lexicon: Logrolling, horse trading, IOUs, and splitting the difference are a few. Proceeding along these lines, bargaining should be regarded as essentially a cooperative enterprise. Certainly, there will be relative winners and losers, but the system of exchange endures presumably because all of the participants are satisfied with its benefits. One important reason for this is that the Constitution and early federal law conveniently segment representation into mutually exclusive states and districts so that politicians within the legislature do not directly compete with one another. There is little reason for conflict, except, perhaps, for greed and the other human foibles that surface whenever a pie is being divided.

The only means of influence proscribed by pluralist theory is coercion. As Dahl and Lindblom noted, "The politician does not often give orders. He can rarely employ unilateral controls. Even as chief executive or a cabinet officer he soon discovers that his control depends upon his skill in bargaining" (1953, 333). Even if politicians or bureaucrats enjoy hierarchical superiority over one another or in some other way could unilaterally preempt another's choice, they should hesitate to use this advantage. That force begets counterforce is a law of political physics. Politicians may be able to avoid tendering compensation one day, but they cannot insure themselves against retribution the next.

Nowhere has the bargaining politician in the United States received a more articulate description than in Richard E. Neustadt's (1980, 28–29) classic treatise on the presidency, originally published in 1960. He observed,

> Status and authority yield bargaining advantages. But in a government of "separated institutions sharing powers," they yield them to all sides. With the array of vantage points at his disposal, a President may be far more persuasive than his logic or his charm could make him. But outcomes are not guaranteed by his advantages. There remain the counter pressures those whom he would influence can bring to bear on him from vantage points at their disposal. Command has limited utility; persuasion becomes give-and-take. . . .
>
> The President's advantages are checked by the advantages of others. Continuing relationships will pull in both directions. These are relationships of mutual dependence. A President depends upon the men he would persuade; he has to reckon with his need or fear of them. They too will possess status, or authority, or both, else they would be of little use to him. Their vantage points confront his own; their power tempers his.[2]

The president is doubtless the Washington community's most prominent and active dealmaker. In addition to his considerable constitutional and statutory assets, the president's appeal to other politicians derives, in large part, from his capacity to provide them with much-needed coordination in assembling coalitions across a broad institutional landscape. Although, as Neustadt reminded us, this task guarantees no more than that he will be everyone else's "clerk," it clearly affords the virtuoso bargainer in the White House an opportunity to parlay real leadership.

The sources and nature of policy disagreements among politicians are less well developed in the literature than are the mechanisms for their resolution. We can stipulate, however, that the policy preferences politicians represent will derive from their constituencies and offices. An important, often-noted feature that distinguishes the priorities of executive from legislative politicians is their dissimilar electoral calendars. A politician's willingness to make unpopular decisions will be inversely related to the time until the next election. Election schedules set in motion the different political rhythms of presidents, senators, and representatives. Otherwise like-minded but differently situated politicians will frequently take different stances on policy questions.

Differences also inhere in the responsibilities of the office and in the needs of constituents. Both incline the president to view policy issues more broadly than legislators do for he alone represents the nation. From the president to the lobbyist, the breadth of politicians' concerns will follow the dictates of the size and homogeneity of their constituencies. Though the distinction can be overstated, these structural differences incline presidents to adopt a more national, public goods orientation to policy questions, while members of Congress must vigilantly weigh a policy's selective costs and benefits for the local constituencies they serve.

The variety of policy perspectives has long been recognized by pluralist theory, but rather than representing a source of conflict, it is exalted as providing a felicitous division of labor. The president is in a position to shoulder principle responsibility for policies that impose costs. Members of Congress, bureaucrats, and others who represent organized constituencies perform an equally valuable service of adapting public policy to the preferences of those whose interests are most affected. Because no actor can claim synoptic rationality, an arrangement that maximizes participation by interested parties not only meets the politicians' different representational requirements, it also makes for good public policy (Braybrooke and Lindblom 1967).

In various ways, pluralist theory constrains the president's efforts to centralize policymaking. This is achieved mainly by denying him sufficient authority to impose his preferences on others. All the Constitution guarantees is that the president will be the most important administrator in the government. To enjoy a measure of success, he must have cooperation from others. This means he must be diligent in providing the goods and services they require. Typically, this takes the form of a distributional game. The president submits national policy, and Congress parcels its divisible parts to the districts and states in the form of contracts, grants, and federal facilities. Even such collective goods as national defense routinely undergo the reconciliation of national and parochial interests. Thus, for example, the navy incorporates political as much as military strategy in its policy to spread out its aircraft carriers so that rarely will two be located at the same port (H. Smith 1989).

A PARTY THEORY OF THE PRESIDENCY

Thus far, I have said little about the place of political parties in fixing relations between Congress and the president—and much less about the special tensions introduced by divided party control. This is because pluralist theory, from which the prevailing view of the presidency is derived, does not offer a clear rationale for political parties. The presidency literature is no exception in this regard. Office and constituency, not political party, are presented as defining the stakes of politicians and their policy differences. These institutional features, not political party, drive the adjustment process toward resolution. To the degree that political parties constrain individual choice in favor of some collective product, they limit the variety of political transactions that can occur.[3] Pluralist theory envisions Washington as the center of a barter economy in which politicians individually engage each other in a commerce of votes, favors, services, and the like to achieve their separate goals. To the extent that party leadership is examined at all, it is typically presented as simply one more source of assets the president can trade on.

A party theory of presidential leadership incorporates much of the pluralist depiction of American politics, if not its underlying rationale. To continue the market analogy, a party model introduces "firms" into the economy. By organizing into political parties, politicians reduce costs both in producing policies and in advertising them to voters. Political parties would be efficient even if their members were only engaged in gleaning local goods from national policy originated else-where. But, in fact, they are vital in producing these goods for which there is a ready market in the electorate—goods that officeholders, individually, are poorly equipped to supply or claim credit for.

Politicians, including the president, act less as individual entrepreneurs than as members of a corporate enterprise. Much of their day-to-day activity resembles that portrayed by pluralist theory. Party politicians bargain with one another in a collective and essentially cooperative search for mutually acceptable policy. A couple of important differences are worth noting, however. The transactions principally occur within the party, and the president's special niche in the division of labor—championing collective goods—is not so pronounced. Instead, all party members share his interest in identifying electorally attractive collective goods.

Across parties, relations are quite different from those envisioned by pluralist theory. The reason, of course, is that rather than pluralist theory's segmentation of constituencies, the parties compete for the same offices. Now, one politician's interest will conflict with another's. At stake are offices and, with them, control over institutions. Majority rule replaces universalism; competition replaces cooperation.

Political parties present themselves to voters as teams. How and how well they arrive at a common platform depend on mechanisms of mutual adjustment, much like those described by pluralist theory. For the representative, the party's positions on national issues ideally would perfectly match those of the constituency. The greater the discrepancy between them, the less loyal the politician can afford to be to his or her party. This suggests a strategic relation between the politician and the party. In making a claim on a member's loyalty, party leaders can seek to offset any electoral liability posed by the party's policy commitments. They can offer selective benefits that will be abundant with a party victory and presumably less available otherwise, and they can minimize the candidate's exposure to defeat with side payments or job guarantees. Nonetheless, the more diverse the constituencies represented among the party's legislative delegation, the more expensive the costs of gaining allegiance will be and the more difficulty the leaders will have in formulating acceptable issue positions. This discrepancy, inherent in the diversity of the nation, is what leads pluralist theory to discount the capacity for party action and instead treat politicians as independent actors.

Party Policy as a Product of Mutual Adjustment

The variety of policy preferences within a congressional party can be represented statistically as the standard deviation of the median voters' positions around the aggregate mean for those districts (or states) represented by the party. A small standard deviation signifies a homogeneous party and an easier task for the leadership in orchestrating party action. Since the 1950s, as the number of southern Democratic seats in the House of Representatives has declined and those that remain have come to resemble national Democratic constituencies, the party has been able to stake out more forthright positions on issues and entrust its leaders with greater discretion in running the institution and conducting external relations, as with an opposition president (Rohde 1991).

The mean of median voters' preferences identifies the optimal policy for the party's members within the institution. But this introduces another problem for party coordination. What happens when these means, or ideal points, differ across institutions? One might wonder whether this circumstance is likely to occur or be so serious as to impair party members in reaching agreement on public policy. As long as the composition of each institution accurately reflects national opinion, should not any differences in their mean preferences be insignificant?

With the Constitution's framers dead set against the formation of stable, governing political parties (Hoftstader 1969), they created different electoral calendars for the president, senators (for which there are several), and representatives as a way of inducing different preferences among members of these institutions. As the electorate's preferences shift over time, so, too, will the policy stances of those party members they elect. One of the most dramatic effects of these differing calendars is the midterm repudiation of the governing party. During the first half of the twentieth century, this alone provided an entrée to divided government.

Another constitutional source of internal party differences on policy across institutions is malapportionment. The framers fully intended that the House of Representatives would be fairly apportioned. But though early federal statutes granted states full responsibility to redraw district boundaries after each decennial census, no guarantees that this would, indeed, occur were included. As a consequence, many districts would go decades without redistricting despite population change. Until the Supreme Court entered this "political thicket" in the 1960s and strictly applied the "one man, one vote" standard to state redistricting plans, the U.S. House was significantly malapportioned in favor of rural over urban voters. Thanks to judicial intervention, the present-day House now fulfills the framers' expectations of it as the representative branch. As a result, the aggregation of individual constituency preferences should produce a result that squares well with the national median.

The Senate is an altogether different story. With its members elected by the state legislatures until 1914, the Senate as a popular institution is a twentieth-century invention. It was originally intended to house the aristocracy of merit (Wood 1969)—individuals who would protect the national interest from the particularistic claims of the House of Representatives. The main enduring vestige of this original concept is the Senate's serious malapportionment. In fact, it is one of the more malapportioned, fully empowered legislatures in the world today. California receives two representatives for its 30 million citizens, but neighboring Nevada enjoys the same representation for a little over 1 million citizens. More generally, the rural and mountain states are greatly overrepresented in the Senate.

In establishing the electoral college mechanism and leaving it to the states to decide how electors would be selected, the framers intentionally removed election of the president from direct popular control. Even after the plurality of the popular vote was instituted everywhere as the mechanism for deciding the electoral vote, the aggregation of preferences remains biased. The small-state advantage inherent in giving every state two votes in addition to its number of House seats has been eclipsed by the unit rule used in each state, which gives the plurality winner all of the state's electoral votes. As a result, voters in large, urban states have disproportionate impact on the outcome of the election (Brams and Davis 1974; Colantoni, Levesque, and Ordeshook 1975). Presumably, this favors presidential aspirants from the liberal to moderate wings of their political parties.

Finally, the Constitution's provision for the separate election of the executive and the legislature allows other discrepancies in a party's policy preferences to crop up across these institutions. In Chapter 4, Gary Jacobson advances an increasingly fashionable argument: Divided government reflects a voting "rule" adopted by a sizable chunk of the national electorate that results in the election of fiscal conservatives (typically Republican) to the White House who will keep a lid on spending and taxes and local representatives (typically Democrats) who will aggressively bring as much federal expenditures to the district or state as possible. Although it is perfectly rational for the individual voter, such a voting rule is highly pernicious to parties in government. It would install legislators and executives who fall on different ends of the policy continuum for many of those issues that dominate these institutions' transactions with one another. The jury is still out on the question of whether substantial numbers of voters are splitting their ballots with this goal in mind. What can be said at this point is that their choices are consistent with this motivation, and transactions between Congress and the president roughly follow this script. Even Jimmy Carter, the one Democrat to win in the most recent presidential elections, had many of his party colleagues in Congress grousing that his budgets were as fiscally conservative as those of a Republican president.[4]

That U.S. politics install party politicians who embrace different policy preferences is a testament to the framers' success: Frustrating the "tyranny of faction" was, after all, their objective. Had they, instead, sought to facilitate the formation of party teams that could formulate coherent policy across the governing institutions, they could have done so by removing malapportionment (or at least by giving much greater authority to the popular branch) and by scheduling elections to occur at the same time. An even easier means to this end was readily available in Britain's parliamentary arrangements, which the framers studied and rejected.

So, once again, we have offices and constituencies generating policy differences. They restore much of the pluralist dynamic of resolving institutionally based policy preferences through bargaining. Here, however, mutual adjustment occurs within and between political parties, not among members independently. Instead of pluralist theory's rudimentary, largely implicit electoral connection in which politicians behave as the delegates of their constituencies, party teams compete over control of policy in order to gain an advantage in the next election.[5]

Unified and Divided Party Control

When government is unified, the consequential transactions are those aligning and coordinating the preferences of the majority party in the different institutional arenas. Everywhere, the minority party is limited to complaining and little more. Circumstances may occasionally arise that make overtures to individual opposition party politicians necessary, but, for the most part, the president and members of the governing party team work through established protocols to achieve their common policy and electoral interests. Members of the president's party in Congress will give him the benefit of the doubt when they deliberate administration initiatives. Conversely, the president will consult with congressional leaders in order to fashion policy proposals that satisfy the particular concerns of his party colleagues in the legislature. The seemingly ubiquitous reciprocity yielding mutual advantage, celebrated in pluralist scholarship, occurs most often and most consequentially among members of party teams.

For the governing party's leaders to allow internal disagreements to erupt into public discord would be flirting with defeat in the next election. Instead, they engage in quiet diplomacy to make the necessary compromises to give the party at least the semblance of unity. During the twenty-year run of unified Democratic governments under Franklin Roosevelt and Harry Truman (with the exception of 1947–1948), informal party mechanisms of mutual adjustment were the fabled institutions of Washington. The Senate's "Inner Club" was mostly composed of the leaders of the different wings of the Democratic party who consulted one another before undertaking major initiatives. The "Big Four" lunches at the White House on Mondays gave the president and Democratic congressional leaders occasion to fine-tune party positions and to coordinate their institutions' schedules. Most workday afternoons, Speaker Sam Rayburn convened the "Board of Education" in a basement room of the House chamber to sip bourbon and compare notes with party colleagues on Capitol Hill (Hardeman and Bacon 1987). Much of the mutual adjustment within and between the branches proceeded through these and other informal avenues, which are based on the comity and trust that arise from futures bound together by a common party label.

When party control of Congress and the presidency is divided, partisan considerations dominate these institutions' relations. On popular issues, party competition may cause a bidding war to erupt between Congress and the president that will even, at times, find the parties championing policies they would prefer to avoid. The overhaul of the tax code in 1987 is an outstanding example. This reform proposal shut down favored tax expenditures, various parts of which were dear to the core con-stituencies of both parties, and for this reason, few aficionados of tax politics predicted much chance of success. But it did succeed because many Republicans (Regan 1988) saw it as offering potentially huge political dividends and Democrats, who agreed on this, decided not to be outdone.

Opposition politicians will sometimes find electoral advantage in frustrating the other side, even when doing so prevents them from satisfying their own policy goals. In 1990, the Democrats in Congress rejected President Bush's overture for mild concessions on a new civil rights bill and sent him legislation he had publicly committed himself to veto (Holmes 1990). The lesson of these tax reform and civil rights legislative histories is that when party politicians seek advantage in the next election through policymaking, they may adopt positions inconsistent with those they would pursue were they simply engaged in serving the interests of their constituencies.

Negotiation must proceed between partisan teams in which each can veto the other's designs. An obvious problem this poses for a president is that the political parties' commitments to their core constituencies will create conflicting policy goals that make compromise difficult. On some issues, there simply may be no middle ground on which both parties can agree. Nonetheless, were policy the only way politicians could satisfy their constituencies, this should not normally create an insurmountable barrier. One can imagine such a setting giving rise to formal mechanisms of mutual adjustment (Lijphart 1968).

More commonly, the conflict and impasse a divided government frequently inspires are not borne of frustration from failing in a sincere search for a mutually acceptable policy; rather, they are more calculated and designed to yield advantage in the next election. No president has surpassed Harry Truman's use of this stratagem, with his extraordinary maneuver of calling the Republican Congress back into special session during the presidential election campaign of 1948. He challenged it to pass the progressive social programs recently endorsed at the Republican party's national convention, knowing full well it would not do so. This incident gave Truman perhaps the most effective issue in his come-from-behind campaign. Gerald Ford played the Republican variant of the game when he went on a veto binge against the 94th Congress and, at its close, campaigned for reelection on his steadfast opposition to the prodigal Democratic majority.

These and other examples instruct us that conflict can serve a party's electoral purposes even when its policy goals are the casualty. Speaking for his party's aggressive opposition to the Democratic majority's policies in 1985, House Republican Whip Richard Cheney explained, "Polarization often has very beneficial results. If everything is handled through compromise and conciliation, if there are no real issues dividing us from the Democrats, why should the country change and make us the majority?" (Oleszek 1991, 99).

THE BARGAINING PRESIDENT
AND DIVIDED GOVERNMENT

In Chapter 1, Gary Cox and I described the hysteria over the specter
of divided government that briefly engulfed Washington following the
1946 Republican landslide. Numerous formal arrangements—such as
regular interparty conferences and "summits" among the leaders—were
proposed to somehow induce a cooperation that the Constitution and
party competition were set against. One distant observer who was
troubled by the clamor for cooperation from Republicans and newspaper
editors was James H. Rowe. Rowe had been the first formal "assistant
to the president," a post created with the new White House Office in
1939. One of his chief responsibilities on behalf of President Roosevelt
had been clearing administration appointees with Congress and the
national party organization. This experience gave him keen insight into
the partisan motivations of politicians.

A month after the election, Rowe wrote Truman an unsolicited,
lengthy memo titled "'Cooperation' or Conflict?" in which he laid out
fully the predicament of divided government and the trap formal
mechanisms of cooperation posed for the president (Oral History
Interview 1969 and 1970). Truman found his argument persuasive, so
much so that he kept the memo in his desk drawer and occasionally
consulted it in the presence of others (Oral History of the Truman
White House 1980). Even though the political circumstances that
prompted Rowe to write to Truman were more precarious for his president
than those to which present-day incumbents are normally exposed,
Rowe's words offer instruction to the current crop of Republican presidents. Truman's predicament poignantly depicts the strategic considerations that govern relations between any president and an opposition
Congress. And Rowe's analysis comes as close as any contemporary
account in explaining President Bush's difficulties with the summit
mechanism employed in the 1990 budget negotiations—the same kind
that Rowe forcefully urged his president to avoid.

The premise of Rowe's argument is that the main business of an
opposition Congress is to prepare for the next election. Accordingly,
the president should disabuse himself of the notion that congressional
Republicans would bargain in good faith: It is simply not in their
interest to do so. Any gains by one side will come at the other's
expense, with the payout coming at the next election.

Instead, Rowe explained, the opposition would spend the next two
years searching for campaign issues. To this end, congressional committees would undertake investigations to ferret out scandal in the
administration, and confirmation committees would grill presidential

nominees in the hearings and reject a few as unfit. On the floor, the Republicans would pass with great fanfare any popular policies that they foresaw causing difficulties for the president, thereby daring him to veto. On none of these matters, Rowe advised, would the president have any control. He must simply endure these and other tribulations, acting all the while as though he were cooperating. True to Rowe's prediction, these stratagems became the trademark of the Republican 80th Congress.

Above all, the president must avoid being suckered into working with Congress as if there might be some common purpose. Political prudence dictated that the president should keep Congress at arm's length and enlist his constitutional resources to become as self-reliant as possible. Summit diplomacy, Rowe warned, is fraught with risks. With both sides eyeing the next election, summitry becomes a game of each party maneuvering the other into a position to be exploited. Furthermore, the presidency plays this game with Congress from a distinct disadvantage. "The office's extremely public nature leaves no room whatever for the private give-and-take, the secrecy and anonymity of compromise, which is the essence of negotiation. . . . The presidency is rigid—when its incumbent speaks the world soon knows exactly what he said" (p. 104).

The awkwardness of visibility recalls President Bush's efforts in the early days of the budget summit negotiation to retract his campaign slogan, "Read my lips: no new taxes." With Democrats demanding a retraction before they would earnestly begin negotiating a budget package, Bush tried to minimize the political fallout by issuing a press release that had the phrase "tax revenue increases" buried among a list of items open for discussion in the negotiations. This phrase, stripped of its circumlocution, won banner headlines in the nation's newspapers and led off each of the network's evening news broadcasts.

By agreeing to compromise, Rowe further warned, "the President yields his one source of strength—the backing of public opinion for his point of view. He brings that opinion to his view only by means of public statements. But reaching agreement with [the opposition] . . . means sitting around the conference table with them and indulging in bargaining and negotiation with them. The agreements would be made public as a combined product and the people would not know which were the contributions—or the concessions—of the . . . President" (p. 109).

One can sympathize with President Bush's predicament when he sat before the television cameras and poorly feigned enthusiasm for a budget compromise at odds with his campaign promise and the out-spoken stance of many House Republicans. No wonder his appeal was brief and tepid and without impact in the country or Congress. The only measurable effect was the president's sharp decline in the public opinion polls.

But the downside of negotiated policy does not end here. "Once having acceded to this proposition of joint responsibility, the President is then unable to resort to his public forum without the accusation that he violated his pledge to cooperate. He has surrendered his leadership of *all* the people and has perverted the principle of executive leadership to congressional procedures" (p. 110).

Added to this, "cooperation is a one-way street. The President can discipline the Executive Branch sufficiently by exercising his right to hire and fire; he can force it to cooperate. The Republican leaders may agree to have co-equal responsibility for executing the agreements reached on policy but they do not have co-equal power to deliver" (p. 109). Again, for Bush, the bipartisan budget that had taken all summer to assemble was quickly dispatched in both chambers within a week of its solemn unveiling. Realizing that he could only cut a deal with the more numerous and more amenable Democrats, Bush reopened negotiations, but by that point, the bipartisan compromise became his initial bargaining position. The partisan discussions revolved around issues that would make it still more attractive to the congressional Democrats.

So, what is the president to do? "Unlike majority Presidents who are able to 'do business' with their own party through judicious use of patronage, the minority Presidents are forced to fall back to their chief weapon—the marshalling of public opinion—which they do through the veto message and the press conference. But such a situation causes conflict. As the conflict deepens, personal bitterness and party suspicion increase on both sides. And these are stated publicly. . . . In such an atmosphere as this . . . talk about 'cooperation' soon disappears" (pp. 106–107).

The answer, according to Rowe, was for the president to pay lip service to cooperation—for which Rowe attached an appendix of mock overtures of cooperation—while aggressively promoting his policies with the public. The president should make a few, broad-gauged recommendations "confined only to major issues and carefully selected solely on the basis of the quantity of public support . . . because the weight of public opinion may force the Congress to accept it, or because making the record is in itself of sufficient importance" (p. 112).

Rowe also urged the president to rely on his constitutional assets, even though here, too, he cautioned that their success depended largely upon the president's ability to gain the public's backing. On the veto, Rowe declared, "This is the weapon of the minority administration. It is almost the only weapon. . . . The veto must, of course, be used strategically but, analyzed, this means only that it should be confined to those issues on which there is public interest and on which public opinion has clearly solidified" (p. 113).

Clearly, Rowe's advice to his president is at odds with the image of the virtuoso bargainer depicted by pluralist theory. For Rowe, the fact of competing political parties, each controlling a branch of government, dominated all other features of a political setting. A politician's desire to achieve policy goals through give-and-take at the bargaining table yields to the strategic dictates of the next election. Formal efforts at cooperation cannot patch over divided government. And cooperation based on mutual advantage and reciprocity gives way to conflict based on mutual threat and retaliation.

But what about coercion and threat as a bargaining device? Like everyone else, Rowe viewed the midterm result as an aberration likely to be erased with a Republican presidential victory two years later. Preoccupied with this more pressing party business, this Democrat did not address the president's capacity to enlist his constitutional assets and public standing to win policy in a stable environment of party conflict.[6] But with present-day divided government a fixture of public life, Congress and the president must now consider the prospects of making public policy across the gulf of party competition.

THE VETO

The veto is easily the most powerful weapon a president has to frustrate the designs of an opposition Congress. Between 1945 and 1990, it was employed 716 times. On only 44 (or 6 percent) of all vetoes did Congress muster the necessary two-thirds majorities in both houses to override. All but 4 came during divided government—12 each in the 80th and 94th congresses, when presidents Truman and Ford and their opposition congresses were busy making records for the next presidential election.

The purpose of giving the executive a strong "negative," as the framers sometimes called it, is clear in the record of the Constitution's deliberations. Desiring to check the excesses of popular government, many of the delegates at the Constitutional Convention preferred an absolute veto to the two-thirds override provision eventually adopted.

On the surface, the veto and its override vote might appear among the more straightforward decisions that Washington politicians ever confront. At the endgame of the legislative process, why should these actors posture or dissemble? They appear simply to be in a position to register their sincere, final preferences. The president decides if, on balance, he prefers the bill sufficiently to sign it into law. And if it is vetoed, Congress's leadership formally canvasses members to see if sufficient numbers support an override. Appearances are deceiving, however. In reality, the veto is bound up in strategic concerns, past and future.

Anticipated responses govern all participants' actions in the veto game. Although the scarcity of successful overrides surely reflects in part the severe hurdle posed by the Constitution, it also arises from presidents adjusting their initial positions on policies to incorporate the preferences of sufficient numbers of Congress's members to sustain their vetoes. And following Rowe's advice to base the veto strategically on "the quantity of public support," presidents will sometimes be reluctant to veto popular legislation that they foresee will be overridden.

Another form of strategic anticipation concerns the next election. The president's party members in Congress who initially supported a popular bill the president vetoed now find themselves cross-pressured in the override vote. In many such instances, the action popular with the home constituency may hurt the party nationally. After President Bush vetoed a couple of bills early in his term that had garnered large majorities in Congress, news reporters scurried over to the White House to get a response to the impending override vote. What they received was a self-assured answer by the president's spokesman, "Republicans in the House and Senate might not like a particular veto . . . but they know that the strength of Bush's veto is the only thing that stands between them and mincemeat" (Dowd 1990). Both vetoes were narrowly upheld on party votes.

Where each political party holds sufficient institutional authority to manipulate outcomes, the veto may, as Rowe warned, have more to do with electoral strategies than with sincere differences over public policy. Congress searches for popular issues with which to embarrass the president and, by association, his party; the president tries to turn the table by spotting flagrant instances of distributional policy that he can veto as he champions the cause of the national and public interest.

Even when elections are left out of the calculus, however, the politics of the veto remain bound up in strategic anticipation. The possibility of a veto insinuates the president's preferences into other politicians' deliberations. It reintroduces bargaining to the institutions' relations— not the cooperative kind based on reciprocity nor its superficial equivalent found in summit negotiation but a more distant kind based on public posturing and mutual threats.

The veto may make the president the most important legislator in government, but it works in a way that confers more influence over policy in some situations than others. For example, the veto does not

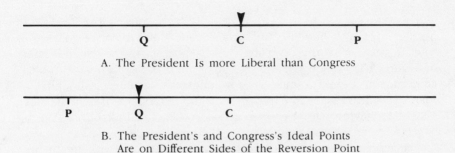

A. The President Is more Liberal than Congress

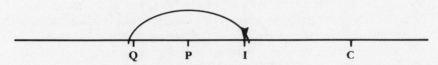

B. The President's and Congress's Ideal Points
Are on Different Sides of the Reversion Point

C. A Liberal Congress Locates Policy
at the President's Indifference Point

P = presidential policy preferences
C = congressional policy preferences
Q = current policy (reversion point)
I = point at which president is indifferent between veto and signing bill

FIGURE 5.1   The Effectiveness of the Veto as a Function of the Distribution of Preferences
(arrow identifies equilibrium outcome)

give the president the wherewithal to pry more out of Congress than
it is willing to give. This is depicted in Figure 5.1,[7] the first of the
several graphs that depict different orderings of presidential, *P,* and
congressional, *C,* policy preferences. When the president's preferred
policy is the more distant of the two from current policy, *Q* (which
we shall assume here is also the reversion point, or the foreseeable
outcome of a veto), all Congress need do is pass its preference.[8] Any
veto threat will be an idle one; in the end, the president will sign *C*
because it leaves him in a better position than the veto would.

Unable to persuade Congress to increase defense expenditures beyond
an inflation adjustment in 1986, President Reagan thought he had hit
upon the solution with the veto. When told of this possibility, House
Democratic leaders responded quizzically that perhaps they would send
him an even smaller appropriation the next time. Eventually, the president
backed off from his threat (McCubbins 1991).

For a president intent on changing the status quo, the veto is not
an especially attractive instrument. Perhaps this explains why the veto
was barely mentioned in scholarship on the presidency during the era
of unified Democratic governments.

The veto can be used more effectively by a conservative president, but here again, it depends upon the location of his policy goals, this time in relation to the reversion point, Q. If, as in the second graph of Figure 5.1, the president seeks to reduce the government's policy commitments while a majority of Congress's members (though less than two-thirds) want to expand them, the outcome will be a standoff. Each side having effectively vetoed the other, the best either can do is reach the reversion point.[9]

The more common and interesting case—and one with potentially perverse results—arises when a moderate president and a more liberal Congress agree to expand policy but disagree on the matter of how much. To identify the point along the policy continuum where the president will be indifferent between signing or vetoing the enrolled bill (point I), an arc describing the various utility payoffs of different policies has been added in the third graph in Figure 5.1. Once Congress identifies the president's position, P, it can then draft legislation that preserves as much of its policy goals while presenting the president with a bill (at I) that is still marginally more attractive than the reversion point. Depending upon where his ideal policy (P) is located on the continuum, this "compromise" outcome may be either near or far from the president's preferred policy. Because the reversion and indifference points are equidistant from the president's preferred policy, the more conservative the president (that is, the closer his position is to the reversion point), the closer final policy (at I) will be to his initial position. The worst scenario for a president arises when his position is midway between Congress's and the reversion point. Now, all the congressional majority need do is pass its preference, and the president will have little choice but to go along.

So, the structure of the veto game gives those presidents interested in defending the status quo greater leverage with Congress than is accorded their counterparts who are willing to venture into new policy commitments. The frustration of being caught in a bind by a strategic opposition Congress explains why Republican presidents persistently ask for a constitutional amendment giving them an item veto in their State of the Union addresses. Occasionally, they even fantasize that the framers intended for them to have one (Lauter 1989). This would allow them to shear away those provisions of enrolled bills being imposed by Congress, thereby bringing the final legislation in closer conformity to their preferences. Not surprisingly, nothing ever comes of these proposals in the Democratic Congress.

So far, public policy has been presented as the structurally induced outcome of the ordering of preferences. There is little place for bargaining or the various other activities attributed to skillful presidents. And yet, we know that under divided government, a high volume of signaling goes on between the president and Congress before legislation is passed. Committee chairs and party leaders announce tentative policy positions, and presidents and their aides respond. Frequently, the response takes the form of a veto threat. By one count, President Bush averaged about six veto-threat messages a month to Congress during his first two years in office (Hook 1990b). Does all this activity represent merely the venting of a president's frustration, or is it a manifestation of a distant bargaining game? Might a skillful president stuck in an unpleasant bind midway between Congress and the reversion point find ways to win a more attractive outcome than I? He would not in the simple game described above, but by relaxing certain of the model's conditions and making it more realistic, opportunities for presidential strategy do open up.

To this point, we have assumed that the president's revealed preferences are sincere. Because it is his ideal point that dictates the outcome in the most common scenarios, we may suspect that, being a strategic politician, he will be tempted at times to misrepresent his ideal point as being closer to the reversion point in order to induce Congress to incorrectly locate I closer to P than is necessary. The trick here is credibility. The president cannot credibly assume stances inconsistent with his record. Nor can he appear to be abandoning the interests of his party's core constituencies. Beyond this, he is free to lie, at least for the moment.

Now, let us relax another generally unrealistic condition—that the transaction is a single-stage game in which the president is presented with a "take-it-or-leave-it" choice and that the outcome has no implication for future decisions. One implication of recognizing the veto game to be a dynamic relationship between the president and Congress is that the latter will find Machiavellian virtue in sincerity. The first time the president engages in false posturing, his ploy may be highly effective because congressional leaders have no basis for suspecting his insincerity. But this will cause them to question his sincerity in future declarations. They will then be inclined to call his bluff and induce vetoes in order to identify where his true preferences lie.

There is yet another, more fundamental constraint on misrepresentation. Highly strategic posturing runs counter to those activities that are central to the president's leadership. His forte is taking positions publicly. The president is the one actor in Washington who commands sufficient visibility and legitimacy to articulate a view of the nation's interest. It is his chief resource, according to Rowe, during divided government. By building support for his policies in the country, the president seeks to make it convenient for other politicians throughout

Washington to sign on to his program. When Senator Arthur Vandenberg reportedly confided to President Truman that the only way he could get his Truman Doctrine policies past the Republican Congress was to "scare the hell out of the country," he was reminding the president of his asset. In the fall of 1990, Democratic Representative Leon Panetta addressed the same aspect of presidential leadership in a national television interview when he questioned whether President Bush's tepid address to the nation on behalf of the summit compromise had "provided sufficient cover" for members of Congress to support the legislation.

The president and his advisers fashion policy initiatives with careful consideration to attracting support in the country and Washington. This often means that his personal policy preferences will be subordinated to politically more attractive public positions. The president's public program, then, will already reflect strategic thinking—but of a kind that will not provide him much leeway for strategic posturing in a veto-based bargaining game with an opposition Congress. If his success involves "providing cover," he cannot afford to develop the reputation for stating policy objectives that are mere artifice.[10]

Relaxing the single-stage game also removes the determinacy of the outcome. Now, the president (and others whose own decisions are tempered by their reading of his) must calculate the future consequences of his decision. An invaluable device for estimating future effects of current actions is the concept of reputation. In the pluralist bazaar where transactions may not be consummated for months or even years, a strong reputation is critical for both attracting trading partners and achieving favorable outcomes. Can the president be trusted to pay his IOUs? Does he mean what he says? These are examples of the kinds of questions politicians in a barter economy must answer for themselves whenever they enter negotiations with the president.

In a partisan veto game played under divided government, the president's reputation is just as important, but the critical questions that shape it are different. We have already considered the question of whether the president's stated preferences are sincere. To this, we can now add the question of whether the president will make good his veto threat. The answer to this question will be informed, via reputation, by what he has done in the past. In the static game with which I began this discussion, this is not an issue because the fixed payoffs of his options are known. Once a veto decision incorporates the future, however, the current payoff may no longer be determinative.

The ideal circumstance for persuading a president to absorb current losses as investments in future negotiations arises, as shown in the third graph, when he proposes a small expansion from the status quo to a more liberal Congress. Confronted with a near dilemma, he will not significantly damage his position by exercising a veto. And as long as he has the votes to sustain his veto, the president will be inflicting more severe losses on Congress because its ideal policy is farther from the reversion point.

There are basically only two structural circumstances that prevent the president's veto threat from being credible. As he nears the end of his second term, he will not be able to postpone even small gains in favor of possibly more attractive future outcomes.[11] Moreover, some policies demand resolution in ways that make the reversion point unacceptable and that will therefore be ill suited for reputation-building strategies. These include statutes facing expiration (such as those containing sunset laws) or those that trigger automatic changes in policy (for example, the Gramm-Rudman Balanced Budget Deficit and Control Act of 1985).

Finally, a president can increase his stake in a particular outcome through a public commitment to veto a bill if specified conditions are not met. For Ronald Reagan, his declared position on tax cuts in 1981 was a "line drawn in dirt," and I have already noted President Bush's "No new taxes" pledge. Whenever a president publicly commits himself to a veto, he is saying to Congress that he will forego the gains of the minimally acceptable policy (I in Figure 5.1) in favor of an objectively less-preferred outcome (Q). What makes a public commitment credible, of course, is that the president has imposed additional costs to his reputation and public prestige by allowing a given policy to become law. Because Congress appreciates these costs as real, the president's declaration places the onus on the opposition either to provide a policy that satisfies his requirements or to call his bluff and be prepared to accept substantially less.

Of course, the president will not want to stake out such positions on most issues.[12] Many policies cannot easily be framed as bifurcated choices. Clear-cut programmatic goals are best suited for this kind of declaration. The issue also must be sufficiently significant so that the commitment is not greeted with disbelief. As with misrepresentation, the president's public commitment is only as effective as it is credible. It should not be overworked: At some point, its overuse might persuade an opposition Congress to force the president to use his veto in order to discourage his heavy reliance on it in the future. And finally, the president had better be prepared to follow through if his bluff is called. As President Bush discovered after "Read my lips" became "Read my hips," backing down from a public commitment will weaken a president's standing in Washington and the country.

Public commitment offers a couple of distinct advantages that commend it to Republican presidents presiding over divided governments.

It neither requires the president to misrepresent his preferences nor become entangled in summit negotiations. Unlike these alternatives, public commitment has the president doing what he does best—taking public stands. And it gives the president, rather than Congress, the initiative in setting the terms of the compromise policy outcome. If one accepts that gaining leverage from commitment is the main reason presidents publicly communicate veto threats to Congress, that they frequently do so indicates this is a standard strategy of presidents facing an opposition Congress.

The tactics of veto-based bargaining reward skill. The first—misrepresentation—is especially risky in that it undermines the president's claim to national leadership. The other two techniques—converting veto politics into a multiperiod game and making public commitments—impose short-term costs, but done well, they offer the prospect of long-term dividends.

CONCLUSION

Students of U.S. politics have long complained of the inadequacies of the Democratic and Republican parties as the purveyors of public policy. With their memberships of ideologically diverse and loosely tethered politicians, America's parties are neither able to formulate coherent policy or present a consistent image to the electorate. Compared to their European counterparts, they appear as little more than hollow structures within which self-directed politicians pursue their own and their constituents' interests.

The party view of the presidency presented here need not claim more for U.S. political parties than is represented by their critics. As long as they compete with each other in the electorate in ways that allow voters to form general impressions about what the parties stand for, the necessary conditions will be satisfied. Within parties, politicians will have sufficient incentive to cooperate, and across parties, they will have sufficient reason to compete. Because the president is more visible than any other politician and is called upon more often to take positions on the kinds of national issues that will inform party images, competing parties will affect him most of all. This is all that is required in order for presidential leadership to entail quite different strategies under unified and divided governments.

Party competition means that a divided government will require the president to draw heavily upon his constitutional prerogatives as he defends his party's positions against the designs of the opposition-controlled Congress. In this circumstance, his leadership depends on self-effectuating behavior. I examined the veto in particular. The president vetoes a bill and frustrates its sponsors, and he requires no more backing than a third of the membership of either chamber of Congress to make his veto stick.

The veto is not the only instrument available to a minority party president. Two of the foremost trends in presidential praxis—the politicization of the bureaucracy and public appeals—share critical attributes with the veto. Neither requires the cooperation of Congress, and both are designed to limit the opposition's options. Consider the following two cases in which Republican presidents have enlisted these strategies against a Democratic Congress.

Within hours of his 1972 reelection, Richard Nixon directed his staff to collect resignation letters from all of his political appointees. Facing a sizable Democratic majority in Congress, the president wanted to assure himself that he would have a wholly loyal group of political executives for the struggle he anticipated over control of the bureaucracy. Eventually, many of these unenthusiastically tendered resignations were accepted. For Nixon's detractors, this maneuver confirmed their suspicion of his "imperious" character. Even his friends expressed misgivings: Would this heavy-handed approach not needlessly demoralize those agency and bureau heads whose cooperation he needed? But subsequent events made this systematic housecleaning appear prudent. The president got his team of administration loyalists to run the bureaucracy. And, to the chagrin of many Democrats in Congress, few bureaucrats later took advantage of the president's preoccupation with Watergate to deviate from the policy course he had set for them.

By the last time Ronald Reagan exhorted the U.S. people to "write and call your congressman, send mailgrams" on behalf of some administration bill, president watchers had stopped counting, and judging by the phone logs and mail counts, the public had stopped responding.[13] But the appeal had not always been so gratuitous a peroration to his radio and television addresses. In the beginning, when only the House of Representatives was under Democratic control, the strategy had paid off handsomely. In 1981, dozens of Democratic members abandoned their leaders and voted with Republicans on budget resolutions and tax cuts. House Speaker Tip O'Neill was given to stoic pronouncements: "If you roll us, you roll us," or "the opinions of the man in the street change faster than anything in this world."[14] Circumstances did become more favorable (and perhaps more quickly than this sage might have foreseen) for he was soon able to pay back the administration for its pressure politics. Within three years, Democratic leaders were pronouncing the president's annual budget to be "Dead On Arrival." The Reagan revolution may have been short-lived, but its impact, most would agree, remains imprinted on public policy.

The politicization of the bureaucracy and the growth of presidential public relations, these two cases illustrate, are widely acknowledged to be the two most prominent trends in presidential leadership. With the president having the prerogative to appoint senior government officials and the Senate having the authority to confirm these appointments, the asymmetry of the veto is reversed. Now, the opposition-controlled legislature is left with the limited and problematic decision of whether a given nominee is the best it is likely to get. And, as with the veto, the significance of this authority melts away under unified government.[15] Public appeals limit opposition actions in a different way. By swinging public opinion to the president's position, opposing politicians must reassess their own positions. As in the case of the Democratic "boll weevils" in 1981, some will find it more attractive to support the president than to adhere to their party's position. By making other preferences more risky, the president may be able to minimize his concessions. A variety of causes for these apparently secular developments have been proposed. Most prominent among them is the weakening of political parties in the country and, in turn, in Washington. And as they assemble governing coalitions in the face of these ever-weakening affinity relations, presidents are increasingly drawn to these alternatives. But, ironically, might both of these developments, as well as greater dependence on the vote, be the result not of weakening parties but of the intensified partisanship that accompanies divided government? If so, the trend toward an increasingly self-reliant presidency would be one of the important consequences of divided government.

NOTES

1. I am borrowing from Charles E. Lindblom's phrase "partisan mutual adjustment" and dropping the first word in order to avoid possible confusion later when I compare mutual adjustment within and between political parties. PMA, as it's sometimes called, received its fullest development in Lindblom 1965.

2. Neustadt 1980, 28–29. Compare with Dahl and Lindblom's earlier observation: "The President possesses more hierarchical controls than any other single figure in the government; indeed, he is often described somewhat romantically and certainly ambiguously as the most powerful democratic executive in the world. Yet like everyone else in the American policy process, the President must bargain constantly—with Congressional leaders, individual Congressmen, his department heads, bureau chiefs, and leaders of nongovernmental organizations" (Dahl and Lindblom 1953, 333).

3. Lindblom 1965, 319. Lindblom's ambivalent discussion of the place of political parties in the pluralist framework illustrated well the parties' uncertain status. Though recognizing the legislative role of party leaders in aggregating

the preferences of their followers, Lindblom came down in favor of less, rather than more, party discipline: "In summary, the argument that party discipline achieves responsibility is in large part an argument against discipline, an argument for permitting legislators and executives to act flexibly and intelligently toward each other and in interchange with the citizenry in order to explore through partisan mutual adjustment, within the legislature as well as elsewhere, all possible opportunities for agreement and acceptable aggregation."

4. Even in an earlier era when public displeasure with federal spending was less salient, James MacGregor Burns noted the tendency for presidential aspirants in both parties to be similarly oriented toward the provision of certain popular public goods, while members of Congress were chiefly concerned then, as today, with local services. To capture those modal institutional differences within the political parties, he described U.S. politics as organized around a four-party system. See Burns 1963.

5. In generating local goods and services, in protecting local interests in the formulation of national policy, and in virtually everything a representative may do, an officeholder is guided by the desire to win reelection, as David Mayhew convincingly argued. On the extraordinary ability of members of Congress to particularize policy, see Mayhew 1974a.

6. In September 1947, Rowe sent to President Truman through intermediaries another advisory memorandum, entitled "The Politics of 1948." Amended by White House aide Clark Clifford, this statement became the blueprint of Truman's come-from-behind victory in 1948. See Oral History Interview 1969 and 1970, Appendix B.

7. These graphs depict a bargaining setting in which institutional preferences differ on a single policy dimension and in which the policy outcome is the product of a single-stage game. After identifying the outcomes in this simple game, I shall consider the implications of relaxing both of these assumptions.

8. By passing no bill, several possibilities are implied, including the status quo, change in policy if the current law is scheduled to expire, or, in the case of appropriations legislation, automatic passage of a resolution to continue funding for programs at current levels. Mathew McCubbins provides a fuller discussion of the reversion point in the next chapter.

9. The same standoff holds when Congress and the president switch places in the second graph of Figure 5.1. Here is the one case where the veto helps the liberal president, and, again, it gains him no more than the status quo. The only historical instance of this occurred in the 80th Congress, when President Truman wielded the veto in response to an only partially successful effort by the new Republican congressional majority to dismantle New Deal programs. The strategic implications of this positioning of preferences are examined by Cox and McCubbins in Chapter 7. See also Kiewiet and McCubbins 1988, 713–736.

10. From his interviews with administration officials, Mark A. Peterson reported that administration officials minimize the extent to which strategic posturing is available to the president. See Peterson 1990.

11. This presents the possibility that his veto threat will unravel. With congressional parties needing to go to the electorate every two years and

presidents reasonably anticipating an eight-year term, the president is in a better position than Congress.

12. For a formal treatment of the conditions that lead to successful commitment, see Ingberman and Yao 1986, 94–96.

13. The three-year course of Ronald Reagan's dealings with the partially Democratic Congress is described in Kernell 1986, 111–114.

14. This remark was reportedly made in a meeting between Reagan and five congressional leaders. It is described in Goldman 1981b, 26–27, and in Church 1981, 10–12. See also Goldman 1981a, 40.

15. Historically, Democratic presidents have surrendered much of their control over these nominations to party members in Congress in order to recruit officials who will work well with the party in both institutions.

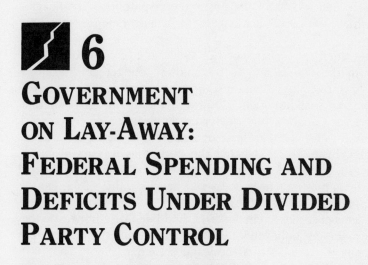

6

GOVERNMENT ON LAY-AWAY: FEDERAL SPENDING AND DEFICITS UNDER DIVIDED PARTY CONTROL

Mathew D. McCubbins

Budget deficits have held a prime spot in the news for over a decade. Everything from a decline in private investment and personal savings to trade imbalances with Japan has been laid at the feet of the deficit, but Congress and the president seem unable or unwilling to find a solution to this problem. Why? Why have national policymakers so consistently defied the down-home logic of budgeting recognized by every family in the United States: that we have to live within our means?

Federal budget deficits are not exactly new, despite the attention they have received of late. Every president in the postwar period has run on a platform that included a promise to bring federal spending under control. Indeed, in only ten of the last sixty years have current-dollar federal revenues exceeded current-dollar expenditures.

Tree-spiking environmentalists must shudder at the thought of the millions of trees sacrificed to print analysis after analysis of the causes and consequences of the runaway deficits of the 1980s. Two explanations for these deficits have received widespread currency. First, many analysts have observed that the plunge into the deficit abyss that followed Ronald Reagan's entry into the White House was a clear break from the four-bit deficits of the late 1970s. Reagan administered over one record deficit after another. From these facts, some analysts have inferred that the runaway deficits of the 1980s were the by-product of the Reagan revolution, which combined tax cuts with sizable defense spending increases.

Others have seen the deficits of the 1980s as a consequence of a trend begun in the late 1970s. To them, these budget deficits arose from a breakdown in congressional restraints on spending. The Congressional Budget and Impoundment Control Act of 1974 established a budget process in Congress that delegated authority to newly created budget committees in the House and Senate. But the congressional budget process, instead of balancing the budget as was its promise, actually unleashed the spending profligacies of Congress from the restraints of the appropriations process and the discipline of the House Appropriations Committee (HAC).

Spending decisions, these scholars said, had been disciplined by the HAC, whose members believed their role was to guard the Treasury from the expensive tastes of their colleagues (Fenno 1966). The 1974 Budget Act, by reducing the role of the Appropriations Committee in determining spending, ruined the incentives for members of that committee to police the spending of their colleagues: Members of the House committee no longer sought to cut executive spending requests but instead tried to secure their own portion of the federal largess.

These explanations represent two fairly common perceptions of U.S. politics. The first is premised on the widely held belief that the president, in the twentieth century, has come to dominate policymaking. The second is premised on a similar belief that congressional committees dominate policymaking. With both explanations skewed toward one branch or the other, neither is attentive to the implications that divided party control of these institutions has for spending policy and the deficit. In this chapter, I reexamine the logic of spending decisions to show that divided partisan control of Congress in the 1980s was the principle cause of the rapid growth in budget deficits seen during that decade.

OF CHECKS AND BALANCES: THE THESIS
OF PRESIDENTIAL ASCENDANCY IN AMERICAN POLITICS

The Constitution provides the House, Senate, and president each with a check on the others' abilities to take action. Careful consideration was given to balancing these checks, to ensure that each department had "the necessary constitutional means and personal motives to resist encroachments of the others" (Hamilton et al. 1961, 321–322). This careful balance, however, has been seen at various times in the republic's history to tilt from one branch to the other. Years with dominant presidents have been interspersed with periods of congressional ascendancy.

But for much of the twentieth century, Congress has been seen to be the declining branch. The greater efficiency of the executive branch and the inability of members of Congress to overcome their diversity of interests led these members of Congress to "abdicate" their responsibilities in many key policy areas (Sundquist 1981, 28, 35–36). However, Congress bounced back in the early 1970s, passing new, important constraints on executive discretion, including limitations on the president's ability to involve U.S. troops in armed conflict in the War Powers Act of 1973 and limitations on the president's ability to impound appropriated funds via the 1974 Budget Act. But Ronald Reagan's election in 1980 quickly reestablished the dominance of his office over a fissiparous Congress. The budget for fiscal year 1982 seemed to set the tone.

Shortly after entering office, Reagan submitted a budget asking for spending of $695 billion, which included $36.6 billion in "cuts," and an *increase* in spending of nearly $100 billion over the last budget submitted by Jimmy Carter.[1] To pass this budget, Reagan needed to wrest control of the budget process from the House Democratic leadership. Though the House Budget Committee rejected Reagan's budget when first offered by Representative Delbert Latta (R–Ohio) in April 1981, presidential pressure and public opinion persuaded sixty-three Democrats (largely conservative southerners) to join with the Republicans on the House floor in defeating the committee's recommendation in favor of Reagan's budget. And though the House Democratic leadership threatened to stop passage of the legislation (termed reconciliation legislation) required to implement the "cuts" mandated in Reagan's budget, twenty-nine Democrats again voted against their party to pass this reconciliation legislation.

The Reagan administration hoped that the large tax cut it also won in 1981 ($100 billion in constant, 1972 dollars) would, by creating unpalatable deficits, cause Congress to go along with its desired cuts in domestic and social spending. The key question I ask here is this: If Reagan was in control of the budget process, why did spending increase so much during the decade? Taxes fell, so why didn't spending?

The presidential ascendancy story, in its strongest form, argues that "strong" presidents can dominate the legislature. But if Reagan—widely regarded in his first term as a strong president—dominated the legislative process, why did this Republican strategy of dragging down domestic spending with a large tax cut fail? If the president controls the political agenda, why was Reagan unable to cut spending or even, simply, to propose balanced budgets via large cuts in domestic and social programs?

Abdication or Delegation?

It is now part of the lore of U.S. politics—a stylized fact—that the president has come to dominate national politics. This thesis is not without merit (see, for example, Binkley 1962; Bryce 1924; Burns 1965; Edwards 1980; Laski 1940; Milton 1965; Neustadt 1980; Schlesinger 1973; and Sundquist 1981). The thesis of executive domination argues that in delegating, Congress actually has abdicated its authority to make decisions. The distinction here between delegation and abdication is a significant one.[2] Congressional abdication implies that members of Congress neither make the policy choices nor even affect the choices being made.

The evidence for this proposition is that policy decisions made by the president are rarely, if ever, challenged in Congress and that policy recommendations made by the president to Congress "are not seriously reviewed" (Sundquist 1981, 12). The complaints of members of Congress with regard to apparent executive usurpations of legislative authority have also been cited as evidence for this interpretation.

But what can we actually infer from these stylized facts? They are entirely consistent with an interpretation that Congress, in delegating, actually has retained all of its authority over policymaking. The argument is as follows: Congress delegates its authority to make public policy to the executive. Members of Congress agree to do so because it is a more efficient way for them to make policy and, therefore, it allows them to make policy on many more areas than they otherwise could. Congress then uses direct and indirect means to discipline those in the executive branch charged with carrying out this delegated authority (Kirst 1969; McCubbins 1985; McCubbins and Schwartz 1984; McCubbins and Page 1987; McCubbins, Noll, and Weingast 1987 and 1989; Weingast and Moran 1983). Through these means, as Congress manages policymaking, members indirectly shape executive decisions as they are being made, thus largely relieving themselves of the need to intervene directly or to challenge executive decisions at a later point. Here, focusing on the nominal decisionmakers in the executive, without considering the incentives and constraints those decisionmakers face in an institutional context, mystifies the policymaking process. Executive branch actors may appear powerful when members of Congress who hold the formal right to direct the executive on policy fail to do so. But inferring that those executive actors are powerful is often a mistake.

Second, because Congress holds the power to veto or amend executive recommendations—such as the president's budget—the executive likely will anticipate members' reactions and accommodate their demands in his proposals before submitting his recommendation. Thus, members are rarely seen to "seriously" review presidential proposals for their demands have already been met. The absence of evidence with respect to congressional influence, again, should not be mistaken for evidence of congressional weakness.

Lastly, as Sundquist noted, forebodings on Capitol Hill with respect to executive ascendancy are most marked when the president comes from a different party than the one that controls Congress. Complaints of executive usurpation, then, may reflect more of a mood toward decreased delegation in the face of partisan conflict than actual foreboding about the collapse of U.S. democracy. Indeed, delegations to the executive seem to expand when both branches are controlled by the same party and to contract when control is divided (Kiewiet and McCubbins 1991). The efforts by Congress to restructure discretion in the 1970s are prominent examples.[3] Members of Congress take on the mantle of responsibility most often when the president is from a different party than the one that controls Congress. This mantle of responsibility, it seems, is delegated only when the president and the majorities in Congress share the same party label.

Although Congress may not have abdicated its authority to the president, its delegations have indisputably expanded the president's authority. Many analysts contend that the delegation of policy initiation, as in the budget, to the president has had a more subtle effect, tilting the balance between the branches toward the president.[4] Thus, Sundquist, for one, argues that the establishment of legislative clearance at the Budget Bureau, created by the Budget and Accounting Act of 1921, has been the principal source of presidential dominance in this century.[5]

But even with an explicit delegation of authority to the president, as in the 1921 Budget Act, Congress need not even consider the president's proposal. Referring to his troubled budgets at a press conference on October 22, 1987, Reagan observed that "every year under the law I submitted a budget program—and as they've done every year I've been here, they've put it on the shelf and have refused to even consider it" ("President Faces Questions" 1987). In response to another question at the news conference, Reagan, though admittedly trying to shirk the blame for the persistent budget deficits of his administration, accurately portrayed the circumstances facing presidents in attempting to influence policy.

> The President of the United States cannot spend a nickel. Only Congress can authorize the spending of money. And for six years now I have repeatedly asked the Congress for less money and they have turned around and given more—given more to spend, and done it in such a way that I can't veto it when they put it all together, instead of appropriations, in a continuing resolution—we haven't had a deficit—or, a budget since I've been here. No—the Congress is the one that's in command, and we have to persuade them that what we've asked for is enough to support the programs, as determined by the people who work those programs and who run them. And every budget I've sent up there has been put on the shelf and I've been told that it's dead on arrival ("President Faces Questions" 1987).

As Sundquist observed, "When the delegation is not a power to act but only responsibility to recommend—the executive budget, for instance—the Congress explicitly retains not only its full authority but also its responsibility to act" (1981, 12). If we are to believe Sundquist in this respect, then delegations such as the ones contained in the 1921 Budget Act have not tilted the balance between the two branches.

What must be remembered is that Congress created the Budget Bureau (now the Office of Management and Budget or OMB), that Congress funds the Budget Bureau, and that Congress manages the activities of the Budget Bureau (Kiewiet and McCubbins 1991; Wilmerding 1943). As a former general counsel to the clerk of the House remarked, "Congress created OMB. Congress can uncreate it—or change it" ("Budget Office Evolves" 1985).

Through all the usual means, Congress has striven to manage its delegations to the president and the Budget Bureau. Nonetheless, presidents do gain some influence over outcomes through the recommendations they make. The president and members of his party in Congress run for reelection based, in part, on how well the party does at implementing its platform. Because their electoral fates are partially linked, the president and his party in Congress will find it in their best interests to cooperate on passing the party's platform. Policy initiation, then, is for them a cooperative process. How much influence is shared by the president in this process is open to debate, particularly when his party is in the minority in both houses of Congress.

Congress generally takes no independent action on an issue prior to the president's request. And on budget, tax, and economic policy, Congress typically enacts legislation that, in its broad outlines at least, is similar to the president's proposal. This does not, however, imply congressional abdication or presidential ascendancy. If presidential proposals are to succeed, the president must anticipate the reaction of members of the House and Senate to his proposals and accommodate their demands and interests. Presidents know this, so they rarely submit proposals that are likely to fail. Those who overlook this lesson have their proposals ignored in lieu of congressional proposals, as happened to Reagan's budgets. Further, if Congress has delegated authority to initiate legislation to the president and thus requests a proposal from him and if the president accommodates congressional interests in his proposal, then members of Congress should be expected to wait for that proposal and to enact something once they get it.

Presidential Power and the Veto

In contrast to the powers delegated to the president by Congress, the veto gives the president a strong position in the legislative process. The president's proposal may matter on some occasions and not on others, but the veto applies to all acts of Congress. Moreover, coming last in the sequence of legislation, the president's veto will affect decisions made in all the previous stages.

Some people, in analyzing presidential vetoes, have inferred that the veto power is ineffective because it is rarely used. Again, in the case of congressional responses to executive proposals in the thesis of presidential dominance, this is a mistaken inference. Members of Congress logically anticipate the president's reaction to their proposals. Their proposals, then, usually are designed to avoid a veto by accommodating the president's demands. Indeed, if members of Congress have good information as to what is and what is not acceptable to the president, there should never be any vetoes!

The influence that the veto gives the president is, however, asymmetrical. The chief executive can use the veto to restrain Congress, to some extent, when he prefers to spend less than do its members. In contrast, the veto gives the president no means of extracting more appropriations from Congress when he prefers to spend more than its members do.[6]

This asymmetry derives from inherent limitations in the veto power. The veto gives the president only the power to reject acts of Congress; it does not provide him with the power to modify these acts. Thus, Congress submits take-it-or-leave-it offers to the president, who is then faced with choosing between the bill and, at best, some future legislation that may or may not be better for him than the current congressional offer.

On spending bills, the president's position is even more precarious: On receiving a bill from Congress, he can either accept the appropriations contained therein or veto it and let Congress write a continuing resolution.[7] Because of the emergency nature of continuing resolutions, they are virtually veto proof. Also, because continuing resolutions almost always contain aggregate spending that is less than that contained in the corresponding appropriations bills, the president is able to reduce spending (to the level in the continuing resolution) through the use or threat of the veto, but he cannot get increased spending from a Congress that does not favor it.

The limited and asymmetric influence conveyed to the president by the veto is illustrated by the budget debates in Reagan's second term. In his budget request for fiscal year 1985, Reagan proposed a 13 percent, inflation-adjusted increase in defense spending for fiscal year 1986. He coupled this with a proposal to slash Social Security and domestic spending and to eliminate cost-of-living adjustments (COLAs) for federal pension payments (including Social Security).

House and Senate forces on Capitol Hill, however, did not favor a package of defense increases and domestic spending cuts. Recognizing that the president's budget was "dead on arrival," Senate Budget Committee Chairman Pete Domenici (R–N.M.) stated his expectation that defense spending would be held to less than a 6 percent inflation-adjusted increase for 1986. Reagan then reduced his defense request to a 5.9 percent inflation-adjusted increase. But he requested steep cuts in domestic spending totaling $34 billion.

The package of domestic spending cuts and defense increases was still unacceptable to Democrats and liberal Republicans. Then, in March 1985, the Senate Budget Committee voted to recommend an inflation-adjusted freeze on defense spending and a freeze on Social Security.

Reagan promised not to compromise on the requested defense increase. However, faced with a projected deficit exceeding $200 billion for 1986 and trying to unite a fractured party, the Senate Republican leadership negotiated with Reagan a 3 percent inflation-adjusted increase in defense spending. The package also included an elimination of cost-of-living adjustments, deep cuts in domestic spending, and some increases in federal pensions. In announcing this new deal, Reagan stated that a 3 percent inflation-adjusted increase was the "rock-bottom level" he would accept (Wehr 1985, 771).

But Reagan was holding the wrong end of the veto stick. Despite his veto threat, the Senate rejected the Republican leadership's package and voted to cut defense and to restore pension COLAs. Ultimately, the Senate approved a budget resolution that reduced but did not eliminate COLAs and boosted defense spending only enough to offset the projected rate of inflation for fiscal year 1986 (4 percent).

On the other side of the Capitol, the House Budget Committee, on a party-line vote, recommended more spending for domestic programs and less for defense than was stipulated in the budget passed by the Senate. The Committee's recommendation sought to freeze defense authorizations without the increase for inflation that the Senate allowed. The House Budget Committee's recommendation also cut defense outlays, but it left Social Security unchanged. The House passed the resolution on a party-line vote. In conference, the House and Senate settled on the higher defense budget authority proposed in the Senate's bill but accepted the House's cut of $27 billion in defense outlays. Moreover, the compromise accepted much of the domestic spending increases advocated by the House, including a (reduced) cost-of-living adjustment for federal pension and Social Security recipients. As expected, Reagan accepted the bills passed under this resolution.

When Congress again slashed his requests for defense in favor of increases in domestic expenditures in 1986, Reagan threatened to veto any bill that contained less than the increase in defense spending that he had requested. In response to a query on this veto threat, Representative William Gray (D–Pa.), chairman of the House Budget Committee, recognizing the asymmetry of influence offered by the veto, countered, "What's he going to do, veto the defense bill because it's too low?" (Bettinger 1986, 1261). Ultimately, again, the answer was no.

The Reagan Revolution and the Determinants of Federal Spending Policy

Though Reagan sought to increase defense spending and decrease taxes, he also wanted to decrease social and domestic spending. Why was he so unsuccessful? If we are to believe that the president dominates Congress, then why did the deficit grow so large under a fiscally conservative president?

The budget for fiscal year 1982 was heralded (or decried) as a victory by a powerful president over an institutionally-weakened Congress. But what sort of victory was this for Reagan? In the first place, the much ballyhooed budget "cuts" of $36.6 billion did not actually reduce spending from fiscal year 1981 levels; rather, they represented reductions relative to Carter's proposed budget for fiscal year 1982 (in which he requested a whopping 17 percent increase in spending relative to that in fiscal year 1981). Although there was much talk of budget cuts in the 1980s, spending nearly *doubled* from fiscal year 1981 to 1989. And, whereas the gross national product, valued in 1972 dollars, grew only 15 percent from 1981 to 1987, spending grew 40 percent.[8] Congress had, in fact, slashed a larger percentage from Carter's previous four budget proposals than the amount cut from the 1982 budget by this action. Indeed, Carter's budget for fiscal year 1981 was smaller than the total appropriations for fiscal year 1980; Reagan's budget, by contrast, requested a spending increase of over 8 percent.

Second, a vast majority of the programs and agencies that suffered cuts in Reagan's budget had previously been cut by the Democrats and Jimmy Carter. Moreover, almost half of these agencies had their budgets reduced not only by Reagan and Carter but also by Democratic congresses when Gerald Ford was president. And those items that were expanded under Reagan's budget (such as defense) had been expanded in Carter's previous two budgets. Thus, though the 1982 budget may have accelerated the spending reallocation, it did not represent a radical change. It largely continued trends of the previous two Democratic budgets.

Third, where Reagan did try to depart from the budgetary consensus of the previous administration, he was rebuffed. In the reconciliation legislation, Senate Minority Leader Robert Byrd (D–W. Va.) successfully offered amendments to keep alive several dozen programs scheduled for termination under the president's budget.[9] Indeed, almost all of the programs scheduled for termination by Reagan survived his tenure in office.

Fourth, due to the recession of 1981–1982, spending for fiscal year 1982 actually exceeded Reagan's budget by $35 billion, thus wiping out his cuts. Finally, Congress chipped away at Reagan's cuts by passing a $4.5 billion supplemental spending bill to fund programs for the Environmental Protection Agency (EPA) that had been cut in the earlier reconciliation legislation and by passing a $14.2 billion supplemental funding bill for agricultural and social programs, as well as a pay raise for government employees. In fact, Congress overrode Reagan's veto to enact the second supplemental bill.

What responsibility, then, does Reagan bear for the runaway deficits of the 1980s? Table 6.1 compares the average change in budget requests for 63 domestic agencies, relative to the preceding year's appropriation, for each president from Truman to Reagan. The table shows that, on average, most presidents (other than Reagan) had requested at least a 10 percent *increase* for these 63 domestic programs. Reagan, in his first three budgets (fiscal years 1983–1985), requested almost an 8 percent *decrease,* on average, for these programs. Moreover, Reagan requested spending cuts for nearly half of the agencies in this sample. Nixon, by contrast, had requested cuts for only 16 percent of these

TABLE 6.1   Average Percentage Change in Budget Requests and Appropriations by Administration for Domestic Agencies, 1948–1985

President	Mean Percentage Change in President's Budget Estimates	Mean Percentage Change in Appropriations	Number of Observations
Truman	17.4	8.2	260
Eisenhower	11.5	8.2	373
Kennedy/Johnson	11.8	8.0	401
Nixon/Ford	11.1	11.5	386
Carter	10.7	10.3	214
Reagan	−7.7	0.6	215

TABLE 6.2   Change in Appropriations by Party Control of Congress

	Republican	Democratic	Split
Appropriations greater than or equal to previous year	57.6% (102)	83.2% (1310)	69.8% (164)
Appropriations less than previous year	42.4% (75)	16.8% (264)	30.2% (71)

agencies, and Eisenhower had requested cuts for 19 percent of these programs.[10]

Nonetheless, Table 6.1 does show that spending growth, for this sample of programs, was slower during Reagan's administration than during any other presidential administration since World War II. Spending growth (in real-dollar terms) for the 63 domestic agencies in my sample was held to less than 1 percent under Reagan. But he did not have to contend with large Democratic majorities in both chambers of Congress, as did Eisenhower, Nixon, and Ford. Indeed, the Republicans owned a majority of seats in the Senate for the first time in over two decades during Reagan's first six years in office.

Table 6.2 demonstrates the differences in spending policies enacted by Republican, as opposed to Democratic, congresses. When the Republicans controlled both houses of Congress (1947–1948 and 1953–1954), they cut appropriations for over 42 percent of the items in my sample of 69 agencies (which includes 63 domestic and 6 defense agencies). When control was split in the 1980s, with the Republicans controlling the Senate and the Democrats controlling the House, spending was cut, on average, for only 30 percent of these 69 agencies. Democratic control of both chambers led to only 17 percent of these agencies, on average, having their appropriations reduced. In fact, the Republican Congress of 1953–1954 cut spending for almost two-thirds of the programs in this sample, more than twice the rate of cuts garnered by Reagan.

Should Reagan have done better? Because most of the programs of the federal government in the postwar era were instituted and supported by the Democratic party (Browning 1986), it is reasonable to expect that Republican control of Congress would bring about reductions in many of these programs. Further, it seems reasonable to expect that a divided Congress would reduce spending for more budget items than would a Democrat-controlled Congress but that it would not reduce spending on as many items as would a Republican-controlled Congress. With the Republicans gaining a majority in the Senate, we would thus expect more and larger cuts, especially in domestic spending, in comparison to the Democratic congresses of the previous two decades, regardless of who occupied the White House. Reagan and the Republicans in the Senate, then, did about as expected, cutting roughly 30 percent of the budget items in my sample (for fiscal years 1982 to 1985). This rate of reductions falls almost dead center between the reduction rate of 17 percent for Democratic congresses and the 42 percent rate for Republican congresses (in fiscal years 1948, 1949, 1954, and 1955).

A roughly similar pattern is evident if we look at presidential success in Congress generally. Democratic presidents facing Democratic congresses win roughly 85 percent of their votes; Republicans facing Republican congresses succeed at roughly the same rate (on average). Republican President Reagan, facing a Democratic House and a Republican Senate (1981 to 1987), won roughly two-thirds of the key votes; whereas Republican administrations facing Democratic congresses won only between 36 and 60 percent of these key votes.[11] During his first year in office, with a Republican majority in the Senate, Reagan won an impressive 85 percent of the votes on which he took a stand. This percentage declined during the next five years to roughly 60 percent in 1986, then dropped dramatically to 36 percent in 1987 (an all-time low for any postwar president), which was the first time he faced Democratic majorities in both chambers of Congress. (His success rate rebounded somewhat in his last year in office, to roughly 47 percent.) Presidential success rates thus appear to be closely associated with the partisan balance in Congress.

The question becomes what was the net effect on spending of Reagan's occupancy of the White House? Certainly, he was no more successful, under the circumstances in Congress, than expected. And, as shown by Table 6.3, Reagan was actually *less* successful than any other postwar president at pushing his spending cuts through Congress. Truman, Kennedy, and Johnson each succeeded in getting Congress

TABLE 6.3   Change in Appropriations by Congress by Presidential Administration, 1948–1988

	Truman	Eisenhower	Kennedy/ Johnson	Nixon/ Ford	Carter	Reagan
PRESIDENT REQUESTED A CUT IN SPENDING						
Congress appropriates more than previous year	0.0% (0)	16.4% (12)	3.3% (2)	26.8% (19)	31.6% (12)	40.4% (40)
Congress appropriates less than previous year	100.0% (27)	83.6% (61)	96.7% (58)	73.2% (52)	68.4% (26)	59.6% (59)
PRESIDENT REQUESTED AN INCREASE IN SPENDING						
Congress appropriates more than previous year	86.7% (202)	90.0% (280)	91.3% (348)	96.1% (347)	96.9% (190)	91.2% (124)
Congress appropriates less than previous year	13.3% (31)	10.0% (31)	8.7% (33)	3.9% (14)	3.1% (6)	8.8% (12)

to enact nearly all the cuts they requested, and Eisenhower succeeded 84 percent of the time. Reagan, by contrast, succeeded less than 60 percent of the time. More generally, his success rate in key congressional votes for each of his eight years in office was less than that of Eisenhower in each corresponding year (Stanley and Niemi 1988, 220–221). Indeed, Reagan's success rate against Democratic congresses in 1987–1988 was less than Nixon's success rate even during the period of the Watergate scandal (Nixon won roughly 60 percent of his key votes that year). Thus, by comparison, Reagan was a weaker president than his predecessors.

What, then, accounts for the budgets of the 1980s? Expenditures on the Great Society programs and the regulatory activities of the federal government started declining under Gerald Ford, and their decline accelerated under Jimmy Carter. The reduction of these programs was therefore begun under a Congress in which both chambers were in Democratic hands and was accelerated when both branches were controlled by the Democrats.

This pattern can be seen in Table 6.4. Spending declined in Reagan's first budget (relative to the budget for 1981) for eight departments and programs: Commerce, Education, Energy, EPA, Housing and Urban Development, Transportation, Interior, and the Post Office (the latter two not shown in table). In two of these departments—Energy and the Post Office—the reduced spending continued declines begun under Carter's 1981 fiscal year budget. Of the other six spending categories, Carter had requested spending cuts for three of them: Commerce, Housing and Urban Development, and Transportation. The remaining

TABLE 6.4 Appropriations for Federal Departments by Fiscal Year, 1947–1986 (in billions of current dollars)

Fiscal Year	Agriculture	Commerce	Defense	Education	Energy	Environmental Protection Agency
1947	0.73	0.19	11.42	0.00	0.00	0.00
1948	0.75	0.19	8.75	0.00	0.00	0.00
1949	0.73	0.18	10.49	0.00	0.00	0.00
1950	0.86	0.27	13.09	0.00	0.00	0.00
1951	0.90	0.71	25.11	0.00	0.00	0.00
1952	1.00	0.87	60.86	0.00	0.00	0.00
1953	0.94	0.80	49.56	0.00	0.00	0.00
1954	1.06	0.86	34.65	0.00	0.00	0.00
1955	0.94	0.97	29.66	0.00	0.00	0.00
1956	1.17	1.27	33.11	0.00	0.00	0.00
1957	2.39	1.43	36.21	0.00	0.00	0.00
1958	4.11	0.60	35.35	0.00	0.00	0.00
1959	3.91	0.98	41.01	0.00	0.00	0.00
1960	4.44	0.90	40.60	0.00	0.00	0.00
1961	4.58	0.69	40.99	0.00	0.00	0.00
1962	6.64	0.79	47.65	0.00	0.00	0.00
1963	6.15	0.79	49.57	0.00	0.00	0.00
1964	6.96	0.80	48.92	0.00	0.00	0.00
1965	5.94	0.73	48.43	0.00	0.00	0.00
1966	7.17	1.29	48.75	0.00	0.00	0.00
1967	7.88	1.27	59.15	0.00	0.00	0.00
1968	5.99	1.03	72.12	0.00	0.00	0.00
1969	6.82	1.11	73.70	0.00	0.00	0.00
1970	8.89	0.96	71.28	0.00	0.00	0.00
1971	9.53	1.16	68.72	0.00	0.00	0.00
1972	12.69	1.40	72.64	0.00	0.00	2.45
1973	13.44	1.72	76.79	0.00	0.00	13.42
1974	11.77	1.51	76.53	0.00	0.00	0.64
1975	14.66	1.72	85.22	0.00	0.00	0.85
1976	14.84	2.29	94.14	0.00	4.50	0.77
1977	13.57	3.91	107.77	0.00	6.34	1.45
1978	15.49	2.33	112.98	0.00	6.82	0.85
1979	25.85	2.61	121.33	0.00	10.80	5.40
1980	21.76	2.46	134.76	0.00	28.66	4.66
1981	24.83	2.92	164.77	14.24	11.29	4.75
1982	26.61	1.84	206.66	12.97	9.31	1.36
1983	36.29	1.83	238.56	15.09	10.65	3.72
1984	39.69	2.05	255.98	15.38	11.58	4.00
1985	37.64	2.20	282.74	17.97	12.12	4.39
1986	45.88	2.23	289.56	18.45	12.38	4.79

Fiscal Year	Health, Education, and Welfare	Health and Human Services	Housing and Urban Development	Labor	National Aeronautics and Space Administration	Transportation
1947	0.00	0.00	0.00	0.14	0.00	0.00
1948	0.00	0.00	0.00	0.09	0.00	0.00
1949	0.00	0.00	0.00	0.01	0.00	0.00
1950	0.00	0.00	0.00	0.02	0.00	0.00
1951	0.00	0.00	0.00	0.21	0.00	0.00
1952	0.00	0.00	0.00	0.25	0.00	0.00
1953	0.00	0.00	0.00	0.22	0.00	0.00
1954	1.82	0.00	0.00	0.26	0.00	0.00
1955	1.70	0.00	0.00	0.39	0.00	0.00
1956	1.99	0.00	0.00	0.42	0.00	0.00
1957	2.22	0.00	0.00	0.43	0.00	0.00
1958	2.51	0.00	0.00	0.40	0.00	0.00
1959	2.97	0.00	0.00	0.54	0.00	0.00
1960	3.47	0.00	0.00	0.55	0.00	0.00
1961	3.82	0.00	0.00	0.55	0.00	0.00
1962	4.58	0.00	0.00	0.64	0.00	0.00
1963	5.12	0.00	0.00	0.34	0.00	0.00
1964	5.23	0.00	0.00	0.35	0.00	0.00
1965	6.70	0.00	0.00	0.57	0.00	0.00
1966	9.18	0.00	0.00	0.70	0.00	0.00
1967	12.11	0.00	0.00	0.64	0.00	0.00
1968	12.75	0.00	1.02	0.63	0.00	1.58
1969	52.64	0.00	2.68	4.79	0.00	7.16
1970	60.58	0.00	7.63	4.90	0.00	7.75
1971	68.16	0.00	3.37	6.35	0.00	11.12
1972	78.33	0.00	3.94	9.01	3.31	8.55
1973	89.97	0.00	4.39	9.60	3.42	7.11
1974	107.39	0.00	4.38	9.18	3.00	23.14
1975	117.50	0.00	50.98	13.87	3.23	19.01
1976	129.39	0.00	27.25	18.71	3.54	7.72
1977	152.91	0.00	19.55	26.14	3.69	12.92
1978	171.51	0.00	38.76	22.88	4.02	13.48
1979	187.26	0.00	32.15	19.88	4.35	16.87
1980	213.94	0.00	33.59	27.66	4.92	17.63
1981	0.00	236.55	37.16	32.16	5.54	25.92
1982	0.00	271.35	22.83	32.86	6.19	19.08
1983	0.00	290.11	12.10	35.12	6.81	34.21
1984	0.00	318.78	13.48	51.64	7.20	27.07
1985	0.00	359.02	12.83	34.10	7.49	28.42
1986	0.00	380.30	16.68	33.61	7.66	26.77

Data for Department of the Interior and Post Office not included.

three departments and programs that declined in Reagan's first budget—Education, EPA, and Interior—constituted new spending reductions and could fairly be attributed to Reagan and the Republicans in Congress. For each of these three departments, however, spending rose quickly in fiscal years 1983 to 1986, undoing much of the reallocation of 1982.

The budget story of the 1980s, then, was not the fiscal contractions so often advertised by Congress and the president. Indeed, the thesis of presidential power suggests that Reagan should have brought down the deficit, but he did not: Evidently, he was not as powerful as has been suggested. To explain the budgets of the 1980s, I must turn elsewhere—to Congress. I will first discuss congressional politics and the effect of the budget process on spending decisions.

COMMITTEE POWER, THE 1974 REFORMS, AND PARTY GOVERNANCE IN CONGRESS

To some analysts of U.S. politics, the runaway deficits of the 1980s were not the unintended result of the Reagan revolution but rather a consequence of a change in congressional procedure. This perception is based on a widely accepted view that Congress is not so much a democratic institution as a "pluralistic leviathan" (Freeman 1955). Central to this view is the thesis, more than a century old, that congressional politics is committee politics.[12]

The "interest group liberalism" (Lowi 1979) that purportedly dominates congressional politics, if it exists, has profound implications for budgeting, as well. As Kenneth Shepsle and Barry Weingast argued:

> The omnipresent electoral imperative induces members of Congress to target expenditures to their electoral constituents or to those who can provide electorally relevant resources. This implies that legislators invent programs, seek funding, and are especially attentive to policy areas that create or maintain jobs within their electoral constituency. . . . Expenditure programs are, as a consequence, biased away from least-cost methods of production so as to favor those methods that yield greater electoral support (1984, 335).

If each subgovernment pursues its policies in the way Shepsle and Weingast describe, the end result could be that the government outspends its receipts.

To mitigate the effects of "interest group liberalism," members of Congress purportedly relied on the members of the House Appropriations Committee to guard the federal Treasury, to make the hard choices between supporting their colleagues' programs and the need to economize spending (Fenno 1966). As David Mayhew concluded, "By cutting budgets they work against the diffuse and primal danger that Congress will spend more money than it takes in. They lean against particularism and also against servicing of the organized" (1974, 153). This system was supported by rules and procedures in Congress that separated authorization from appropriations. And the system appeared to work reasonably well, producing small but manageable deficits through the 1950s and 1960s.

This all changed with the Congressional Budget and Impoundment Control Act of 1974. Many viewed the new budget process established by the act as a way to coordinate spending and revenue decisions between the various subsystems in order to cut the deficit. But by transferring authority for establishing overall spending limits to the budget committees, the budget process so weakened the House Appropriations Committee that it could no longer act to guard the Treasury. Instead, its members seemingly became claimants on the federal Treasury, rather than its protectors. And because the budget process itself failed to work, there has been no restraint on spending in Congress.[13]

Two assumptions underlie this explanation of the deficit crisis. First is the belief that "power in Congress has rested in the committees or, increasingly, in the subcommittees," and thus, as a consequence, "throughout most of the postwar years, political parties in Congress have been weak, ineffectual organizations" (Dodd and Oppenheimer 1977, 50). Second is the belief that the House Appropriations Committee, once the "guardian of the federal Treasury" (Fenno 1966, 353), is now only a subdued guardian. I will examine these assumptions in turn, arguing that congressional parties and party leaders exercised more control and greater influence in congressional politics—and in budgeting, in particular—than commonly has been perceived. I will then seek to explain the budgetary decisions of the 1980s in light of this new understanding.

The Institutions of Agency: Parties and Committees

The common view of weak parties and autonomous committees in Congress, in its logical form, is identical to the view of presidential dominance presented earlier in this chapter. The membership of each house has delegated to the committees in each house wide-ranging authority to write legislation, hold hearings, and oversee the executive branch. But this delegation, as was the case in interpreting delegation to the executive, has been mistaken for abdication.

This view of committee and subcommittee power was developed to explain a set of generalized observations on congressional behavior. It explains, for example, why coalitions within Congress are seemingly universal and nonpartisan: The reason is that all members face the same necessity to bring home particularistic benefits, and the institutions are geared toward establishing and enforcing vote trades across projects and benefits. It also follows, for the same reason, that party discipline will be very lax—the vote trades cross party lines. Committees also use their powers, particularly their ex post veto (Shepsle and Weingast 1987), to ensure that amendments rarely get offered to their bills; when they are offered, few, if any, are successful. Further, committees can withhold legislation from consideration even in opposition to concerted floor majorities. Lastly, because committees are central to the policy-making process, committee members spend most of their time and effort in their committee work.

But again, are not these observations consistent with party control of committees? If congressional party organizations controlled committee decisionmaking, we would expect to observe all of the things typically recounted in support of the subgovernment model of congressional politics. Indeed, none of the things listed above discriminates between the two views.[14] And, in fact, we do observe obvious violations of this cozy view of subcommittee autonomy. Multiple referrals, where legislation is sent to several subcommittees, are increasingly common in the House.

The influence of congressional parties and their leadership may be indirect rather than direct and overt. It is important to consider how congressional majorities retain their authority to make decisions: Members of Congress design their institutions to fit their purposes. Students of U.S. politics have tended to focus on those aspects of congressional institutions that enable members to bring home private goods (projects or programs for their own districts). And studies of congressional behavior have focused largely on how members secure water projects, military bases, roads, and post offices for their districts and on the consequences of these activities for their political survival. These studies, of course, assume that voters appreciate projects in their district and that members can build reputations as good providers of the federal pork.

But party affiliations are also an important ingredient in voters' decisions: Party labels signal information that is otherwise very expensive for voters to obtain about the policy positions of candidates. As a result, politicians, in seeking office, also establish reputations as partisans and, moreover, have an incentive to enhance the collective reputation of their party. Thus, politicians adopt a mixture of collective (i.e., partisan) and individual (i.e., district-oriented) activities in seeking reelection.

It follows that members will seek to structure Congress in a way that will facilitate both of these activities. Party organizations, their leadership, and the committees that serve them provide the institutional means for pursuing the collective goals of party members. This leads to the enactment and implementation of policies that affect a large proportion of congressional districts for which the members of the majority party can claim credit.

But these pursuits do not preclude individual, district-oriented benefits. It is in the interest of all members of the majority party to establish a system that enables party members to secure the individual, district-oriented benefits they need to enhance their own reputations. Thus, the majority party leadership uses its agenda powers, in concert with the agenda powers assigned to committees, to secure the omnibus pork-barrel logroll so familiar to congressional scholars.

The congressional parties, of course, delegate much of the authority to make these kinds of decisions to the leadership and to committees, though the Democratic caucus has, at times, sat down as a whole and made policy for the Democratic majority. In delegating, the congressional parties encounter the agency problems ubiquitous to human experience: For a variety of reasons, intentional or not, the persons to whom authority is delegated may not carry out their authority in the best interests of those doing the delegating. So pernicious are these problems that their existence has led many scholars to conclude that the congressional parties have, in fact, abdicated their authority to the standing committees and subcommittees of Congress.

The abdication conclusion, however, ignores both the efforts by the congressional parties to mitigate these delegation problems and the effects their efforts have on structuring choices and outcomes. Those in authority, holding positions of trust within the party organization, are compensated for their efforts. Sanctions, of course, can also be applied to those who misuse the authority delegated to them. Further, one often-noted feature of the legislative game as it is currently structured is the multiplicity of veto points. Both authorizing and appropriating committees, as well as the party leadership, have a say in the passage of legislation. This system can be viewed as follows: Both committees and leaders are agents of the majority caucus; one of the techniques used to control these agents is to give them mutual checks on each others' actions. In essence, like the separation of powers designed into the structure of the federal government, party organizations—in particular, the party leadership—and the system of standing committees form a separation of powers—a system of checks and balances—that protects members of Congress from opportunistic behavior on the part of their agents.

Another important avenue through which parties mitigate these problems with respect to standing committees is appointments. Both parties have committees that appoint their members to standing committees. It does not seem likely that those in the party responsible for making committee assignments would merely sell committee posts to the highest bidders. Rather, we should expect that they would use committee assignments to further their substantive interests. Indeed, appointments to the control committees—Appropriations, Rules, and Ways and Means—and transfers from the lesser committees to the major committees are strongly affected by the leadership's desires and are determined, to an extent, by past party loyalty (Rohde and Shepsle 1973; Shepsle 1978; Cox and McCubbins 1991).

Another common means of constraining committee activities is through procedural restrictions. In this regard, procedures can have two effects. First, reporting requirements make it difficult for committees to hide information relevant to the evaluation of their recommendations. For example, the Government in the Sunshine Act opened up committee hearings so that committee members could no longer have access to information that others did not; committees are also required to report their findings when submitting major legislation to the floor. Second, procedures can establish access points for selected representatives and constituencies to have input into committee decisions, and moreover, they can be used to establish a system of checks on committee decisions.

Some standing committees, of course, will receive greater scrutiny of their activities via appointments and procedures than will others. A few committees have jurisdiction over issues that are encompassed, at least implicitly, in the meaning of the party label. Because the party's label is a collective good for its members, the actions of these committees affect everyone in the party, and, collectively, the party and its leaders have a greater interest in mitigating the agency problems that arise vis-à-vis these committees. Social Security, for example, has been a core Democratic program since the New Deal, and the Committee on Ways and Means, which was delegated jurisdiction over this program, has been an important committee for the Democrats.

Not all committees, however, have jurisdiction over areas for which their actions have large external effects on other members. Some standing committees have jurisdiction over issues unrelated or only minimally related to the issues that voters identify with the party. These are usually committees whose jurisdiction covers topics affecting only a minority of members, such as Post Office (since World War II), Interior, or Merchant Marine and Fisheries. The legislation proposed by these committees has few external effects: The effects are primarily limited to those members whose districts are targeted for projects or benefits in the bill.

The majority party caucus will treat these various committees differently. Those committees whose jurisdictions overlap with the issues that identify the majority party will be subject to greater scrutiny and more careful screening: The appointment committee will seek to ensure, through the appointments it makes, that these standing committees will pursue the majority party's agenda. Committees like Ways and Means, Appropriations, Rules, and Budget will be subject to the greatest control efforts because of their policy jurisdictions. Committees like Agriculture (since 1960 at least) or Merchant Marine and Fisheries, on the other hand, may escape serious efforts to "stack" their assignments.

Sanctions against committees and their chairs are, of course, rare because they are a clumsy and very expensive form of discipline and because a word to the wise (or an occasional public hanging, as demonstrated by the removal of Wright Patman, W. R. Poage, Edward Hebert, and Mel Price and the threatened removal of Les Aspin) is usually sufficient. But party caucuses do take measures to ensure that committees act in a manner responsible to the will of the majority party, especially on issues that will affect the collective reputation of the party.

Again, in the conventional view of committees, delegation (in this case, from the majority party caucus to the standing committees of Congress) has been mistaken for abdication (Cox and McCubbins 1991; Kiewiet and McCubbins 1991). If committees are agents of party caucuses, then we expect that most of the decisions in Congress would be made in committee—that is, after all, their function—and that committee members would acquire expertise in the committee's jurisdiction (which is why, after all, they were delegated the jurisdiction in the first place). We don't expect these functions to be uncontrolled, however, and we witness many and varied attempts by majority party caucuses and their leadership to control committees. Further, having anticipated the reaction of the majority party to its proposals, the committee can expect that few of its bills will be amended or rejected on the floor. The absence of amendments to committee bills by floor majorities is, in fact, equally good evidence that committees are efficient and responsible agents of the majority party. We also expect members to spend most of their time in Washington, attending to their committee duties—it is their job, as delegated by the majority party caucus.

The Role of the House Appropriations Committee

In Richard Fenno's classic account, the House Appropriations Committee was depicted as a budget-slashing "guardian of the federal Treasury" (1966, 353), protecting the House from the budgetary excesses of its own committees and from budget-maximizing bureaucrats. This model of the committee was based upon Fenno's interviews with members of Congress and on a comparison of committee decisions and presidential requests for the period from 1947 to 1962. For the 36 bureaus on which he collected data, Fenno reported that the amount recommended by the House Appropriations Committee for a given bureau was less than the amount requested by the president in 73.6 percent of the 575 cases in his data set (1966, 353, Table 8.1). For a set of 69 agencies and programs (including almost all of Fenno's 36 bureaus) during a period extending from 1948 to 1985, I found that the House Appropriations Committee cut the president's requests for 70.4 percent of the 1,983 cases in my data set.[15]

But do these statistics constitute evidence that the "dominant pattern" (Fenno 1966, 353) for the HAC is to guard the Treasury? What would be expected of the committee's recommendations were it not guarding the federal Treasury? If the procedural restrictions on the Budget Bureau work to constrain the bureau's ability to revise agency budget estimates and if agencies compile estimates in accordance with the legislation that authorized their activities, then presidential requests will reflect, to a large extent, the level of funding preferred by the authorizing committees in Congress.[16] These figures, of course, are often revised according to the president's policy guidelines. If many committees can be expected to prefer more spending on items within their jurisdiction than would be preferred by the House as a whole or by the majority as a whole and if the HAC is relatively representative of the House and the majority party,[17] then the members of the HAC will often prefer to spend less than the members on the committee that authorized the item. Consequently, the HAC will often cut the spending requests made for agencies by the president. Thus, even if they are not guarding the federal Treasury, the members of the HAC can be expected, in most years, to cut most executive budget requests.

In Fenno's account of the HAC, party politics plays essentially no role. I have argued here and elsewhere (Cox and McCubbins 1991; Kiewiet and McCubbins 1991) that the partisan contingents on the committee are agents of their parties and that, as a result, the committee functions as an agent of the majority party, pursuing the collective goals of that party's membership. These goals may sometimes be to cut the budget, but they are not necessarily so. Consequently, the varying goals of the parties controlling the White House and the House of Representatives determine, for example, the treatment afforded the president's budget requests by the HAC, with Democratic majorities favoring higher spending on domestic programs than do the Republican majorities. As shown in Table 6.5, how often the committee cuts the president's requests is determined by partisan factors.

In the table, the committee's treatment of the president's request for an agency or program (whether the committee's recommendation is less than, equal to, or greater than the president's request) is tabulated against partisan factors (a cross-match of the partisan control of the executive branch by the partisan control of the House). The table shows that the House committee is most likely to cut the president's requests when the president is a Democrat and the House is controlled by the Republicans (cuts amount to 93 percent of actions taken); that the committee is somewhat less likely to cut the executive's requests when the same party controls both bodies (whether controlled by Democrats or Republicans, the committee cuts nearly 80 percent of the requests in my sample); but that a Democratic committee is far less likely to cut a Republican president's requests (only 57 percent of requests were cut by the committee under these circumstances). Further, when the Democrats hold a majority in the House but the president and a majority of the Senate are Republicans (as in Reagan's first six years), the committee ends up cutting only 38 percent of the president's requests and actually proposes *increases* for 55 percent of the items. Fenno described such changes as "mood" swings, where the committee would shift from an "economy mood" to a "spending mood." The pattern in Table 6.5 suggests that the mood toward executive budget requests by the House Appropriations Committee is determined in partisan differences between the House, the Senate, and the executive.

Further, if the guardianship hypothesis were correct, I would never expect the House, in its amendments, to decrease the committee's recommendations. The committee, after all, is supposedly holding back spending. What I find, however, is that for the spending recommendations made by the committee for individual agencies and programs, more than 58 percent of those recommendations that were amended by floor action were decreases, and only 42 percent were increases. Of the appropriations bills amended by the House that I examined, 106 (or 43 percent) reduced the totals recommended by the House Appropriations Committee.

Has the 1974 Budget Act changed the House Appropriations Committee from the Treasury guardian it once was to the subdued guardian who now seeks its own claims on the federal Treasury? Actually, there is no evidence that it ever was a guardian or that its function has, in

TABLE 6.5 House Appropriations Committee (HAC) Treatment of Presidential Budget Requests by Partisan Control of Government

	President—Republican Congress—Republican	President—Republican Congress—Democratic	President—Republican House—Democratic Senate—Republican	President—Democratic Congress—Republican	President—Democratic Congress—Democratic
HAC<Pres	73 (80.2)	486 (67.1)	90 (38.5)	80 (93.0)	667 (78.7)
HAC=Pres	12 (13.2)	104 (14.4)	14 (6.0)	4 (4.7)	70 (8.3)
HAC>Pres	6 (6.6)	134 (18.5)	130 (55.6)	2 (2.3)	111 (13.1)
Column Total	91 (4.6)	724 (36.5)	234 (11.8)	86 (4.3)	848 (42.8)

Chi-square (8 df) = 270.3

Chi-square test is a statistic used for a general "goodness of fit" test, which compares (in this case) the observed cell frequencies to expected cell frequencies (where the expectation is that observations occur with equal probability in each row).

HAC<Pres=HAC appropriation bill calls for less than presidential request
HAC=Pres=HAC appropriation bill equal to presidential request
HAC>Pres=HAC appropriation bill calls for more than presidential request

fact, changed. It was and still is a check upon the authority of the other standing committees in the House, a check used by the majority party leadership to ensure that the policies pursued by the other standing committees in the House reflect the collective goals of the membership of their party (Kiewiet and McCubbins 1991). This suggests that it is not a change in the behavior of members of the HAC nor is it a change in the spending process that wrought the deficits of the 1980s.

The Congressional Budget Process in the 1980s

The budget process created by the act has three key components. First, it creates budget committees to draft a budget policy, which sets guidelines for all aspects of federal spending and revenue. Second, it requires authorizing committees to "reconcile" policy in their respective jurisdictions with the budget guidelines. Third, if a committee fails to offer sufficient reconciliation legislation, the act empowers the budget committees to write their own reconciliation bills.

Members of the budget committees are hand picked by the party leaderships and do not accrue seniority on these committees, nor do they gain secure tenure. The party leaderships, by these procedures, have relatively greater control, year in and year out, over the composition of their partisan contingents on the budget committees than they do over the composition of any other committee, which allows the majority party leadership to use the budget process to inject its priorities into the decisions of every committee.

Indeed, from the perspective of floor majorities in the House and Senate, the budget process was strikingly effective in the 1980s. In 1981, a coalition of House and Senate Republicans and some conservative Democrats used the budget and reconciliation process to cut some $36.6 billion in spending authority for fiscal year 1982.[18] The first budget resolution called for the House Agriculture Committee to write legislation bringing about cuts of $2.2 billion in fiscal year 1982 budget authority; it required the House Banking and Urban Affairs Committee to cut budget authority in its programs by $12.9 billion; and it required Education and Labor to reduce authority by $13.5 billion, Energy and Commerce, by $6.4 billion, and Public Works and Transportation, by $6.6 billion. This "conservative coalition" outmaneuvered the House Democratic leadership in the budget process, forcing the HAC to work within the spending parameters set by these budget limits. Its success demonstrated how effective the new process could be at subjecting congressional committees to the will of floor majorities. It also marked the only time since the passage of the act that the House Democratic leadership was defeated.

The first budget resolution in 1982 for fiscal year 1983 required cuts of only $2.2 billion in budget authority, compared to the previous year's $36.6 billion. This time, as the amount indicates, the House Democratic leadership, using inventive procedures, such as the King of the Mountain rule,[19] reasserted itself.

The House Democratic leaders then used the budget process in 1983 to draft their own budget blueprint as an alternative to the Republican budget submitted by Reagan. The Democrats' budget added $33 billion in domestic spending to Reagan's proposal, requested $30 billion in new revenues, and cut Reagan's defense request by $16 billion. The final conference agreement added $5 billion to the House's defense proposal and reduced, usually by small amounts, most of the House's domestic spending recommendations.

Whereas the Senate Republican leadership used the budget process to give direction to the Senate committees, the House Democrats used it to unite the party behind a common program, with the House Budget Committee holding hearings with the entire Democratic caucus.[20]

Ultimately, the result of these efforts by caucuses to control the product and actions of committees was to make spending policy reflect the desires of the majority party in each chamber. Indeed, the single best predictor of changes in spending policy for almost the whole range of federal programs and agencies is party control of Congress and the White House (Kiewiet and McCubbins 1991). This analysis suggests that policy is influenced, to a far greater extent than commonly believed, by party politics.

THE PARTISAN ROOTS OF DEFICIT SPENDING

Having rejected the two most common explanations of the spending growth of the 1980s, how then, can I account for this growth? To explain deficits, I first need to explain federal spending policies and how they are affected by divided government.[21] The approach I take to explain budget deficits is quite different from the course set by Robert Barro, whose explanation assumes that government spending is exogenous and fixed and that taxpayers are indifferent between debt and tax financing of public spending (Barro 1979).

With regard to federal spending decisions, it can be shown that, at every stage of the spending process, such decisions reflect party politics (Kiewiet and McCubbins 1985a, 1985b, 1988, and 1991, Chapter 8). Indeed, in the appendix to this chapter, I demonstrate that there is, in fact, a strong relationship between party control of government and spending policy. Domestic agencies, for example, do better under Democratic administrations and Democratic congresses than under Republicans. Defense and high-technology programs, on the other hand, do better under Republican administrations and Republican congresses than under Democrats.

When the president is a Republican and both houses of Congress are in Democratic hands, spending on domestic and social programs is somewhat restrained but is close to the levels that would have been adopted had the Democrats controlled the White House as well. In such instances, though the Republican presidents act as a restraint on domestic spending, the ability of Congress to package various spending items into an omnibus bill makes it difficult for even the most ardent Republicans to restrain spending (Kiewiet and McCubbins 1988 and 1991, Chapter 8).

But what happens when control of Congress is divided—when a Democratic majority controls the House and a Republican majority controls the Senate? This has happened several times, for example, from January 1981 to January 1987.

The Constitution established a bilateral veto game between the two chambers, with each chamber holding a check on the actions of the other. But the cooperation and coordination necessary to overcome these constitutional checks and balances is frequently inadequate.[22] Policies that have a large collective component are frequently adopted by the congressional parties and serve to define their collective reputations. Neither congressional party is likely to go along with a solution to a problem such as the deficit for which the other party can claim credit, and each will use its institutional position and the veto granted it by its control of one house of Congress to defeat the other party's attempts to solve the problem. What is implied by divided control, then, is that the cooperation to solve collective problems, like the deficit, will largely be nonexistent.

What, then, will be the equilibrium to this bilateral veto game? In an effort to model this game, I make a simplifying assumption about the preferences of the members of each party. I assume that there are two types of programs—domestic programs favored by the Democrats and defense programs favored by the Republicans. The preferences of the two parties over budgetary allocations to these two goods is given in Table 6.6. The Democrats, I assume, prefer most that spending on their programs be increased, while spending on the Republicans' programs be decreased (denoted D,r in the table). Further, Democrats next most prefer that spending on all programs be increased (denoted D,R). Democrats are then assumed to prefer decreases in both their own programs and the Republicans' programs (denoted d,r) to a decrease

TABLE 6.6   Party Ranking of Spending Allocations, Most Preferred to Least Preferred

Democrats	Republicans
D, r	d, R
D, R	D, R
d, r	d, r
d, R	D, r

D = increased spending on Democratic programs
R = increased spending on Republican programs
d = decreased spending on Democratic programs
r = decreased spending on Republican programs

in their programs with an increase in the Republicans' programs. I assume that Republican preferences are similar with respect to their own programs.

In bilateral veto games, the reversionary outcome if no solution is adopted determines what, if any, cooperative solution will be an equilibrium. (The reversionary outcome is that which obtains if no agreement is reached between the players in the game—i.e., the level of spending to which appropriations revert.) The spending reversion point for most federal programs is zero. Congress must enact legislation annually to appropriate money for most of these activities if they are to continue. Typically, however, Congress will pass a continuing resolution that pegs spending at some low baseline level (the "Fenno Rule") if no appropriations bill is enacted. Continuing resolutions typically yield little or no growth in spending and may even entail a modest decrease in spending (adjusting for inflation) for the programs covered by the resolution. Thus, the reversion, if no spending policy is agreed to by the two parties, is to decrease appropriations for all programs (i.e., the outcome denoted d,r in the table is the reversion point).

The only alternative in the table that is preferred by both parties to the reversionary outcome (and thus will not be vetoed by one or the other party) is the outcome in which spending for the programs of both parties is allowed to increase (denoted D,R). Thus, under conditions of divided control, I expect overall spending to increase. In the appendix, I offer a test, in a study of postwar budgetary policy, that supports this proposition.

Fiscal year 1984 reconciliation legislation, for example, did not cut budget authority in any area. And Fiscal year 1986 reconciliation legislation passed by Congress and signed by the president, though requiring cuts in agriculture, defense, energy, Medicare, and ten other programs, increased spending for the EPA's Superfund, income and

Social Security programs, veterans' affairs, and· three other programs. The following year, there again were no significant cuts in any area.

Throughout the decade, the Democrats in the House and the Republicans in the Senate forged a union that enacted policies contrary to the basic tenets of Reagan's budget policy. In his second term, as was seen in Table 6.4, this "coalition" enacted increases in social and education programs and cuts in defense spending, despite Reagan's strenuous opposition.

I have already noted that spending increased during Reagan's two terms in office—nearly doubling in current-dollar terms during these eight years. Though some areas of domestic spending were reduced (primarily those that were under pressure in earlier decades), other areas increased tremendously. Defense spending also increased during Reagan's first term. As expected, this spending compromise was abrogated once the Democrats regained control of the Senate. With unified party control of Congress, the Democrats could undertake to cut back on those programs favored by the Republicans, namely, those tied to defense.

Taken together, the effect of divided government on revenue (Cox and McCubbins, Chapter 7 in this volume) and on spending decisions and the effect of the tax cut of 1981 produced the runaway deficits of the 1980s. The pattern was not new; it has recurred throughout the twentieth century. Since 1929, divided government has yielded sizable increases in the national debt (a test of this hypothesis for fiscal years 1929 to 1988 is provided in the appendix). Indeed, the increase in the debt attributable to divided government exceeds the effects of national unemployment and inflation by an order of magnitude. If the Democrats continue to hold majorities in the House and Senate and the Republicans continue to occupy the White House, then little progress will be made toward reducing the national debt.

CONCLUSION

Drawing from the literature on U.S. national government, two explanations for the runaway deficits of the 1980s have received widespread comment. The first is that the president did it—that Ronald Reagan, on his way to forging a revolution in U.S. politics, put into place policies that pushed the nation over the deficit precipice. The second has its roots in Congress—finding that the Congressional Budget and Impoundment Control Act of 1974 led to the unraveling of fiscal restraints in Congress and unleashed the spendthrift, committee-centered, policy subgovernments. Both of these explanations have, at their core, a perception that congressional parties are merely shells within which policy is bartered and to which no control over policy is granted.

Congressional majorities, in these models, are believed to have abdicated their collective responsibilities over national policy to the president, on the one hand, and to congressional committees and subcommittees, on the other.

Evidence cited for this abdication includes the apparent neglect of oversight and policy review by congressional majorities. In one case, although Congress cuts presidential budget estimates for nearly every item in the budget, the policy priorities of the president seem to emerge from Capitol Hill little changed. In the other case, on most legislation, the House and Senate rarely amend the work of their committees, and most members are unaware of and unconcerned about the activities of committees other than the ones to which they are assigned.

What appears to be a neglect of oversight and review, however, is really a preference for a more effective form of delegation, a form in which the structure of the delegation—through fire-alarm oversight, procedural restrictions, and checks and balances—in fact alleviates the necessity for active oversight and review. The absence of oversight and review, then, is not evidence of abdication; rather, once the structure of the delegation is understood, it is evidence that the delegation is serving the purposes of those who structured it (in this case, congressional majorities). Thus, contrary to the presumption common to the scholarship on presidential power and on policy subgovernments, delegation need not be abdication, so long as delegates are properly constrained and disciplined.

The rapid spending growth of the 1980s was the consequence of a structural problem: divided government. Just as the framers of the Constitution intended, the divided partisan control of the executive and legislative departments has created a kind of stalemate. The compromise required to overcome the mutual checks held by the House Democrats and the Senate Republicans over each other's spending programs led to increased spending on nearly every function of government. The Democrats' return to unified control of Congress in 1987 meant that the stalemate on spending was weakened—defense spending was slowed and likely will stay close to zero or negative growth, barring a major war—and the Democrats' domestic programs will continue to grow, albeit at a slower rate than would be expected under unified Democratic government.

APPENDIX

The central thesis of this chapter is that parties exert substantial control over the policymaking apparatus in Congress. It follows that divided government will lead to increased budget deficits. In this appendix, I examine the effects of party politics on federal spending allocations in the postwar period and on the level of the deficit for the period from 1929 to 1988.

On Measuring Changes in Spending and Deficits

Before describing my test and results, however, it is important to discuss some measurement issues. The first has to do with choosing baselines in comparing fiscal policy from one year to the next. For example, is it possible to compare the defense budget in the 1950s to the defense budget in the 1980s? There are many potential pitfalls. Several data transformations are commonly used to facilitate this comparison. Budget figures are deflated to account for price increases; changes in budgets are described as a percent of total spending or of gross national product (GNP). Each transformation serves a purpose, and each introduces errors, distortions, and biases into the comparison. Using data transformation willy-nilly, especially in making comparisons across many years, can introduce more confusion than clarity (Muris 1989).[23]

On a more abstract level, without explicating a specific theory of the demand for government goods and services, we can make use of the general properties of demand functions as an approximation and apply the Slutsky equation. It states that changes in the demand for a commodity can be decomposed into a substitution or price effect and an income effect.[24] To avoid these problems in the text, I compare spending figures over time for federal programs in constant (1972) dollars.

The second measurement issue concerns how to measure the deficit. It may seem odd that this is problematic. The deficit, it seems, should just be the difference between how much the government spends and how much it takes in. Something akin to this is the measure commonly reported by the government as the deficit.

But this measure of the deficit minimizes its apparent size. The current surplus in the Social Security trust fund is used to offset the deficit in spending on other items. Doing so, however, ignores the obligations created by the Social Security system. The surpluses in the Social Security trust fund are not treated as tax revenue for general obligations—the Social Security administration uses them to purchase Treasury bonds. Yet, these bonds must be repaid if the Social Security system is to remain solvent. Thus, although the deficit measure commonly used by the federal government treats Social Security contributions as general revenue, in actuality the surplus in contributions just adds to the debt that, in this case, the government owes to the Social Security trust fund.

Another measure that treats the bonds held by the Social Security trust fund (and other federal agencies) as debt instead of revenue examines changes in the national debt from one year to the next. This measure captures all government borrowing from private and public sources, and it gives an indicator of how far government expenditures exceed general revenue. I examine both measures here.

On the Determinants of Spending

I will only outline the logic of my model of spending decisions here (for details, see Kiewiet and McCubbins 1985a, 1985b, 1988, and 1991). My model has two stages: First, I model how changes in voters' preferences alter the activities of officeholders; second, I model how the individual choices of officeholders are mapped into a collective choice over spending. In this model, I assume that the incentives of political actors are forged through the electoral connection and that different politicians confront different reelection problems, so that their incentives and actions will be shaped somewhat differently. I also assume that the organization of Congress—the rights and authority granted party and committee leaders—induces an equilibrium over policy choices (Shepsle 1979) and that this equilibrium is responsive to the changing preferences of members of Congress.

In this model, parties play a key role. In the first place, candidates within each district and state are franchiseholders for one of the two major parties. Much like manufacturers' brand names, party labels allow candidates to convey complex information about their issue positions to voters—information that might otherwise be unavailable or too expensive for voters to acquire. Candidates affiliated with one of the two major parties, then, have a competitive advantage relative to someone who has no such affiliation and must therefore bear the full costs of informing voters about his or her issue positions. Parties also organize Congress. The majority party in each chamber appoints members to standing committees, writes the rules and procedures of collective choice within the chamber, and schedules debate and votes over legislation. Through these actions, the parties enforce their franchise rights and make public policy that reinforces the informational value of their party label (for a full discussion of this model, see Kiewiet and McCubbins 1991; Cox and McCubbins 1991).

If there are appreciable differences in the policy platforms of the two parties, then it will matter which parties organize the upper and lower houses of Congress. Because most programs of the federal government were created by Democratic congresses, I assume that the Democrats prefer to spend more on these programs than do the Republicans. The Republicans, on the other hand, have an alternative spending strategy, which largely entails cutting the Democratically created programs and supplanting them with their own (primarily in the realm of national defense). Thus, domestic programs will expand more quickly when the Democrats control Congress, and they will contract or expand more slowly when the Republicans hold majorities in both chambers, all else constant. The same comparative static holds with respect to presidential budget estimates and party control of the White House. Under conditions of divided control, as I hypothesized in the text, spending should increase across virtually every program in the federal budget.

Factors other than the collective reputations of the two parties that affect voters' evaluations of incumbents (i.e., that affect the personal reputations of these incumbents) should also affect policy decisions. Variables representing these factors are included in my regression below. The electoral calculus underlying these variables can be found in Kiewiet and McCubbins (1985b).

To test these hypotheses, I examined data on federal spending for 69 agencies and programs (see Kiewiet and McCubbins 1991 for a list of these agencies and programs).[25] I estimated the equation described in Table 6.7, pooled across the agencies and programs in my sample, for changes in congressional appropriations. Virtually all accounts of the appropriations process stress that key decisionmakers within both branches consider proposed budgetary figures primarily in terms of the changes such figures represent over the previous fiscal year (Fenno 1966; Wildavsky 1974). I therefore performed a transformation that is roughly equivalent to percentage changes. In this transformation, I divide the current-dollar spending choice for each agency by the real-dollar appropriation it received in the previous fiscal year and then take the logarithm of this division (multiplying the result by 100).

Decisionmaking in the appropriations process is sequential: The executive branch (since the Budget and Accounting Act of 1921, the president) submits budget requests to the committees on appropriations in each chamber; the two chambers of Congress then use these requests as a baseline for their spending decisions. In this process, the outcome at each stage is a function of the outcome at the previous stage. And because actors at each stage are assumed to be sophisticated, the choices at each stage reflect expectations about what will happen at later stages. In each case, spending choices, when they enter an equation as independent variables, are endogenous, and some sort of instrumental variables technique must be employed to ensure that my estimates are

TABLE 6.7 Two-Stage Estimation of Final Congressional Appropriations Pooled Cross-Sectional Time Series of Sixty-nine Agencies, 1948–1985

Regression of $\Delta CONG_{it}$ by: Dependent Variable	Estimated Coefficient	Standard Error
Constant	−4.743	2.105
$\Delta PRES_{it}$*	0.612[a]	0.107
$\Delta DEBT_{it}$	−0.061	12.913
E_t	1.732[a]	0.628
U_{t-1}	1.238[a]	0.445
I_{t-1}	−0.099	0.103
DEM_t	6.291[a]	1.466
$DIVIDED_t$	5.779[a]	3.087
$KOREA_t$	−2.702	1.755
$VIETNAM_t$	0.570	0.984

N = 1980
Adjusted R^2 = 0.637
Standard error of the regression = 13.696
[a]the coefficient is significant with the probability greater than or equal to .99

$\Delta CONG_{it}$ = log of the appropriation received by agency i in fiscal year t as a proportion of the appropriation that agency received in the previous fiscal year.

$\Delta PRES_{it}$* = an instrumental variables estimate for the appropriation requested for the same agency as a proportion of what the agency received the previous fiscal year.

$\Delta DEBT_{t-1}$ = partial log of the total federal debt (reported in the Department of Commerce's *Historical Statistics, Historical Tables, Budget of the United States Government* for fiscal 1990, and the *Economic Report of the President* for 1989) in year $t-1$, i.e., if $DEBT_t$ is the debt in year t, then $\Delta DEBT_{t-1}$ = log[$DEBT_t/DEBT_{t-1}$].

E_t = a dummy variable that takes on a value of 1 in congressionsl election years and 0 otherwise.

U_{t-1} = the average rate of unemployment during the six months prior to the end of the fiscal year, as reported in the Department of Commerce's *Survey of Current Business.*

I_{t-1} = the (annualized) percentage change in the consumer price index during the six months prior to the end of the fiscal year, as reported in the Department of Commerce's *Historical Statistics* and *Survey of Current Business.* For FY 1965, for example, this measure would register the rate of inflation during the last half of calendar year 1963.

DEM_t = a dummy variable that takes on a value of 1 when the Democrats control both houses of Congress and a value of 0 otherwise.

$DIVIDED_t$ = a dummy variable that takes on a value of 1 when the House is controlled by the Democrats and the Senate is controlled by the Republicans, 0 otherwise.

$KOREA_t$ = a dummy variable that takes on the value 1 for fiscal years in which the United States was engaged in armed conflict in Korea (fiscal years 1952 to 1954), 0 otherwise.

$VIETNAM_t$ = a dummy variable that takes on the value 1 for fiscal years in which the United States was engaged in armed conflict in Vietnam (1967 to 1974), 0 otherwise.

The instrument for $\Delta PRES_{it}$ was derived in a regression of that variable against all of the exogenous variables in this equation and a similar equation, not reported here, estimating $\Delta PRES_{it}$ (for details, see Kiewiet and McCubbins 1991).

consistent and efficient. The model I specify for congressional appropriations is overidentified, and I thus used two-stage least squares to
construct instruments for the endogenous choice of presidential request.
This method permits consistent and efficient estimates.

One further econometric note: My full time series is thirty-eight
years; for some programs, the number of observations is less than that.
For this reason, I pooled the data across my sample of programs. Pooling
creates additional diagnostic problems and requires special care in
estimation; for example, test statistics on the residuals for the equation
described in Table 6.7 indicated a significant degree of heteroskedasticity.
To correct for heteroskedasticity, I used the heteroskedasticity-consistent
covariance matrix procedure of Halbert White (White 1980; MacKinnon
and White 1985). A battery of tests did not suggest any other significant
violations of the Gauss-Markov assumptions, leading me to believe that
considerable confidence can be placed in these results.

The results are reported in Table 6.7. I report the variables, their
definitions, the estimated coefficient for each, and the standard error
for each coefficient. The results support most of the comparative static
hypotheses, relative to domestic agency appropriations, that I outlined
at the beginning of this appendix. Importantly, the dummy variables
for Democratic control of Congress and for divided party control of
Congress are large, positive, and significant. This regression also supports
the hypothesis of an electoral appropriations cycle; Congress appropriates
nearly 2 percent more in election years than in nonelection years to
this set of agencies. Though there appears to be no response to changes
in the inflation rate in the spending decisions here, increasing unemployment leads to sharply increased spending for my sample of programs.
Wars and budget deficits, however, seem to have no impact on congressional spending patterns. A complete test of the divided government
spending model described in the text would require me to test a
specification similar to the one above, with changes in defense spending
as the dependent variable. I will not undertake such a test here; however,
given the above results on domestic spending, I can extend my empirical
examination of the theoretical model by estimating a model of changes
in the deficit. Such a test is offered below.

On the Determinants of the Deficit

In the 1980s, the annual increments to the national debt (i.e., the
budget deficit) became larger than the entire budget of just a few years
earlier. To test my hypothesis that divided government leads to increased
budgetary imbalances, I estimate a model of the choice of the deficit,
derived from models of spending and revenue developed elsewhere

(Kiewiet and McCubbins 1991; McCubbins 1990). The estimation involves income effects (modeled as GNP and unemployment) and substitution effects (various political variables, including dummy variables corresponding to periods of divided government, wars, and inflation). The model is represented by the independent variables listed in Table 6.8.

The estimation in Table 6.8 was affected by a few econometric problems, the most serious of which was autocorrelation. In each case, I included a set of lagged dependent and independent variables to correct for potential inefficiencies. Other details of the estimation can be found in McCubbins (1990).

In Table 6.8, I estimate a model of deficit determination using three different measures of the deficit. In column 1, I estimate the model using the common definition of the deficit that is reported each year by the federal government (measured in constant dollars). This measure is simply the difference each year between federal expenditures and federal revenues from all sources (including, for example, Social Security). In column 2, I estimate the model using as a measure of the deficit the percentage change from one year to the next in the size of the (constant-dollar) federal debt. This measure has the advantage of including purchases of Treasury Notes by Social Security, which, in fact, must be repaid by future taxes, as part of the debt and therefore as part of the deficit.

From previous research on spending decisions, I expected increasing unemployment to lead to increased spending. I therefore expect increases in the unemployment rate, all else constant, to lead to increased deficits and thus, U to have a negative coefficient in column 1 (deficits are measured as negative numbers; surpluses as positive numbers) and positive coefficients in column 2. I have no prediction about how changes in the rate of inflation, I, will affect budget deficits. Wars increase defense and related spending and seem to have a mixed effect but no net decrease on domestic spending. Consequently, I expect the wartime variables (WWII and KOREA), all else constant, to yield negative coefficients in column 1 and positive coefficients in column 2. A dummy variable for the Vietnam war was dropped from the specification; all tests showed that its effect was insignificant.

If spending has increased faster than revenue as the economy has grown, then the coefficients for the two GNP measures will be negative in column 1 and positive in column 2. My model of party politics implies that deficits will not increase (Republican majorities might decrease spending and therewith the deficit) when both houses of Congress are controlled by the same party (the majority party in Congress will control the agenda over spending and taxes), even when the

TABLE 6.8 On the Determination of the Federal Budget Deficit, 1929–1988

Independent variables	Dependent Variables	
	DEFICIT Estimated Coefficient	ΔDEBT Estimated Coefficient
Constant	28.69	−0.06
WW II$_t$	−84.39^a	0.45^a
KOREA$_t$	−9.40^a	0.02
PRES DEM/CONGRESS REP$_t$	2.81	−0.08^a
PRES REP/CONGRESS DEM$_t$	−2.68	0.01
PRES REP/CONGRESS DIVIDED$_t$	−26.99^a	0.09^a
U$_t$	0.50	0.01^a
I$_t$	0.07	−0.00
GNP$_t$	−0.17^a	
POSTWAR GNP$_t$	0.12^a	
ΔGNP$_t$		0.29
POSTWAR ΔGNP$_t$		0.13
DEFICIT$_{t-1}$	0.09	
DEFICIT$_{t-2}$	−0.09	
ΔDEBT$_{t-1}$		−0.02
Number of observations	58	58
Adjusted R^2	0.89	0.68
Sum of squared residuals	6945	0.22

Note: Throughout this analysis, where possible, data were collected as reported by government sources in constant 1972 dollars. However, constant-dollar data reported during the 1980s generally is expressed in a different base year (1982, for example). These data were adjusted algebraically to base-year-1972, constant-dollar data in order to maintain comparability.

^{a}Indicates that the coefficient is significant with probability greater than or equal to .95.

DEFICIT = the constant-dollar (1972) federal budget deficit, calculated from the current-dollar figures (reported in the Department of Commerce's *Historical Statistics of the United States* and summary tables in OMB's *Budget of the United States Government*) and the Implicit Price Deflator for federal government purchases of goods and services (reported in Commerce's *Survey of Current Business*).

ΔDEBT = the percentage change in the constant-dollar (1972) federal debt (expressed in partial log format, as was ΔCONG$_{it}$ (in Table 6.7), using the Implicit Price Deflator for federal government purchases of goods and services to deflate the current debt figures (reported in Commerce's *Historical Statistics, Historical Tables, Budget of the United States Government* for fiscal 1990, and the *Economic Report of the President* for 1989).

WW II$_t$ = a dummy variable that takes a value of 1 for the fiscal years of World War II (1943 through 1945) 0 otherwise.

KOREA$_t$ = a dummy variable that takes on a value of 1 for the fiscal years 1952 and 1953, 0 otherwise.

PRES REP/CONGRESS DEM$_t$ = a dummy variable that takes on a value of 1 when the presidency was held by a Republican and the Congress was controlled by the Democrats (fiscal years 1956–1961, 1970–1977, and 1988), 0 otherwise.

PRES DEM/CONGRESS REP$_t$ = a dummy variable that takes on a value of 1 when the president was a Democrat and the Congress was controlled by the Republicans (1948–1949), 0 otherwise.

PRES REP/CONGRESS DIVIDED$_t$ = a dummy variable that takes on a value of 1 when the president was a Republican and control of the two houses of Congress was divided (fiscal years 1932–1933 and 1982–1987).

U$_t$ = the unemployment rate during the fiscal year, as reported in *Survey of Current Business*.

I$_t$ = the rate of inflation during the fiscal year, calculated as a change in the consumer price index, as reported in *Historical Statistics* and *Survey of Current Business*.

GNP$_t$ = the constant-dollar (1972) GNP, as reported by *Survey of Current Business*.

POSTWAR GNP$_t$ = a variable that is equal to GNP$_t$ for fiscal years after the end of World War II (1946–1988), 0 otherwise.

ΔGNP$_t$ = the percentage change in real GNP (in partial log form).

POSTWAR ΔGNP$_t$ = a variable that equals ΔGNP$_t$ for 1946–1988, 0 otherwise.

president is of a different party, all else constant. Thus, *PRES DEM/ CONGRESS REP* and *PRES REP/CONGRESS DEM* should be nonnegative in column 1 and nonpositive in column 2. Importantly, however, divided control of Congress should yield higher deficits: That is, *PRES REP/ CONGRESS DIVIDED* should be negative in column 1 and positive in column 2.

The results here strongly support the hypothesis that divided control of Congress leads to increased deficits: In both equations, the coefficient on divided control of Congress was significant and in the predicted direction. We have had two occurrences of divided congressional control in this century, once in the latter half of the Hoover administration and then for the first six years of the Reagan presidency. In an auxiliary regression, I estimated two dummies (one for each occurrence), which both yielded significant estimated coefficients. Otherwise, divided control of government, holding constant the effect of divided control of Congress (and the tax act of 1981), either shows no effect on deficits or confirms that Republican control of Congress produces decreased spending and therewith decreased deficits. The coefficients for unemployment and GNP had the predicted sign, but they were not always significant. The war dummies always had the right sign, and the dummy for World War II was always significant.

NOTES

I thank Neal Beck, Gary Cox, Gary Jacobson, Rod Kiewiet, Sam Kernell, Sam Popkin, Mike Rothschild, Brian Sala, and Barry Weingast for their comments and criticism. I acknowledge the support of the National Science Foundation, grant no. SES-8421161.

1. The federal government has an unusual way of defining a cut. Though claims that tens of billions had been "cut" from the budget were made during the Reagan presidency, the budget actually increased from $600 billion to $1.2 trillion. Indeed, rarely was spending actually reduced; "cuts" referred to changes in authorization, so that spending was less than it would have been had the law not been changed. This was true even if spending ultimately was greater than it had been the year before. For example, "cuts" in Medicare were said to exceed $50 billion for the 1980s, but Medicare outlays actually grew from $32 billion to $94 billion (Muris 1989).

2. For a contrary view, see Sundquist (1981, 12), who described the difference between delegation and abdication as merely semantic, saying that any delegation by Congress is abdication.

3. Measures included the impoundment controls of the 1974 Budget Act, a requirement that heads of OMB be confirmed by the Senate, and the War Powers Act, among others. See, for example, Sundquist's 1981 discussion of congressional "resurgence," Kiewiet and McCubbins 1991, and Aberbach 1990.

4. A different explanation for why members of Congress delegated the authority to propose legislation to the president was explored in Kiewiet and McCubbins 1988. Essentially, they argued that Congress will always delegate to someone the jobs of fact-finding and drafting legislation. The choice is between an executive agency or department, which will be heavily influenced by congressional committees, or the president, who is independent of such "iron triangles." When the members want to establish a check on their own committees, they must secure information from sources independent of those committees. Only one official in the federal government satisfies the requirements—the president.

Though the president has a vague constitutional mandate to present proposals to Congress, most successful proposals arise as a result of congressional delegation. Compare, for example, the success rate on proposals for executive reorganization, which are not requested by Congress and which are almost never approved, against the success rate for spending or tax proposals, on which Congress almost always passes a bill.

5. As Louis Fisher pointed out (1975), it was the House Appropriations Committee that first requested the Budget Bureau to undertake legislative clearance. And, as Kiewiet and McCubbins noted (1991), the extent of clearance exercised by the Budget Bureau was limited and structured in several pieces of legislation.

6. For a theoretical development and some empirical validation of this point, see Kiewiet and McCubbins 1988.

7. Continuing resolutions are joint resolutions that may provide temporary funding for affected agencies when Congress fails to complete action on one or more regular appropriations bills before the start of a fiscal year (Oleszek 1989). Disputes over program funding levels in continuing resolutions are resolved by application of what Kiewiet and McCubbins (1991) have called the "Fenno Rule," a conventional solution that pegs line items to the lowest amount available from appropriations bills passed by the House and Senate or from the previous year's appropriation.

8. Defense spending grew by almost 30 percent (in 1972 dollars) and accounted for roughly one-quarter of the spending increase during the period. Social Security spending roughly matched the growth rate of defense. Another large chunk of the increase in spending resulted from a near doubling (in real terms) of interest payments on the national debt. The remaining growth in the budget, accounting for 30 percent of the total budget growth, came in other domestic programs.

9. In each of his budget requests, Reagan sought to terminate several dozens of programs. In 1985, for example, he sought to end 26 programs, ranging from the Job Corps to Amtrak to the Small Business Administration to urban mass transit subsidies and Rural Water and Waste Disposal Grants. But such cuts were not part of the Democratic-Republican compromise on spending: Congress voted to terminate only the U.S. Travel and Tourism Agency and to sell Conrail. Indeed, of those programs Reagan sought to terminate, only half even had their budgets reduced.

10. In Table 6.7 in the appendix, I present results that compare the effects of all postwar presidents on budget requests. The regression reported there shows that Reagan, on average, requested far deeper spending cuts than any postwar president, all else constant. Further, Republicans requested greater cuts in spending, all else equal, than did Democrats, with the exception of Carter.

11. The figures are based on the number of votes for which the president announced a position. See Stanley and Niemi 1988, 220–221.

12. Woodrow Wilson first said it in *Congressional Government* (1885).

13. The purpose and function of the 1974 Budget Act have been greatly misunderstood. If the budget process was created to reduce the budget, it is hard to explain the special rules devised for the selection of committee members, as well as the unprecedented prohibitions against members being granted tenure on the committee and against the use of seniority in the leadership succession on the budget committees. An alternative interpretation of the 1974 Budget Act sees its budget committee provisions as part of a larger context with other committee reforms enacted in the early 1970s. Two schools of thought have emerged in the literature: One sees the committee reforms as part of a process of strengthening the democratic caucus and the party leadership as the party became more homogeneous—as southern Democrats became more like their northern comrades (Rohde 1991). The other sees the reforms as part of a much longer trend of party decline and a process of decentralization of power on the floor of the House (Steven Smith 1989; Smith and Deering 1984; Davidson and Oleszek 1977). This second view suggests that out-of-control spending was an unforeseen—or unavoidable—consequence of transferring power away from the House Appropriations Committee.

In my view, as elaborated later in this chapter, the budget committees were created to be (and have operated as) new "control" committees, dominated by the majority party leaderships in the two chambers. The new budget process was tied to new congressional prohibitions against presidential impoundments of funds; by creating new leadership committees with extraordinary powers to "reconcile" authorizing legislation with party budget policy, congressional Democrats significantly increased their ability to manage spending policy against the contrary wishes of a president. Far from weakening the House Appropriations Committee, the act strengthened the leadership's oversight of authorizing committees. By encouraging firm leadership parameters for spending, the act should, in fact, have made the HAC's job easier.

14. For some critical tests, see Kiewiet and McCubbins 1991; Cox and McCubbins 1989.

15. The obverse, of course, is that the committee increased spending for over 19 percent of the budget items that came before it, and they granted an amount equal to the president's request in almost 10 percent of the cases. The proportion of times the committee recommended an increase for one of these items over the president's request ranged from 0 percent in fiscal year 1947 to over 13 percent in fiscal years 1959–1961 to a high of 51 percent in 1984.

16. This, of course, is implicitly Mayhew's (1974a) model of agency estimates. If we are to believe that the committee is protecting members from themselves,

the estimates the committee deals with must be a reflection of the members' own desires. If they were not, then the committee would be protecting members from the executive branch, not from themselves.

17. On the unrepresentativeness of many House committees, see Cox and McCubbins 1991. On the representativeness of the House Appropriations Committee, see Kiewiet and McCubbins 1991.

18. Freshman Democrats at the December 1982 meeting of the Democratic Caucus voted unanimously to recommend that Phil Gramm of Texas be dropped to the bottom of the Democratic seniority list because of his consistent support for President Reagan's economic policies in the 97th Congress. In 1981, Gramm was a cosponsor with Delbert Latta (R–Ohio) of the Republican alternative to the Democrats' 1982 budget.

19. Under this rule, adopted by the House in May 1982, seven budget alternatives were considered (and sixty-eight perfecting amendments), with the House Budget Committee's recommendation being voted last. The rule requires that the last alternative to win a majority is the plan that prevails. This is just one example of the extraordinary rule changes used by the Democrats to control the budget process and the conservative "Boll Weevil" faction. In 1982, none of the alternatives won a majority. The rule was used again in 1983 when the Democratic House Budget Committee's plan prevailed.

20. The Republicans obviously had less about which to disagree: Because most domestic government programs were created by the Democrats to further their own policy goals, most Republicans could agree to cut those programs. The Democrats had a more difficult time deciding what to cut and what to protect.

21. I address only spending policy here, leaving deficits for the appendix. Gary Cox and I use a similar approach to explain federal revenue policies in Chapter 7 of this volume.

22. For a number of discussions of this problem, see the various essays in Chubb and Peterson 1988.

23. In modeling fiscal policy decisions, most analysts have included GNP as an explanatory variable (Kiewiet and McCubbins 1991, Barro 1979). Dividing one's dependent variable by an independent variable tends to cause problems for estimation. Therefore, I have not included debt as a percentage of GNP as an independent variable in my analysis.

24. On the Slutsky question, see any textbook in microeconomics.

25. Data was collected from the annual Senate document entitled, "Appropriations, Budget Estimates, Etc."

7

DIVIDED CONTROL
OF FISCAL POLICY

Gary W. Cox and Mathew D. McCubbins

Republicans and Democrats have differed over tax policy since the creation of the Republican party before the Civil War. The broad outlines of these differences can be seen by briefly reviewing tax policy in four different periods: the period of Republican dominance from the end of Reconstruction to 1913; the period of Democratic control during World War I; the period of Republican control during the 1920s; and, finally, the New Deal era of Democratic dominance.

Policy differences between the parties were somewhat obscured during the Civil War due to the absence from Congress of the southern Democrats but emerged in stark outline with the return of party competition after Reconstruction. At that time, the Republicans had had unfettered control of the federal government for well over a decade— and were to remain the hegemonic party until 1913.[1] During this long period of ascendancy, the Republicans had ample opportunities to set tax and spending policies; even when they temporarily lost control of the House, Senate, or presidency, they retained enough power to veto any significant changes in the tax system that they had instituted (Stewart 1989 and 1991).[2]

The Republican tax system emphasized excise taxes on tobacco and alcohol (which fell most heavily on southern Democratic farmers) and tariffs on manufactured imports (which protected Republican industrial constituents). The ample proceeds from these high excise taxes and tariffs quickly retired the debt incurred during the Civil War, largely paying off Republican bondholders. Although the Democrats pled for tax relief, the Republicans found that by continuing to levy taxes at a high rate, they could increase the pensions of the Grand Army of the Republic—another solidly Republican constituency. Contrary to their image in this century, Republicans in the nineteenth century sought both higher taxes (O'Halloran 1990) and higher spending (Stewart 1989; Kiewiet and McCubbins 1991) than did the Democrats.[3]

The Republicans maintained their traditional reliance on excise taxes and tariffs for the first twelve years of the twentieth century, but Democrats and progressive Republicans began to push, with increasing force, for a constitutional amendment allowing the establishment of an income tax. Finally, as part of a deal to get progressive votes for the Payne-Aldrich Tariff of 1909, the old guard Republicans agreed to introduce an income tax amendment, believing that it would not pass. However, they miscalculated: Not only were the Republicans weakened by the 1910 elections and swept from power in the 1912 elections, the income tax amendment was ratified by the states in 1913 (Studenski and Kroos 1963, 272).

On coming to power in 1913, the Democrats moved quickly to de-emphasize tariff rates, shift excise taxes to manufactures, and introduce an income tax. From fiscal year (FY) 1914 to FY 1921, tariff receipts as a percentage of total federal receipts declined from 40 percent to 5 percent, excise tax receipts fell from 42 percent to 21 percent, and income tax receipts took up most of the slack, rising from $71 million in 1914 (9 percent of total receipts) to $3.2 billion in 1921 (58 percent).[4]

As World War I drew to a conclusion, the Republicans regained control of Congress and, in 1921, the White House, as well. By FY 1922, the Republicans were in a position to change the tax and spending programs that had been enacted by the Democrats over the previous eight years. They slashed expenditures from $6.2 billion in FY 1920 (the first postwar budget) to $2.9 billion in FY 1925 and continued to hold expenditures below $4 billion throughout the remainder of the decade (all figures are given in current or nominal dollars; see Studenski and Kroos 1963). They also passed four successive tax reductions—in 1921, 1924, 1926, and 1928. As a result, income tax receipts fell from $4 billion in 1920 (59 percent of total federal receipts) to $2.3 billion in 1929 (50 percent of receipts). Tariffs and excise taxes rose correspondingly in percentage terms.[5]

The Democrats retook control of both Congress and the White House in 1933. During the period of Democratic hegemony that followed, tariffs and excise taxes remained relatively low, despite the repeal of Prohibition, and income and payroll taxes became the increasingly predominant form of revenue.

Since World War II, instead of the alternation in partisan control of the prewar period, we have witnessed an alternation between extended periods of divided control, on the one hand, and periods of unified Democratic control, on the other (the one exception being 1953–1954, when the Republicans held majorities in both chambers of Congress and the White House). Divided control in the postwar era has consisted mostly of Democratic congresses facing Republican presidents, with only the "Do Nothing" 80th Congress (held by the Republicans and facing Democrat Harry Truman in the White House) and the split congresses of Ronald Reagan's first six years breaking the pattern.

The effects of divided control on tax policy are not obvious and even have the potential to be quite perverse, as each party endeavors to use its institutional leverage to adjust tax policy to its liking. Yet, for the most part, extant theories of fiscal policymaking ignore the possibility of divided partisan control of government. Some theories abstract away from the political process entirely, and those that do not either conclude that there are no substantial differences between the parties or assume that there is unified control. Nonetheless, there are reasons to expect fiscal policy in periods of divided control to differ from that observed in periods of unified control. In this chapter, we provide statistical evidence of the impact of divided control on the overall level of taxation in the period 1934–1988 (which coincides with the era of Democratic congressional hegemony).[6]

We will first review some of the literature on the determinants of governmental fiscal policy, noting that none of it takes explicit account of the possibility of divided partisan control of the policymaking apparatus. We will then consider the impact that divided control might have on tax levels, using the notion of "reversion points" familiar in the spatial modeling literature (Romer and Rosenthal 1979). Later sections will specify and estimate a time series regression to test whether the ideas we have developed hold any water for the period 1934–1988. Finally, we will offer some brief conclusions.

THE DETERMINANTS OF FISCAL POLICY

The literature on the determinants of tax levels is quite diverse. We divide it here into two main branches: first, those studies that focus on economic fundamentals (what kinds of policies will have what kinds of macroeconomic effects?); second, those studies that focus on political fundamentals (what kinds of incentives do fiscal policymakers face?).

Among the economic models of fiscal policy, we mention just two as examples: John Keynes's theory of countercyclical spending and Robert Barro's theory of tax smoothing. Keynes, of course, was concerned with how fiscal policy *ought* to be conducted, not with predicting how governments actually behave. The gist of his prescriptions is captured in the familiar injunction that government taxation and expenditure should be countercyclical. That is, governments ought to raise taxes and lower expenditures during upturns in the business cycle, in order to prevent inflation, but lower taxes and raise expenditures during downturns, in order to prevent recession.

The normative injunction that fiscal policy should be countercyclical becomes a positive prediction about any particular government's behavior only if that government buys into Keynesianism. Not all do. There are other theories about how to manage the macroeconomy from which a government might choose, and these other theories sometimes prescribe quite different behavior in response to the fluctuations of the business cycle. Barro (1979) has even argued that countercyclical policies can never work, that governments know this, and that they therefore avoid any attempts in this direction.

The gist of his argument is that deficit spending of the kind advocated by Keynes will not increase real growth rates.[7] The reasoning behind this assertion is that rational economic agents, seeing an increase in the deficit, know that it will have to be financed eventually with higher taxes; they therefore reduce their own spending (in order to save enough to defray the coming increased taxes), and this reduction in private spending exactly counterbalances any public deficit. Thus, the real growth of the economy will be invariant with respect to the government's choice between higher taxes and higher debt, and no government will have any incentive to engage in countercyclical policies.[8]

Keynes's and Barro's models do not focus on the political processes underlying fiscal policy. To the extent that they touch on the issue, however, they seem to assume either unified partisan control of government or minimal differences between the parties. Keynes's assumptions in this regard are less clear than Barro's, but if one supposes that the government is under divided control and that the parties differ over the advisability of countercyclical policy, the question naturally arises of whether such a government could or would implement countercyclical policies. Barro's assumptions about government are quite clear. He explicitly assumes that the government's only goal is to minimize the discounted present costs of collecting taxes and that what all the money collected is to be spent on, now and in future, has already been decided.[9] In the present context, this means either that both parties have adopted the same expenditure policies or that only one party will ever control government.

It is understandable that models of fiscal policymaking whose primary focus is on the macroeconomic effects of different policies would not devote much attention to the political process whereby fiscal policy decisions are made. Thus, it is not surprising to find that political details, such as whether the various branches of government are controlled by a single party, are largely ignored. It is somewhat more surprising to find that even models of fiscal policymaking that are primarily political in orientation also ignore the issue of divided government. We can illustrate this by, again, considering two examples: the electoral cycles model and the median voter model.

The electoral cycles model is based on a very simple notion: that incumbent governments will seek to ensure, in any way they can, that the economy is on the upswing around election time.[10] In principle, this might be achieved in any number of ways, but the relevant way in the present context is the preelection tax cut.

The various versions of the electoral cycles model typically assume unified control of government. If there is divided control, however, the issue of how the electorate assigns blame and credit arises, and, depending on how this issue is resolved in the minds of politicians, incentives to prime the pump at election time may disappear. For example, if it were commonly believed that (1) all credit for a healthy economy accrues to the party of the president and (2) the health of the economy is the primary determinant of votes in congressional elections, then a party controlling the legislature but not the presidency would have little incentive to cooperate in any preelection manipulation of the economy.

The median voter model has a rather different starting point than the electoral cycles model. Although it, too, is concerned with the electoral incentives that politicians face, it views economic policy primarily as something over which the parties compete in campaigns rather than as something that the party in power implements. Each party is envisioned as advocating a particular fiscal policy (e.g., "taxes and spending should be cut back to a lower level") that can be located along a single left-right spectrum. The parties are assumed to choose fiscal policies in order to appeal to the largest number of voters and, hence, maximize their vote totals. The median voter model's conclusion, enshrined in the famous "median voter theorem," is that competition between vote-maximizing parties will drive both to adopt the position of the median voter.[11]

In research into fiscal policymaking, this theorem has been used to justify a concentration on the tax price faced by and the preferences of the median voter.[12] Issues of divided government do not arise naturally in research motivated by the median voter theorem because both parties end up advocating identical policies—hence, there should be little difference between periods of unified and divided control (or, for that matter, between periods of unified control by one party and periods of unified control by the other).

The median voter model is, of course, an extremely simplified theoretical construct and one that has been criticized from a variety of perspectives. For our purposes, the most pertinent critiques have come from two directions. First, many scholars have noted that the median voter model overstates the incentives for the two major parties to converge at the center of the electorate.[13] Agreeing with these critiques, we shall take as a premise that the parties differ significantly on fiscal policy, in ways elaborated in the next section. Second, Romer and Rosenthal (1979) have criticized the median voter theorem's neglect of budgetary "reversion points." They point out that spending levels typically revert to some prespecified level (zero or last year's level, for example) in the absence of a new budget agreement. The existence of such a reversion point changes the strategic opportunities considerably from those recognized in the median voter theorem.

The original example of how reversion points change the strategic context actually concerns elections in which party competition does not play much of a role: votes on propositions to finance Oregon schools. To simplify matters, we can pretend here that the Oregon school budgets are voted upon directly by the voters every year. A straight application of the median voter theorem would lead one to expect that budget levels (and corresponding tax rates) would be set at a level that appealed to the median voter: Any proposal that was not set at such a level could be defeated by one that was. Romer and Rosenthal, however, point out two things (which we will again simplify here): that budgets are made by an interested party—in this case, the school system administrators—and that voters know the consequence of voting down a budget is not that another will spring up closer to the median voter's ideal but rather that the school budget for that year will be set to zero—the schools will close, in other words. The existence of such a draconian reversion point changes the calculation of Oregon voters considerably. They do not vote solely on the merits of the budget in question; instead, they ask, "Do I prefer this budget to the reversionary budget of zero?" This change in perspective leads to a considerable change in the kind of budgets that can be expected.

Romer and Rosenthal's work has motivated careful attention to reversion points in a variety of models.[14] The issue of reversion points is relevant to fiscal policy, too—as will be seen in the next section.

DIVIDED CONTROL AND FISCAL POLICY

In the last section, we reviewed four theories bearing on the process of fiscal policymaking, all of which essentially ignore the issue of divided partisan control of government. In this section, we indicate the grounds on which one might expect partisan division in control of the policymaking apparatus to have a systematic effect on fiscal policy.

Our basic premise is simply that the major parties in the United States differ meaningfully on what constitutes appropriate fiscal policy. They differ most obviously on the appropriate incidence of taxation—i.e., on what groups in the population pay what share of the total tax bill. But they also differ in the sense that, for any given incidence of taxation and any given program of expenditure,[15] they will disagree over the optimal level of taxation. Thus, for example, if the incidence of taxation and program of expenditure are chosen by the Democrats, then the Republicans will probably want a substantially lower level of taxation than do the Democrats. If, however, the Republicans get to choose where the money comes from and where it goes, they may be the ones willing to set higher tax levels.[16] More generally, as the incidence of taxation and program of expenditure change, each party's appetite for tax revenues will also change.

The potential consequences of partisan disagreement over fiscal policy are several. One possibility is suggested by Samuel Finer's (1975) "adversary democracy" model. If the two parties alternate in full control of the government and if they differ significantly over fiscal policy, then one can expect a seesaw pattern across the budgetary board: Expenditure will be set first in a Democratic pattern, then in a Republican pattern; taxes will have first a Democratic incidence, then a Republican one; tax and expenditure levels will be set first to Democratic liking, then to Republican liking.

Naturally, there are many inertial elements that parties may find difficult to change, so the degree of continuity is larger than a pure "adversary democracy" model might predict. Nonetheless, the basic prediction—of an alternation in policy with any alternation in power—is a straightforward consequence of the initial assumption that parties differ (along with an ancillary assumption that they can act on their preferences once in office). This seems to tally reasonably well with the facts of early twentieth-century politics.

What happens when the parties do not simply alternate in power but, instead, alternate between the unified control of a dominant party and divided control? This, of course, is characteristic of most of the post-1933 era in the United States, with the Democrats playing the role of the dominant party.[17]

One might expect that the transition from unified Democratic to divided control would have little impact on fiscal policy. After all, the post-1933 tax code is largely a Democratic construction. When the Republicans secure control of a branch or two of government, they may very well *want* to change tax levels, but the Democrats can use their branch to veto any change and preserve the status quo.[18]

This point is well taken as far as it goes, but it fails to recognize several ways in which the Republicans might succeed in dragging real tax levels down. First, tax systems are always subject to evasion and to the invention of new methods of evasion; absent explicit legislative responses to newly invented techniques to avoid payment of taxes, real yields may decline. But the Republicans can prevent such legislative responses when they hold a veto over tax legislation, so they may be able to offer the real equivalent of tax cuts without explicit legislation.[19] Second, when Republicans hold the presidency, they can reduce the allocation of resources to the Internal Revenue Service, loosen audit procedures, and in other ways lower the probability that taxpayers will get caught bending or breaking the rules of the tax code. This, too, offers the real equivalent of a tax cut without the need for a legislative enactment. Third, when the Republicans control at least one branch of government, they are in a better position to bargain with the Democrats; the bargain may take the form of lower taxes in exchange for some other policy goal that the Democrats alone cannot achieve. Thus, the chances of a real tax cut effected through legislation are higher under divided control than under unified Democratic control.

In addition to these general considerations, it should be noted that there is one situation of divided control—that in which the Republicans control Congress and the Democrats control the presidency—that is likely to yield particularly large tax cuts. Indeed, under certain conditions, one expects even larger reductions in real tax levels when Democratic control gives way to divided control of this kind than when Democratic control gives way to unified Republican control.

The conditions under which this expectation holds true involve three plausible assumptions about partisan preferences and one regarding the status quo after an extended period of Democratic control. The assumptions about preferences deal with how a party's ideal level of taxes depends on the tax incidence, the pattern of expenditure, and the level of expenditure:

1. Other things being equal, a party will prefer a lower level of taxes when the incidence of taxation is less to its liking.
2. Other things being equal, a party will prefer a lower level of taxes when the pattern of expenditure is less to its liking.
3. Other things being equal, a party will prefer a lower level of taxes when the level of spending is lower.

Our assumption about the nature of the status quo after an extended period of Democratic control is simply that the incidence of taxation, the pattern of expenditure, and the level of expenditure will largely be to Democratic liking.

These assumptions, together with some observations about the strategic situation of the parties when the Republicans seize control of Congress after an extended period of Democratic control, yield the desired result. Consider, to begin with, the courses of action open to the Republicans in the hypothetical situation envisioned. They are faced by assumption with an unattractive array of spending programs and an unfavorable incidence of taxation. Yet, they cannot initiate new expenditure programs because this requires authorizing legislation and is hence subject to the president's veto.[20] Similarly, they cannot change the incidence of taxation on their own. They can, however, cut spending because the reversion point for spending policy is either zero or some low amount defined by the Fenno Rule, so that the president's veto threat is not credible: If he does not accept the Republican cuts, even worse cuts will ensue (see Kiewiet and McCubbins 1988).

Accordingly, one can expect that Republicans in the situation posited above will cut spending. After they do so, however, both parties will—other things being equal—want to cut taxes. Moreover, under some circumstances to be specified presently, they will agree on a level of taxation lower than that which would have obtained under unified Republican control. Hence, the expected tax cut will be larger than that which would have occurred had the Republicans taken full control.

Consider first the Republicans. We shall denote the level of taxes that they would have most preferred had they secured full control of the government as $R(Rep)$ and the level that they actually prefer, given that they control Congress and the Democrats control the presidency, as $R(div)$. Assumptions 1–3 allow us to conclude that $R(Rep) > R(div)$. To see why this follows, consider the difference between full Republican control and Republican control of Congress only. Under full control, the Republicans can improve the incidence of taxation and the pattern of expenditure much more than they can under divided control. Under both situations, they can cut spending—but they are likely to achieve larger net cuts in spending under divided control because they cannot initiate new spending programs as readily. Thus, the incidence of taxation is worse, the pattern of expenditure is worse, and the level of spending is lower under divided control, and assumptions 1–3 imply that the Republicans will want a lower level of taxation.

Consider next the Democrats. Denote their most preferred level of taxation after the Republican spending cuts as $D(div)$. If this level is less than $R(Rep)$, then the argument is complete, because the final outcome will be some compromise between $D(div)$ and $R(div)$, both of which are lower than $R(Rep)$. There is some reason to expect that $R(Rep) > D(div)$ because the Republicans' appetite for spending (and hence for taxes) would no doubt be increased were they able to establish their own programs and finance them with taxes that fell mostly on Democratic constituencies. But it might well take more then one term in full control before the transformation from antitax out party to proservice in party were complete. Even if $R(Rep) < D(div)$, however, the final outcome under divided control could still be less than $R(Rep)$. All that is necessary for this conclusion is that $R(Rep) > D^*$, where D^* is the lowest tax level that the Democrats prefer to the status quo level, $D(Dem)$. When this condition holds, the Republicans in Congress can offer a take-it-or-leave-it deal to the Democratic president: Accept either a level—namely, the larger of D^* and $R(div)$—that is lower than $R(Rep)$ or get nothing. If the president vetoes the offer, the reversion point is the status quo level—$D(Dem)$. But, by definition, the president prefers D^* to $D(Dem)$; hence, he will not veto the Republican offer, and the level of taxes will end up lower than it would have been under unified Republican control.

The line of argument just sketched is, of course, highly simplified. In particular, it ignores the possibilities of veto overrides and bipartisan logrolling of one kind or another. It should therefore be regarded not as a general model but as an illustration of what might happen under a particular form of divided government. Nonetheless, there are some general features to the illustration: In particular, we think it is generally true that the Republicans in the situation posited will *prefer* even larger tax cuts than they would if they were to secure full control.

If we compare the predictions in the model to the actual sequence of events during the only post–New Deal instance of divided government in which the Republicans controlled Congress, we find some real differences—for example, the tax bills offered by the Republican-controlled 80th Congress were all vetoed by President Truman, with the last passed over his veto. The model seems to have predicted preferences correctly, however: The Republicans wanted very substantial cuts, and Truman was willing to go along with some cuts once the Republican spending reductions that he had been forced to accept had caused the federal budget to go into (prospective) surplus. But the president disliked the alterations in incidence that the Republican bills would have effected, and he was also worried that a tax cut would exacerbate the bout of inflation that the postwar economy was suffering at the time. In other words, all other things being equal, the lowered spending that the Republicans had forced through may have led Truman to prefer lower taxes. But other things were not equal: The bill changed tax incidence to some extent, and Truman, a good Keynesian, thought that a tax cut in the face of serious inflation was not good policy. Thus, he vetoed the bill, and it was passed over his veto with the help of southern Democrats. Nonetheless, the result was one of the largest tax cuts in the post–New Deal era.[21]

AN ECONOMETRIC MODEL OF TAX RECEIPTS

We have suggested several hypotheses about how differing constellations of partisan control of government might affect federal tax policy. These hypotheses can be organized in the context of a model that predicts change in the level of real federal tax receipts as a function of which party controls what branches of government: Is there unified Democratic or Republican control? Do the Democrats or Republicans control just the presidency? Is there split control of Congress? We shall also include, as controls, variables that indicate major wars and changes in real income.

The primary economic data we use in our estimations consist of time series on annual federal tax receipts and real income (GNP) from fiscal year 1934 to fiscal year 1988. Using the implicit price deflator for federal purchases and the GNP price deflator, we converted both series into real or constant dollars.[22]

We then created dummy variables to identify varieties of party control of government. In all cases, attention focused on fiscal rather than calendar years—and in interpreting what follows, it should be remembered that changes affecting the tax code in fiscal year t will typically be passed in calendar year $t-1$.

We recognize five different varieties of party control: (1) unified Republican control of both the presidency and Congress, designated by the variable *UNIF-REPUBLICAN* (equal to 1 in fiscal years 1954 and 1955, 0 otherwise); (2) unified Democratic control of government, designated by the variable *UNIF-DEMOCRATIC* (equal to 1 for fiscal years 1934 to 1947, 1950 to 1953, 1962 to 1969, and 1978 to 1981, 0 otherwise); (3) Republican control of the White House and Democratic control of Congress, designated by the variable *P-REPUBLICAN & C-DEMOCRATIC* (equal to 1 for fiscal years 1956 to 1961, 1970 to 1977,

TABLE 7.1   Partisan Control and Federal Tax Receipts, 1934–1988

Partisan Control	Number of Fiscal Years	Average of $100 \times (Receipts_t/Receipts_{t-1})$ in those fiscal years[a]
Unified Democratic control	30	13.7
Unified Republican control	2	−5.1
Republican president, Democratic Congress	15	2.2
Democratic president, Republican Congress	2	−10.4
Republican president, split Congress	6	2.8

[a]$Receipts_t$ is total real federal tax receipts in fiscal year t.

and 1988, 0 otherwise); (4) Democratic control of the presidency together with Republican control of Congress, designated by the variable *P-DEMOCRATIC & C-REPUBLICAN* (equal to 1 in fiscal years 1948 and 1949, 0 otherwise); and (5) Republican control of the White House and Senate together with Democratic control of the House, designated by the variable *P-REPUBLICAN & C-SPLIT* (equal to 1 in fiscal years 1982 to 1987, 0 otherwise).

This categorization catches all of the observed constellations of partisan control in the period since 1932. Table 7.1 shows what the mean percentage change in real federal tax receipts has been under each constellation. As can be seen, tax receipts have increased, on average, by 13.7 percent per fiscal year under unified Democratic control. When the Republicans have controlled both houses of Congress, in contrast, tax receipts have declined, on average—by 5.1 percent in the two years when they also held the presidency and by 10.4 percent in the two years when they did not. Finally, when the Republicans have controlled the presidency, tax receipts have increased, on average—by 2.8 percent in the six years when they also held the Senate and by 2.2 percent in the fifteen years when they did not.

These figures may delight Republican campaign strategists, but they do not fairly represent partisan differences in tax policy. After all, the Democrats were in control during World War II, when the largest single run-up in taxes in U.S. history occurred. It seems plausible that, had the Republicans been in office when Pearl Harbor was attacked, taxes would still have gone up dramatically. Moreover, simple averages do not control for fluctuations in the economy, which, of course, have an important impact on tax receipts.

Accordingly, we included in our regressions both a variable indicating percentage changes in real GNP and a series of dummy variables identifying major wars: *WWII*, equal to 1 for fiscal years 1943 to 1946, 0 otherwise; *KOREA*, equal to 1 for fiscal years 1953 and 1954, 0 otherwise; and *VIETNAM*, equal to 1 for fiscal years 1967 to 1970, 0

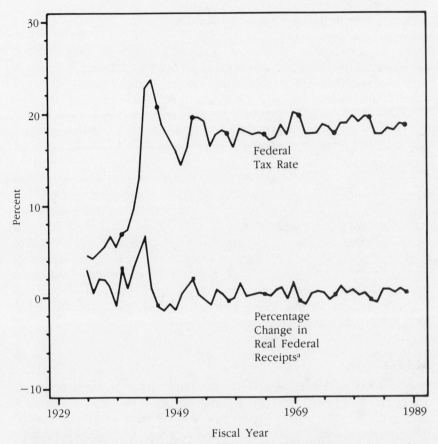

Fiscal Year

[a] Calculated as the log (Receipts$_t$ / Receipts$_{t-1}$). In this presentation, the resulting figures have been reduced by a factor of 10.

FIGURE 7.1   Federal Tax Rates and the Percentage Change in Real Federal Receipts, 1934–1989

otherwise. The impact of World War II can be seen clearly in Figure 7.1: Tax revenues jumped dramatically in fiscal year 1942 and since then have remained very high, relative to the prewar period, as we have amortized the cost of the war. As it turned out, the impact of the Korean and Vietnamese conflicts was small enough that we dropped the associated dummy variables from the final specification reported in the next section.

A few other features of our specification should also be noted. First, the dependent variable, $\Delta RECEIPTS_t$ is the partial logarithm of real receipts, rather than the simple percentage change.[23] Second, the model does not incorporate the economic models—of countercyclical or flat tax rates. Were we to accommodate these theories, all that would change is the specification of the *GNP* variable, which should be independent of which party controlled what branches of government; thus, at most, we lose efficiency.[24] Third, we exclude the *UNIF-DEMOCRATIC* variable from our specification, thereby throwing its effects into the constant term. That is, the value of the constant term coefficient can be taken to represent the average percentage change in tax receipts (in partial log terms) during years of Democratic control, when real income does not change and no major war is under way.

We expect that Republican control of any part of the policymaking apparatus will yield decreases in real tax receipts, relative to the baseline level of change in Democratic years. Thus, the coefficients on *UNIF-REPUBLICAN, P-DEMOCRATIC & C-REPUBLICAN, P-REPUBLICAN & C-SPLIT,* and *P-REPUBLICAN & C-DEMOCRATIC* are all expected to be negative. We also expect that the coefficient of *P-DEMOCRATIC & C-REPUBLICAN* will be larger in magnitude than the coefficient of *UNIF-REPUBLICAN,* which will, in turn, be larger in magnitude than the coefficient of *P-REPUBLICAN & C-SPLIT,* which will, in turn, be larger in magnitude than the coefficient of *P-REPUBLICAN & C-DEMOCRATIC.* Our results are given in Table 7.2.[25]

RESULTS

The findings in Table 7.2 do not cause us to reject our hypotheses. The pattern of coefficients in the first equation (column 1) shows a clear partisan difference on tax policy. The constant term, representing the average increase in tax receipts during years of unified Democratic control is, as expected, nearly zero and statistically insignificant: The Democrats, for the most part, hold the line on taxes, at levels they have had the largest hand in choosing. Unified Republican control, in contrast, produces nearly a 10 percent decline in federal tax receipts, relative to the Democratic baseline. When the Republicans hold majorities in both houses of Congress but do not occupy the White House (i.e., fiscal years 1948–1949), we see the steepest mean decline in federal tax receipts, all else constant; this decline, moreover, cannot be chalked up simply to postwar readjustments during the Truman administration.[26] Finally, when the Republicans control the executive but do not hold majorities in both houses of Congress, there is some evidence of decline in tax receipts, but the decline is relatively small.

The results in the second equation reported in Table 7.2 (see column 2) provide a clearer contrast between those cases when the Republicans control both houses of Congress (whether or not they also hold the presidency) and when they do not. Instead of the four partisan dummy

TABLE 7.2 Divided Government and Federal Tax Receipts, 1934–1988 (Dependent Variable: ΔRECEIPTS$_t$)

Equation 1

Independent Variables	Coefficient	Standard Error
Constant	0.015	0.02
UNIF-REPUBLICAN	−0.095	0.02[a]
P-REP & C-SPLIT	−0.033	0.02
P-DEM & C-REP	−0.169	0.05[a]
P-REP & C-DEM	−0.038	0.02[b]
GNP$_t$	0.362	0.188[b]
WW II	0.242	0.09[a]
Autoregressive Variables		
GNP$_{t-1}$	1.363	0.31[a]
RECEIPTS$_{t-1}$	−0.180	0.14
adj R^2	0.64	
Standard Error	0.086	

Equation 2

Independent Variables	Coefficient	Standard Error
Constant	0.014	0.02
C-REPUBLICAN	−0.130	0.04[a]
P-REP & H-DEM	−0.036	0.02[b]
GNP$_t$	0.375	0.19[b]
WW II	0.237	0.09[a]
Autoregressive Variables		
GNP$_{t-1}$	1.352	0.31[a]
RECEIPTS$_{t-1}$	−0.164	0.136
adj R^2	0.65	
Standard Error	0.085	

[a]Significant at 0.01 confidence level.
[b]Significant at 0.05 confidence level.

C-REPUBLICAN = a dummy variable that takes on a value of 1 when both chambers of Congress are controlled by the Republicans (fiscal years 1948–1949 and 1954–1955), zero otherwise.
GNP$_t$ = the constant-dollar (1972) GNP as reported by *Survey of Current Business* for year t (or $t-1$).
P-REP & C-DEM = a dummy variable that takes on a value of 1 when the presidency is held by a Republican and both houses of Congress are held by the Democrats (fiscal 1956–1961, 1970–1977, and 1988), zero otherwise.
P-REP & C-SPLIT = a dummy variable that takes on a value of 1 when the presidency is held by a Republican and control of the two houses of Congress is divided (fiscal 1982–1987), zero otherwise.
P-REP & H-DEM = a dummy variable that takes on a value of 1 when the presidency is held by a Republican and the House of Representatives is controlled by the Democrats (fiscal 1956–1961, 1970–1977, and 1982–1988), zero otherwise.
P-DEM & C-REP = a dummy variable that takes on a value of 1 when the presidency is held by a Democrat and both houses of Congress are controlled by the Republicans (fiscal 1948–1949).
RECEIPTS$_t$ = total federal tax receipts for year t, as reported in *Historical Tables, Budget of the United States Government.*
UNIF-REPUBLICAN = a dummy variable that takes on a value of 1 when both the presidency and Congress are controlled by the Republicans (fiscal 1954–1955), zero otherwise.
WWII = a dummy variable that takes on a value of 1 during the fiscal years of the war (1943–1946), zero otherwise.

variables used in the first equation, the second uses only two: *C-REPUBLICAN*, equal to 1 when the Republicans hold majorities in both houses of Congress, 0 otherwise (that is, the variable is equal to 1 for FY 1948 and 1949 and for FY 1954 and 1955) and *P-REPUBLICAN & H-DEMOCRATIC*, equal to 1 when the president is a Republican and the Democrats hold a majority in the House of Representatives, 0 otherwise (this is the union of two earlier dummies, *P-REPUBLICAN & C-DEMOCRATIC* and *P-REPUBLICAN & C-SPLIT*, because there are no cases of a split Congress with Republican control of the House; the variable is equal to 1 for FY 1956 to 1961, FY 1970 to 1977, and FY 1982 to 1988).

As can be seen, the coefficient on the first dummy variable is significantly smaller (a larger negative) than the coefficient on the second (the difference yields a t-test of 2.99), suggesting that the most important determinant of changes in tax policy is which party controls Congress. Republican control of both the House and Senate produces cuts in tax receipts of 13 percent (in partial log terms) below the Democratic baseline, and Republican control of some parts of government but without majorities in both houses of Congress produces relatively small cuts in tax receipts below the Democratic baseline.

The control variables work about as would be expected. An increase of 1 percent in GNP yields an increase of slightly more than one-third of 1 percent in tax receipts, all else being constant. Further, the war years between FY 1943 and 1946 saw, on average, a 24 percent increase in tax receipts. The costs of amortizing World War II produced a permanent increase in tax receipts: The increases in tax receipts for the war were not followed by decreases of a similar magnitude in the postwar period.

Though for simplicity of presentation we do not provide the results here, we estimated the equation in column 1 including a dummy variable for election years. The coefficient of the election year term was significant and negative, though including it (or excluding it) has no significant effect on the remaining coefficients. This finding offers some support for a political-taxation cycle: Tax receipts fall, on average, in election years.[27]

CONCLUSION

Which party controls the presidency has been shown to be important in previous studies of U.S. monetary and fiscal policy (Hibbs 1987). In this study, we have adopted a finer categorization of the possibilities for control, looking not just at control of the presidency but also at control of the two houses of Congress. In principle, each of the three legislative branches—House, Senate, and presidency—can be controlled by either of the two parties, yielding eight possible constellations of partisan control. In the period since Franklin Delano Roosevelt's first election, only five of these eight possibilities have been observed, but three of them involved divided partisan control of government.

The motivation for looking at a finer categorization of partisan control is that the U.S. system empowers each branch separately with its own veto. Depending on which party controls which branch of government and what policy will be in force in the absence of new legislation, a variety of different bargaining contexts are established. In the period since 1932, the potential variety of such contexts has been reduced by the continuing congressional hegemony of the Democratic party. We have thus focused our theoretical attention on questions about the likely consequences of *interrupting* Democratic control with bouts of either Republican control or some kind of divided control.

The chief notions driving the theoretical discussion are simple: that the parties differ significantly on tax policy and that any party will wish to set a lower tax level when it finds tax incidence or expenditure patterns to be suboptimal, rather than when it finds them to be optimal. The findings are straightforward. First, when Democratic control is interrupted by Republican control of all branches, there is a substantial decline in real federal tax receipts, relative to the baseline rate of growth established under unified Democratic control. Second, when Democratic control is interrupted by Republican control of either the presidency alone or of both the presidency and the Senate, the decline in tax receipts relative to the Democratic baseline is substantially less than in the first case but still significant. Third, when Democratic control is interrupted by Republican control of Congress but not the presidency, there is an even larger decline in tax receipts than in the first case. We have argued that this especially large decline may reflect what congressional Republicans can and cannot do. They can cut spending, but they cannot as readily alter the incidence of taxation or the pattern of spending. They thus want even larger tax cuts than they would were they in full control (and hence able to adjust the incidence of taxation and pattern of expenditure more to their liking). Success in getting large tax cuts is likely because Democrats will prefer a lower level of taxes after the Republicans have forced through their spending cuts. Although this line of argument makes some abstract sense, there has been only one postwar instance of Republican control of Congress coupled with Democratic control of the presidency. Thus, the empirical evidence for our speculations regarding parties' desires for especially large tax cuts when tax incidence and spending patterns are suboptimal is necessarily slight.

The results reviewed in the previous paragraph suggest two simple lessons about divided control of government and fiscal policymaking. The first is that, for some purposes, control of Congress may be more important than control of the presidency; the Republicans, in any event, have achieved far larger cuts in spending and taxes when they have controlled Congress than when they have controlled the presidency.[28] The second lesson is that, in some cases, divided control of government can produce even larger changes in policy than would occur under partisan alternation in office, due to the particular bargaining situation that the structure of our government provides.

NOTES

1. The Republican party held unified control of government in the 37th–43d (1861–1875), 47th (1881–1883), 51st (1889–1891), and 55th–61st (1897–1911) congresses. The Democrats gained control of the House in the 44th–45th (1875–1879), 48th–50th (1883–1889), and 52d (1891–1893) congresses; of both the House and Senate in the 46th (1879–1881) and 53d (1893–1895) congresses; and of the White House in 1885–1889 and 1893–1897 (Grover Cleveland's two terms). In the entire period from the creation of the Republican party in 1854 to the inauguration of Woodrow Wilson in 1913, the Democrats enjoyed unified control of government for only a single Congress, the 53d (1893–1895).

2. Grover Cleveland and the House Democrats, for example, prepared a modest reduction in the average tariff in the 51st Congress, but the Republican-controlled Senate would have none of it.

3. The Democrats meanwhile advocated, without success, a reinstitution of the income tax that had first been enacted during the Civil War, along with a reduction in the excise taxes and tariffs besetting their constituents. Democrats such as Grover Cleveland characterized tariffs in particular as a "vicious, inequitable, and illogical source of unnecessary taxation" (Studenski and Kroos 1963, 208).

4. U.S. involvement in World War I, of course, played an important role, in that amortizing the cost of the war required a large and permanent increase in revenues. For our purposes, however, the important point is that this increase came almost entirely in the form of income taxes. In contrast, the Civil War had been paid for chiefly by tariff revenues and excise taxes.

5. A complicating factor for the Republicans was the ratification of Prohibition and the passage of the Volstead Act in 1919, which eliminated a major source of excise tax revenue.

6. On the roots of Democratic hegemony in the House, see Jacobson 1990a.

7. This is the so-called "Ricardian invariance theorem," first advanced by David Ricardo.

8. Barro deduces from the Ricardian invariance theorem various conclusions about "tax smoothing"—that is, the maintenance of a constant tax rate when

government expenditures are fully anticipated and the financing of unanticipated expenditures by permanent, one-time adjustments in the tax rate.

9. The future stream of government expenditures is assumed to be exogenously fixed at some (presumably optimal) levels.

10. The literature on electoral cycles in government policy and in the health of the economy is vast. See, for example, Beck 1982b; Hibbs 1987; Kalecki 1943; Kiewiet and McCubbins 1985a; Tufte 1975; and Nordhaus 1975.

11. For a full statement and proof of the median voter theorem and a review of its history, see Enelow and Hinich 1984, Chapter 1.

12. Quantitative testing of the median voter theorem in the finance literature has been confined, for the most part, to single-service local governments, such as school boards, and to cases of direct voter control over budgets. See Pommerehne 1978 and Inman 1978 for reviews and critiques of this literature.

13. This criticism is embodied in several branches of the spatial literature—in, for example, the branch that stresses the role of primary elections (Aranson and Ordeshook 1972); the branch that stresses that parties seek not just office per se but also specific policy outcomes (Wittman 1973, 1983, and 1990; Cox 1987); and the branch that investigates how entry by third parties is deterred (Palfrey 1984). To these, one might also add the branch that stresses the multidimensionality of the policy space. The convergence of candidates to the "center" of the voter distribution is still observable in some such models (Nicholas Miller 1977; McKelvey 1986; Cox 1987), but it is convergence to an area rather than to a single point. Hence, some room for divergence is left.

14. See Rosenthal 1990 for a review of the literature using the reversion point notion.

15. By a "program of expenditure," we have in mind here a complete budgetary specification of how much will be spent on what, not just a single project.

16. It might be recalled that in the late nineteenth and early twentieth centuries, the Republicans, not the Democrats, were the "tax and spend" party (see O'Halloran 1990 and Chapter 9 by Charles Stewart in this volume).

17. They have lost control of all three—House, Senate, and presidency—only once since Franklin Roosevelt's first election.

18. This is where fiscal and expenditure policy differ crucially from a strategic point of view. The reversion point in tax policy is last year's tax code. For most expenditure programs, however, spending is determined by annual appropriation, for which the reversion point is zero.

19. Of course, two can play at this game. Bracket creep in the personal income tax increased the real yield of taxes for many years without requiring new legislation.

20. We are assuming that the Republicans do not have a large enough congressional majority to override any veto.

21. For a review of tax legislation in the 80th Congress, see Hartmann 1971; Studenski and Kroos 1963.

22. Total federal revenue for 1934 to 1988 is drawn from OMB's *Historical Tables, Budget of the United States Government Fiscal Year 1990*, Table 2.1,

pp. 24–25. These figures were deflated using the implicit price deflator for federal government purchases of goods and services, as reported in the Department of Commerce's *Survey of Current Business* (1972=100; i.e., 1972 is the base year for the deflator and is set equal to 100, and all other years are scaled relative to the base). Current dollar GNP is drawn from the Department of Commerce's *Historical Statistics* (through 1970), vol. 1, series F1, p. 224; Commerce's *National Income and Products Accounts of the United States 1929–1974, Statistical Tables;* Commerce's *National Income and Product Accounts of the United States 1976–1979, Special Supplement* (for 1975 to 1979); and subsequent issues of Commerce's *Survey of Current Business* (1971–1988). These figures were deflated using the implicit price deflator for GNP, as reported in the Department of Commerce's *National Income and Products Accounts of the United States 1929–1974, Statistical Tables* and *National Income and Product Accounts of the United States 1976–1979, Special Supplement* (for 1975 to 1979), and calculated from implicit price deflator figures reported in subsequent issues of Commerce's *Survey of Current Business* (1972=100).

23. The dependent variable is $\Delta RECEIPTS_t$, equal to log ($Receipts_t/Receipts_{t-1}$) where $Receipts_t$ equals the total real federal tax receipts in fiscal year t. This transformation yields a statistic that closely approximates percentage changes. But whereas percentage change scores are asymmetric (they cannot be less than 0), these scores have the advantage that the distribution of change scores is symmetric. The percentage change in real GNP is calculated in the same manner.

24. Similarly, the model does not incorporate "median voter" variables, in part because we can't get information on tax level preferences of the national electorate, in part because the criticism of the unidimensionality assumption seems more telling at the national level, and in part because the Romer-Rosenthal critique seems plausible and our model more or less incorporates their view.

25. Our first cut at this regression revealed that the errors were first-order autoregressive. (We used a series of Lagrange multiplier tests, as detailed in Harvey, p. 169, in testing for autocorrelation.) We therefore included, as additional independent variables, the first-order lags of the dependent variable and of the percentage change in real GNP. With this respecification, the errors were no longer autoregressive.

26. As Figure 7.1 shows, the tax rate did not decline after the war to anything like its prewar levels. Moreover, if one puts in a dummy variable specifically for the "postwar wind-down period," defined as fiscal year 1946, nothing of consequence changes in the regression. If the wind-down period is defined as fiscal years 1946–1947 or 1946–1948, the regression results do change, but the coefficient on the variable under consideration—*P-DEMOCRATIC & C-REPUBLICAN*—does not. So, the large negative value of this coefficient cannot be chalked up simply to postwar readjustments.

27. The election year term was defined to be 1 in odd-numbered years (to reflect the realization of tax policy enacted in election years) and 0 otherwise.

The coefficient of this dummy variable was −0.04, with a standard error of 0.02, yielding a significant t-statistic (in a one-tailed test) of −1.76. The standard error of the regression is reduced to 0.085. Neither the sign nor the significance of any of the other variables was changed by the inclusion or exclusion of this variable.

28. Hibbs (1987) studied fiscal policy in the period 1955–1987. During these years, there were no cases of a Democratic president and Republican Congress nor of unified Republican control. Thus, classifying by "control of the presidency" essentially divides the cases into two groups: unified Democratic control, on the one hand, and divided control with the Democrats holding at least the House, on the other. Thus, Hibbs's use of the party controlling the presidency as the key variable makes sense as a way of identifying Republican intrusion into the policymaking process for the period he studies.

PART THREE
COMPARATIVE PERSPECTIVES

8
DIVIDED GOVERNMENT IN THE STATES

Morris P. Fiorina

Divided government has been defined and discussed primarily in national terms: The Republicans consistently win the presidency while the Democrats win Congress or at least the House of Representatives. This national emphasis is understandable enough. Although the states are more important than many realize, as a practical matter the national government is much more important. Consequently, national politics dominate the perspective of contemporary political discussion.

But developments in the states merit our attention, as well. In retrospect, it appears that the contemporary era of divided national government began in 1954 during Eisenhower's first term, solidified when Nixon emerged as the choice of a badly split electorate in 1968, and became the norm in the 1980s. Although little noticed, developments in the states have been somewhat parallel. Unified control in the states declined sharply after the 1952 elections, stabilized at a lower level in the mid- to late 1960s and declined still further in the 1980s (Figure 8.1).[1] These developments are interesting in themselves, but they also have important implications for explanations of divided national government. Discussions of presidential-congressional splits naturally em-

179

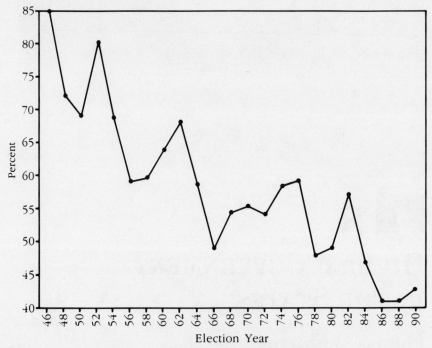

FIGURE 8.1   The Decline of Unified State Government, 1946–1990

Source: Statistical Abstract of the United States, various years (Washington, D.C.: Government Printing Office).

phasize national-level factors—House incumbency, the Democratic presidential nomination process, and so forth. But trends in state elections parallel to those in national elections raise suspicions that more general forces are at work and that existing explanations of divided government are too level specific. Put a bit boldly, whatever the disparity in practical importance, each state's experience is as interesting as that of the nation from the standpoint of democratic theory. The states share the larger cultural context and have similar institutional structures and political processes. The national experience is but one observation among fifty-one—a case study, actually.

I will begin by noting the striking disassociation of recent state legislative and gubernatorial outcomes. Then I will describe the patterns of party control in the states since World War II. This survey identifies a number of questions that will be the focus of some new hypotheses and some preliminary analysis. The discussion is very much of an exploratory nature: It is clear that multiple forces are at work, and the discussion in this chapter can only be regarded as suggestive.

TABLE 8.1   Gubernatorial and Legislative Victories in 1978, 1982, and 1986

	Governors		Legislatures	
	Number	Proportion	Number	Proportion
Democratic	90	.62	93	.64
Republican	56	.38	32	.22
Split	—	—	21	.14

	Patterns of State Governmental Control		
	Number	Proportion	Expected Proportion
Unified Democratic	58	.40	.40
Unified Republican	14	.10	.08
Divided, with Democratic governor	32	.22	.22
Divided, with Republican governor	42	.29	.30

Source: Calculated from *Statistical Abstract of the United States.*

THE ILLUSION OF DEMOCRATIC DOMINANCE IN STATE ELECTIONS

Election postmortems in the 1980s regularly emphasized the shallowness of Republican victories. Not only did the Republicans fail to crack the House of Representatives but, in state elections, the Democrats typically captured more than 60 percent of the governorships and legislative seats. Such outcomes leave a natural impression of Democratic dominance of state government. Commenting on the 1984 elections, for example, Chubb and Peterson (1985, 2) remarked that "a sizable majority of state governments remain solidly Democratic." In fact, such impressions of Democratic dominance of state governments are mistaken. As Burnham (1989) observed, after the 1988 elections almost three-quarters of the U.S. population lived in divided states. A complete tabulation reveals that Democrats controlled a majority of state governments for only six years between World War II and 1992 (the two years following their landslide presidential victory of 1964 and the four years following the 1974 Republican debacle). How does this fact square with the over 60 percent success levels in state elections? The answer is that Democratic successes in gubernatorial and legislative elections have become decoupled to a truly remarkable degree.

Table 8.1 charts patterns of party control resulting from the 1978, 1982, and 1986 elections (three-quarters of the states now hold gubernatorial elections in the off years). The Democratic party held 64

TABLE 8.2   Gubernatorial and Legislative Victories in 1948, 1952, and 1956

	Governors		Legislatures	
	Number	Proportion	Number	Proportion
Democratic	72	.54	56	.42
Republican	61	.46	59	.44
Split	—	—	18	.14

	Patterns of State Governmental Control		
	Number	Proportion	Expected Proportion
Unified Democratic	48	.36	.23
Unified Republican	47	.35	.20
Divided, with Democratic governor	24	.18	.31
Divided, with Republican governor	14	.11	.26

Source: Calculated from Statistical Abstract of the United States.

percent of the legislatures and 62 percent of the governorships after these three elections. Now, if party success in one arena had absolutely nothing to do with party success in the other, one could construct the expected distribution of unified and divided governments by simply multiplying the respective marginal probabilities of party control. Of course, such a null model would strike most analysts as absolutely ridiculous. But as the table shows, recent gubernatorial and legislative majorities are, in fact, completely independent ($p > .99$, X-square test). Consequently, although the Democrats do win more than 60 percent of the governor's races and a similar number of state legislatures, they *control* only 40 percent of the state governments.

This noteworthy disassociation between gubernatorial and legislative control has existed for some time. Not until we go back to the 1950s do we find some semblance of the expected relationship between gubernatorial and legislative control. Table 8.2 shows that in the 1950s, even with pluralities of the governorships and legislatures in opposite party hands, there was a significant ($p < .01$) relationship between party control in the two arenas.[2]

Findings such as these generally are discussed under the heading of party decomposition.[3] Certainly, party is less of a unifying force in the behavior of voters now than a generation ago, but such an observation takes us only so far. Party decline allows other factors to work but does not in itself determine those factors or explain their operation. At the national level, we have identified various considerations that apparently have grown in importance as party has declined, but it is far from clear how such considerations might apply to the states. Consider North Dakota. Democrats controlled the governor's mansion from 1960–1980; Republicans controlled the lower house for the same period.[4] National-level arguments might lead us to ask whether North Dakota Republican legislators have developed an incumbency advantage that enables them to withstand the Democratic gubernatorial tides? Does the North Dakota Republican party have a fractious gubernatorial nomination process that prevents them from uniting behind an executive candidate? Have the North Dakota Republicans cunningly gerrymandered Democrats out of a fair share of legislative seats? Or, finally, do North Dakota Democratic executives benefit from a reputation as effective macroeconomic managers while North Dakota Republican legislators benefit from a reputation as fair, compassionate protectors of the people? Each of the preceding arguments has been offered as an explanation of presidential-congressional splits, but it is not obvious that they apply to North Dakota. Perhaps such arguments do have some relevance for state outcomes, but some modification of those arguments clearly will be necessary.

My belief is that, when suitably generalized, some of the considerations offered as explanations of national divided government do apply to the states. As a way of motivating those generalizations, I will review the patterns of election outcomes that have developed in the states. Several of these patterns suggest directions in which to proceed.

PATTERNS OF PARTY CONTROL IN THE STATES

The Aggregate Picture

Figure 8.1 raises an obvious question: To what extent does the decline in unified state government reflect the breakup of the once-solid South? Figure 8.2 separates the southern and nonsouthern states. Evidently, the South is not much to blame for the decline in unified state government. The breakup of the solid South at the state level did not begin until the 1960s, by which time the decline of unified government in the non-South was well under way. Variations in unified government after that time move together in both the South and non-South, including the decline of unified government in the 1980s. Neither early nor later drops in unified government appear to be merely a by-product of party realignment in the South.

Figures 8.1 and 8.2 also address another question. One might naturally suspect that changes forced by the Supreme Court's apportionment

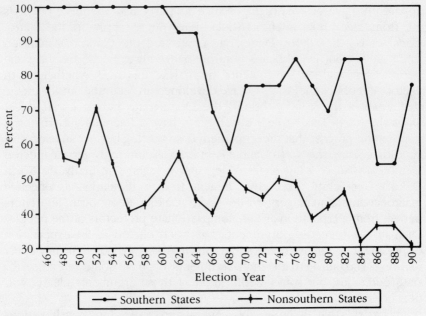

FIGURE 8.2   Unified Government: Southern Versus Nonsouthern States

decisions of the mid-1960s somehow underlie the decline in state unified government.[5] The data suggest otherwise. Much of the decline occurred prior to the court decisions, and there is actually a slight *resurgence* of unified government in the late 1960s, consistent with Robert Erikson's suggestion that reapportionment would lead to *less* divided government.[6] All in all, it is difficult to argue that the reapportionment decisions had much to do with the increase in divided government.

Thus, the broad outlines of divided government in the states suggest the most basic question for further inquiry:

What factors have led to the decline of unified state government, especially the large drop in the first half of the postwar period?

Disaggregating the Trend: Parties and Institutions

With the exceptions of the unified Republican episode of 1952–1954 and the Democratic-headed divided government episode of 1946–1948, the past half-century of national elections has yielded either unified Democratic government or divided government with Republican presidents. The states provide much more variation. More than half the states were unified Democratic after the 1974 elections; less than one-

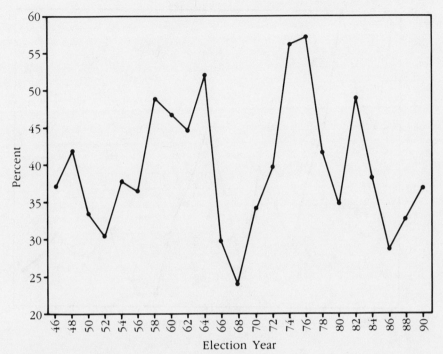

FIGURE 8.3   Unified Democratic Government

quarter were after the 1968 elections. More than half the states were unified Republican after the 1952 elections; less than 5 percent were after the 1974 elections (Figures 8.3 and 8.4). Divided governments of both kinds (Democratic executives, Republican executives) are present in some numbers.

Although there has been quite a bit of fluctuation over time, Figures 8.3 and 8.4 indicate that the decline in unified state government largely reflects a fall in unified *Republican* state government: There is no trend in unified Democratic government, with comparable highs and lows before and after the 1968 trough, whereas the Republican figures show a sharp decline that parallels the national trend.[7]

Unified government is a concatenation of gubernatorial and legislative outcomes, so the logical next step is to examine those outcomes separately. Gubernatorial outcomes show little trend, though they are highly variable (Figure 8.5). The Republicans held more than 60 percent of the governorships following the 1952 and 1968 elections and less than 30 percent following the 1958 and 1974 elections. Democratic outcomes are the mirror image, of course, save for an occasional independent. Legislative outcomes reveal a different picture, however

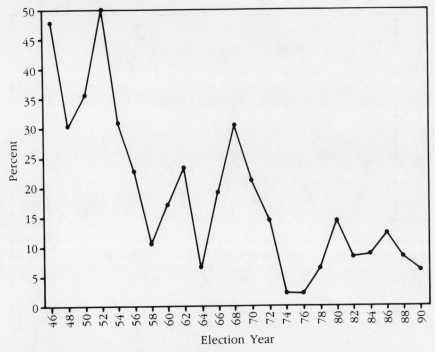

FIGURE 8.4   Unified Republican Government

(Figure 8.6). There has been a clear increase in unified Democratic legislatures or, almost equivalently, a decline in unified Republican legislatures.[8] In the early postwar years, Republicans controlled the legislatures of nearly half the states, but that figure dropped to less than one-quarter during the 1980s, with intermediate low points following the elections of 1958, 1964, and 1974–1976. Thus, the inability of Republicans to capture the U.S. House of Representatives since 1952 finds a reflection in the declining ability of Republicans to win legislative majorities in the states.

As a consequence of these developments, divided government with a Republican executive (the contemporary national pattern) and divided government with a Democratic executive (unknown on the national level since 1946) have become the second and third most common patterns of party control in the states (Figures 8.7 and 8.8). The obvious starting point in any explanation of these changing patterns of government control appears to be the precipitous decline in unified *Republican* state government, which, in turn, largely reflects a decline in Republican *legislatures*. Even without the decoupling of executive and legislative outcomes, the sharp decline in Republican legislatures

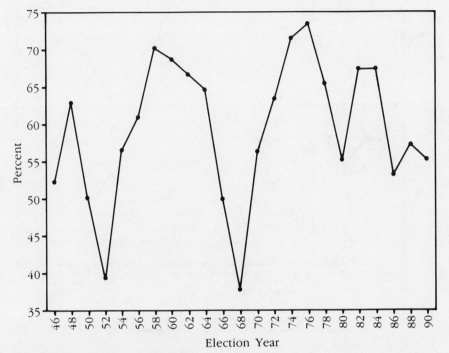

FIGURE 8.5 Democratic Governors

together with no trend in gubernatorial outcomes would have produced a decline in unified government, ceteris paribus. Thus, we have a second question for future research:

What factors have contributed to the decline in Republican state legislatures?

Disaggregating the Trend: States

Measured by the percentage of years unified, the top ten unified government states include nine southern states, plus Hawaii.[9] The second ten most unified states and the ten least unified states are listed in Table 8.3.

Aficionados of state politics may detect some subtle patterns, but for most of us, these listings offer no obvious clues. South Dakota is unified; neighboring North Dakota is divided. Maryland is unified; neighboring Delaware is divided. Indiana is unified; neighboring Ohio is divided. Heterogeneous California is unified; heterogeneous Illinois is divided. The two groups seem indistinct.

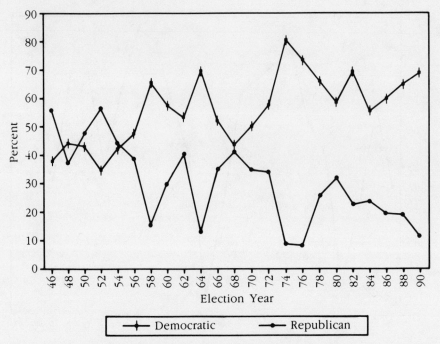

FIGURE 8.6   Unified Legislatures

Some clues emerge, however, upon differentiating between the Democratic-headed and Republican-headed divided states. With the decline in Republican state legislatures, the modal pattern of divided government has become like the national pattern: Republican executive/Democratic legislature. But there are also numerous examples of the opposite pattern—North Dakota is not unique. The ten most divided states of each type are listed in Table 8.4.

The Michigan and Nevada cases apparently reflect intensely competitive state party systems.[10] The remaining cases, however, stimulate two observations. First, the Democratic-headed divided category includes more smaller states than the Republican-headed category—a total of 92 congressional districts in the former, as compared to 110 in the latter (as of the 1981 apportionment). Second and more intriguing, in many cases gubernatorial outcomes in these states run counter to their popular national images, especially in the Democratic-headed divided government category. We think of the mountain states as rock-ribbed Republican, but they have elected Democratic governors almost half the time since World War II.[11] The same is true for Maine. On the other side, few states are more Democratic than West Virginia, but citizens there show a certain fondness for Republican governors.[12] In

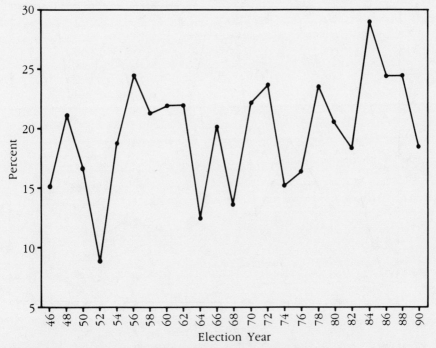

FIGURE 8.7   Divided Government with Democratic Governor

fact, outside the South, there is an interesting correlation between a state's partisanship and patterns of party control. The more partisan the state, the more years of unified government under the advantaged party *and* the more years of divided government under an executive of the disadvantaged party.[13] Again, note the analogy to the national pattern, where a Democratic advantage in partisanship has long coexisted with Republican presidential majorities. Thus, we pose a third question for future research:

Relative to the partisan compositions of their states, why do minority party executive candidates seem to do better than expected?

POTENTIAL EXPLANATIONS

The foregoing survey raised three questions that provide a narrower focus for future explorations. What explains the shape of the postwar decline in unified state government—a sharp early decline, a leveling-off, and a smaller 1980s decline? What explains the sharp decline in

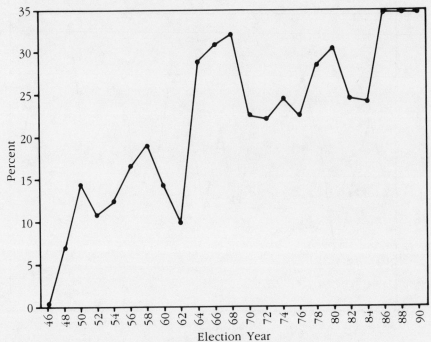

FIGURE 8.8   Divided Government with Republican Governor

TABLE 8.3   Second Ten Most Unified States and Ten Least Unified States (percentages)

Second Ten Most Unified		Ten Least Unified	
South Dakota	81[a]	Michigan	14[a]
North Carolina	77	Nevada	19
Virginia	77	Montana	24
New Hampshire	76	Illinois	27
Maryland	73	Alaska	29
Oklahoma	73	Ohio	33
Tennessee	71	North Dakota	36
Minnesota	67	Maine	36
California	65	Delaware	36
Indiana	64	Utah	41

[a]Percentage of years unified.

Republican legislatures? And what explains the relative success of minority party executive candidates?

Generally, answers to timing questions emerge from attempts to answer other more substantive questions. In this case, whatever explains the decline of Republican legislatures and the increase of divided governments headed by the minority party probably will help to account

TABLE 8.4 Democratic-headed and Republican-headed Divided States (percentages)

Democratic-headed Divided		Republican-headed Divided	
North Dakota	59[a]	Oregon	54[a]
Colorado	55	Delaware	46
Wyoming	50	Washington	46
Idaho	46	California	41
Kansas	46	Illinois	41
Michigan	46	Michigan	41
Nevada	46	Montana	36
New York	46	Nevada	36
Ohio	46	New Mexico	36
Maine	45	West Virginia	36

[a]Percentage of years under this form of government.

for the shape of the unified government decline. I will devote the remaining part of this chapter to those questions.

The Decline of Republican Legislatures

Republican prospects in state legislative races clearly rise and fall with national election outcomes. Relative low points were reached in the Democratic landslides of 1958, 1964, and 1974, and relative high points were reached in the lean Democratic years of 1952, 1968, and 1980 (Figure 8.6). A complete analysis should bear out the state-level variation that reflects national forces (Chubb 1988). Over and above national electoral impacts, however, Republican legislatures clearly have been in decline during the postwar period; at the state legislative level, the Reagan tidal wave of 1980 did not even match the narrow Nixon victory of 1968, and the "personal" Reagan victory in 1984 had nowhere near the reverberation of Nixon's "personal" victory in 1972.

One possibility that merits investigation is that Republican legislatures have declined as a by-product or unintended consequence of "progressive" reforms. Consider two polar cases.

Case 1: Wyoming, 1950

Wyoming is a glorious state, but service in its legislature has never been one of its notable attractions. In the early postwar years, representatives were paid $12 a day and received a $6 per diem during the session. This did not amount to much because the legislature met every two years and was limited to a forty-day session. No major perks went along with office. Not surprisingly, turnover was about 50 percent per election (Shin and Jackson 1979).

Since 1950, the responsibilities and compensation of Wyoming legislators have increased, of course. By 1990, they received $75 per day
with a $60 per diem, and the legislature may now meet for twenty
days during the even years, as well as forty during the odd years. But
relative to other states, the Wyoming legislature continues to occupy
a position on the amateur end of the amateur-professional continuum.
Turnover remains relatively high—about 33 percent per election (Niemi
and Winsky 1987). Perhaps coincidentally, perhaps not, in the postwar
period, Wyoming has never elected a Democratic House, and only twice
(1958, 1964) has it chosen a Democratic Senate.[14]

Case 2: California, 1990

The contemporary California legislature epitomizes the professional
pole of the amateur-professional dimension (though passage of a terms-
limitation initiative may alter this fact). By 1990, its members received
salaries of $40,816, $88 per diems, state-leased automobiles, and generous
retirement benefits. Like Congress, the California Assembly meets more-
or-less year-round, and the members have full-time personal staffs. Not
surprisingly, turnover is less than 20 percent per election (Niemi and
Winsky 1987).

Even in the early postwar years, California legislators were relatively
well supported by national standards, with $3,600 annual salaries and
$12 per diems. Session limits were relatively loose—120 days per year,
with an additional thirty-day budget session permitted in even years.
Turnover rates were about half those of Wyoming (Shin and Jackson
1979). Perhaps coincidentally, perhaps not, Democrats took control of
the legislature by 1958 (for the first time since 1938), and since then,
they have never lost the House (a tie in 1968) and lost the Senate
only in 1968.

These examples differ across many important dimensions; nevertheless, they suggest a hypothesis that can be examined in a systematic
fashion: Other things being equal, amateur legislatures favor Republicans, and more professionalized legislatures favor Democrats.

Candidates who hope to serve in amateur legislatures differ in
systematic ways from those who seek to serve in professional legislatures.
Because service is part time and poorly remunerated, candidates must
have independent sources of income and/or the freedom to take time
away from primary occupations without major financial or career costs.
Conversely, the candidacies of individuals with little discretionary
income and jobs that require their regular presence will be discouraged.
Certainly, those who work for wages are in no position to take a month
or two off each year. Thus, amateur political settings advantage the

independently wealthy, professionals with private practices, independent business people, and others with similar financial and career flexibility.[15] As Nike spokesman Mr. Robinson would say, "How do you spell Republicans, boys and girls?"

Professional legislatures generate quite different incentives. Average compensation in California, New York, Massachusetts, and other professionalized legislatures exceeds the median household income of U.S. citizens (about $38,000), and generous expense allowances, tax deductions, and leadership bonuses can add significantly to their salaries.[16] For many capable Democrats, service in such a legislature would be an alternative career that is more attractive than others open to them.[17] Conversely, as legislative service becomes a full-time pursuit, it becomes less attractive to Republicans who are unable or unwilling to abandon more lucrative careers in the private sector, even for comparatively well-compensated legislative positions.

Thus, as legislatures professionalize—as they become full-time institutions, with respectable salaries and perks, professional staffs, and responsibility for overseeing billion-dollar state expenditures—there should be an erosion of the recruitment advantage Republicans enjoy in more amateur situations. And the Democratic candidate pool should grow in both quantity and quality. This logic is analogous to that advanced by European parties of the Left when they advocated salaries for parliamentarians, and it goes back at least as far as Aristotle.[18]

One final observation is in order. There is a growing movement in this country to limit by statute or constitutional provision the length of legislative service. Voters in California and Colorado adopted such proposals in the 1990 elections, and more attempts are likely. Most academic analysts are skeptical of such proposals, arguing (1) that the terms-limitation movement errs in presuming that high legislator reelection rates reflect unresponsiveness or corruption and (2) that terms limitation will have negative consequences that outweigh any good that might result. If the legislative professionalism argument advanced here is correct, terms limitation will have an additional "unanticipated" partisan consequence: It will help Republicans in legislative races. What proponents of terms limitation refer to as "citizen" legislatures are what political scientists refer to as "amateur" legislatures. Recall the case of Wyoming.

The Minority Advantage in Gubernatorial Elections

As noted, divided government most commonly occurs when a state elects a governor of its minority party along with a majority party legislature. Before considering substantive explanations for this tendency, we should consider the possibility that it is an artifact.

To explain, assume that a state's elections are entirely determined by the underlying partisan distribution and that the latter is such that any candidate of the majority party has a 60 to 40 chance of winning. Then, the probability that a minority party candidate will win a governor's race is, by definition, .4. But the probability that the minority party will win 26 or more seats in a 50-member upper house is a faint .04, and the probability that it will win 101 or more seats in a 200-member lower house is effectively zero.[19] These statistical truisms simply reflect the operation of the law of large numbers: The smaller the number of minority successes needed for control, the more likely minority control is. Obviously, the proposed null model is not very realistic, but it is sufficient to make the point that there are nonsubstantive reasons for expecting minority party governors more often than minority party legislatures.[20]

In light of this fact, we need to identify empirical regularities not predicted by an artifactual model before investing much effort in formulating alternative substantive explanations for minority party governorships. Before proceeding to this task, note that an artifactual explanation does not appear to account for the national-level results. Between 1952 and 1990, the Democrats won an average of 60 percent of the seats in the House of Representatives. If these thousands of outcomes reflected the underlying probability of Democratic victory, then the probability that Republican presidential candidates were simply on a hot streak since 1952 is .042 (7 of 10 victories/probability = .4)—within the realm of possibility, but not likely.

This latter observation suggests a counterfactual implication inherent in an artifactual explanation of the minority party governor phenomenon. According to an artifactual explanation, episodes of minority-headed divided government would be occasional and sporadic, rather than frequent and persistent, with such episodes being less common and less persistent the more one-sided a state's partisanship. Though the minority party should win an occasional gubernatorial race, its underlying partisan disadvantage should prevent it from retaining the governor's mansion for a long period. Of course, real-world factors like incumbency might make two-term minority governorships reasonably common, but can we find state-level analogies to the national pattern, where, against the odds, the minority party wins the executive more frequently and more persistently than partisanship would suggest? The answer is a clear yes.

A study of the election outcomes between 1954 and 1990 reveals some interesting patterns. There is, of course, North Dakota. On the

Erikson-McIver-Wright partisanship measure, the state ranks eighth in Republican partisanship. But for twenty consecutive years (1960 to 1980), the Democrats held the governorship while the Republicans held the lower house and usually the upper, as well. Kansas ranks third in Republican partisanship and, until 1990, had elected a Democratic lower house only once in the period of this study; yet, the Democrats controlled the governorship of Kansas for twenty-two of the years between 1946 and 1992. Idaho (second in Republican partisanship) had a Democratic governor and Republican legislature between 1970 and 1990, as did Wyoming (sixth) since 1976. California is an interesting case. From 1940 to 1956, Republicans owned the legislature; from 1958 to 1966, the state was unified Democratic; and from 1966 to 1990, it resembled the national pattern, with sixteen years of Republican governors and Democratic legislatures.

On the other side, the examples are less striking but still plentiful. The southern states, of course, had the highest Democratic partisanship scores, but in all of the following cases, the Democrats had an advantage in state party identification. Oregon had a Democratic upper house between 1958 and 1990, but these Democratic majorities had to work with Republican governors in twenty-four of thirty-four years. Neighboring Washington had a Republican governor and Democratic lower house for sixteen of the past twenty-eight years. Delaware and Illinois had Republican governors and Democratic upper houses between 1976 and 1990, and Missouri had a Republican governor and Democratic legislature from 1980 to 1990. Finally, in West Virginia (seventh in Democratic partisanship), the Republicans did not capture either house of the legislature during the period of our study, but they controlled the governorship for sixteen of forty-six years.

In sum, patterns of divided government in the states seem to reflect something more than the random successes of minority party gubernatorial candidates. There appear to be too many such victories, and the resulting strings of divided government seem too long to be explained as the sporadic occurrence of unlikely events. What, then, accounts for these patterns? Consider the case of Massachusetts.

Case 3: Massachusetts, 1990

The Massachusetts legislature was under Democratic control between 1958 and 1990, but from 1964 to 1974, the Republicans controlled the governorship. In 1974, the Democrats won the governorship, inaugurating a string of sixteen years of unified Democratic government. During the 1980s, conditions in the state were so good that an incumbent Democratic governor parlayed the "Massachusetts Miracle" into the presidential nomination of his party. By 1990, however, conditions had changed dramatically. With revenues growing rapidly during the 1980s, there had been little need to set priorities, let alone to make hard choices to slow ballooning expenditures in accounts like health. As a result, state expenditures outpaced revenues by the end of the decade. Although signs of trouble were clearly apparent by the late 1980s, the exigencies of presidential politics led top state officials to discount bad indicators, accept optimistic forecasts, and otherwise postpone the day of reckoning. By 1990, recession had set in, taxes had been raised twice, the legislature was paralyzed by the need for yet another, larger increase, and the lame duck Democratic governor had become a pariah.

Feeling misled and manipulated, the population reacted predictably. Levels of distrust and resentment reached record highs.[21] A Draconian tax-limitation initiative led in the polls until the general election campaign, when it wilted under a ferocious assault by a unified front of the media, public officials, interest groups, and the Catholic church. The 1990 elections took place against this backdrop of popular frustration. In the September primaries, the party-endorsed gubernatorial candidates both lost decisively. John Silber, a Texas emigrant who had voted for Reagan twice and for Bush, won the Democratic primary despite (or because of) a series of "Silber shockers" that insulted the entire range of Democratic constituency groups. Democratic voters did not stop there. The party-endorsed speaker of the assembly was defeated in his attempt to move up to state treasurer. Even the attorney general (former Congressman Jim Shannon) was swept away by the anti-incumbent tide. Interestingly, although that tide rolled through the ranks of candidates for executive positions, it stopped short on the steps of the legislature. Only a handful of incumbents lost primaries.

In the general election, the electorate completed its revenge. Republican William Weld defeated Silber, ending sixteen years of unified Democratic government. A Republican won the patronage-rich treasurer's office for the first time in forty years. Meanwhile, in the legislative elections, the Republicans gained seats but still emerged on the short end of 123 to 37 (House) and 24 to 16 (Senate) party divisions.

A disinterested observer watching the Massachusetts campaign could not help being struck by the irony of it all. For twelve of sixteen years, the state had been led by a governor of unquestioned personal integrity, considerable intelligence, and administrative skill.[22] Yet, a majority of the electorate believed that corruption, incompetence, and misman-agement were rampant in the state.[23]

The explanation, I think, lies in Lord Acton's classic dictum that "power tends to corrupt." Reflecting such sentiments, the folk wisdom of political science emphasizes the salutary effects of two-party competition and the cleansing properties of party alternation in office. In retrospect, Massachusetts nicely illustrates the traditional wisdom. After sixteen years of Democratic rule, the statistics indicated that state government had gotten corpulent, the budget crisis suggested all-around incompetence, and there were a few prominent indications of outright corruption. It was time for a change.

How could Massachusetts voters implement such a change? Transforming the partisan composition of the legislature was an impossible task. With 128 to 31 (House) and 31 to 9 (Senate) majorities, no one in the state could expect anything but continued Democratic dominance of the legislature. And even if the disparities had been smaller, a major Republican seat gain was never in the cards. Much like U.S. representatives, Massachusetts state legislators maintained close personal ties with their constituents, separated themselves from an unpopular administration, and ducked the responsibility as best they could.

Although Massachusetts certainly is an extreme case, changing a legislative majority is both difficult and chancy in general. In the first place, there is a coordination problem. Not only must voters defeat the majority party candidate in one district, they must do so in coordination with voters in enough other districts to change control of the legislature. Changing legislative control often entails changing *many* majorities. In Massachusetts, for example, Republicans would have had to win 50 Democratic-held districts (of 128) to take control of the lower house.

In the second place, partial success in changing a legislative majority can be costly. If only one district changes its party representation, an experienced member of the majority party is replaced by an inexperienced member of the minority party, with a possible loss in constituency service and district benefits. Enough districts must change representation to shift the legislative majority; with anything short of that, the changing districts lose (Zupan 1991).

Neither consideration applies to executive offices. Only one majority need be changed to shift control of the governorship. And the question of putting one's district at a disadvantage if control does not change simply does not arise. Thus, voters who wish to end unified control will generally find voting for the gubernatorial candidate of the minority party to be the simpler and more efficient way to achieve their aim.

Of course, the force of the preceding argument will vary with particular features of each state. In general, the more entrenched legislative majorities appear to be, the more a popular desire for change will focus on the executive. This argument has at least three testable implications. Other things being equal we would expect the governor to be the agent of change in more one-sided legislative majorities (the more majorities that must be changed) and when majority party leg-

TABLE 8.5   How Unified Governments Ended, 1946–1990

Duration of the Unified Government	Lose Chamber	Lose Governorship	Lose Both
2–4 years	29	24	6
6–8 years	8	22	1
10–40 years	1	27	0

islative control has existed for a longer period (what has been will probably continue to be). Some evidence consistent with the second proposition appears in Table 8.5. Unified government episodes of two to four years are more likely to be ended by changes in legislative majorities, rather than in executive majorities. Beyond four years, however, termination of unified control is very likely to be the result of a change in gubernatorial control, and beyond ten years, it is almost a certainty that unified state governments will end via a minority-party gubernatorial victory. Ironically, secure legislative majorities may pose an electoral disadvantage for executive candidates of the majority party.[24]

The third testable implication involves the argument about legislative professionalization introduced earlier. Professionalization makes at least some contribution to the increased advantage of incumbency in the U.S. House of Representatives: Members intent on reelection and in possession of considerable resources have the motive and opportunity to build individual coalitions based on personal contact and district service (Cain, Ferejohn, and Fiorina 1987). These "personal" constituencies partially insulate them from the winds of electoral change that blow across the presidential landscape (Ansolabehere, Brady, and Fiorina 1988). Professionalized legislatures, whether national or state, are probably more electorally insulated than less professionalized ones (Asher 1978; Dodd and Kelly 1990). Thus, we would expect the governor to be the agent of change in the more professionalized state legislature.

The preceding theory is consistent with but more general than two other proposed explanations of divided national government. Gary Jacobson (1990b) argued that U.S. citizens view the Republican party as superior to the Democratic party in the realms of macroeconomic management and foreign relations. Meanwhile, he said, the Democrats enjoy an advantage when it comes to the fair distribution of national benefits and burdens. Given that the modern presidency is preeminent in foreign relations and economic management and that Congress is traditionally concerned with distribution, the present pattern of divided national government follows. Jacobson's argument is plausible, but though national survey data are consistent with it, persistent Democratic-headed divided government in North Dakota, Wyoming, Colorado, and Idaho would seem to be beyond the scope of his explanation.

Mark Zupan (1991) offers a more complex theory that includes a "prisoner's dilemma" dynamic. He contends that the ideology of the Democratic party places more emphasis on local benefits while that of the Republican party stresses national benefits. Thus, voters who elect Republicans to legislative office forego benefits. If the majority of other districts are not so self-sacrificing, then the districts that elect Republicans are "suckers" who pay for the local benefits of other districts but receive none of their own. When it comes to executive office, however, no such considerations apply, and the more that Democratic legislatures have logrolled for local benefits, the greater the incentive is to support Republican executives.

The logic of my argument resembles Zupan's, though I do not posit any association between the parties and particular issues or ideologies. Such associations are not necessary to explain the national and state data. One need only posit that continuous party control results in a buildup of waste, fraud, and abuse (WFA), which eventually leads majorities to opt for change. When that time comes, it is generally easier to make the executive the agent of change than the legislature. Of course, Zupan's ideological model provides another explanation for the Republican disadvantage at the state legislative level, whereas I offer a separate explanation (increasing professionalization) for that situation. On the other hand, Zupan's theory appears silent when it comes to explaining Democratic-headed divided governments.

Still, the preceding theory fails to provide a complete explanation of state election patterns for it does not explain why divided government persists. That is, periodic minority party gubernatorial victories may be useful instruments for flushing out WFA, but why should divided government become a more-or-less permanent state of affairs? One possibility is that, for most voters, the policymaking role of state government is sufficiently limited so that guarding against WFA is more important than the greater policymaking efficiency that unified government might bring. Another possibility is that persistent divided government reflects the kind of balancing considerations I have proposed as an explanation of divided national government (Fiorina 1988 and 1991). That is, voters whose preferred policies lie between those advocated by two polarized parties will split their tickets in order to balance the parties and bring about a more moderate outcome.[25] Because testing such notions requires data on the policy positions of state parties relative to those of state electorates, I will not pursue this argument any further here, but some such argument may be necessary to explain the notable persistence of some divided state governments.

CONCLUSION

As mentioned at the outset, this chapter is an exploratory effort, a quick tour through some rarely examined electoral data. But that exploration will have served its purpose if it convinces readers of two things. First, divided government is not a unique feature of U.S. national government; rather, it has become pervasive in state government as well. There is a great deal of variation in state patterns of divided government, so that state data provide students of divided government with considerable analytical leverage. In the end, we may conclude that the national and state patterns are totally different in their causes, but that should be the *conclusion* of a great deal of research, not the starting assumption.

Second and more generally, I hope that this chapter convinces at least some readers that state politics are both interesting and important to study. For too long, the area of state politics has been a neglected stepchild of the U.S. politics subfield. In his great works, *Southern Politics* (1949) and *American State Politics* (1956), V. O. Key, Jr., demonstrated that state politics were a rich source of theoretical ideas about the operation of democratic political systems. It is a lesson worth recalling. The varied experiences of the states force us to transcend our nationally determined patterns of thinking. And state experiences stimulate us to consider further the possibility that electorates act as if they have some appreciation of institutional interconnections when they choose among the candidates on their ballots.

NOTES

I wish to thank Alberto Alesina, Gary King, and Paul Peterson for helpful comments on an earlier version of this chapter. Special thanks to James Lavin, who compiled most of the data presented here.

1. Divided government exists when the governorship and both houses of the legislature are not controlled by the same party (states with nonpartisan legislatures—Minnesota before 1972 and Nebraska—are omitted from the tabulations). The reported figures indicate the presence or absence of unified government following the state elections of that year (or the preceding year in states holding elections in odd-numbered years), but the number of states that actually elected both governors and legislatures in that year varies. That is, in 1952, some 32 states held gubernatorial elections in presidential election years. This number fell to 12 by 1966 and remains at 12 today. Also, during the period under study (1946–1990) 20 states extended the terms of their governors, and some extended legislative terms, as well.

2. Because most of the states held gubernatorial elections in presidential years in the early 1950s, this comparison is based on three presidential-year elections (see Note 1).

3. Thus, Clubb, Flanigan, and Zingale (1990, Chapter 6) discussed declines in unified state government as aspects of the party decomposition phase of realignments.

4. The Republicans controlled the North Dakota Senate for sixteen of the twenty years; Democrats captured the Senate in 1964 and achieved a tie in 1976. Although unified Republican for two years after the 1980 and 1984 elections, the pattern of divided government otherwise continued in the 1980s.

5. The seminal decision was *Baker v. Carr*, 369 U.S. 186 (1962). Others soon followed.

6. Although reapportionment helped the Democratic party gain seats in state legislatures, the effect was not as large as many expected (Erikson 1971), possibly because rural Republicans lost seats to suburban Republicans. As for divided government, Hofferbert (1966) found that malapportionment between 1952 and 1962 was unrelated to divided control.

7. Following the 1990 elections, only South Dakota, New Hampshire, and Utah were under unified Republican control.

8. The two trends are almost mirror images because split legislatures are relatively rare (generally between 12 to 18 percent of the total) and show no trend.

9. Tabulations for Hawaii and Alaska are based on the years from 1958 to 1988; for Minnesota, from 1972 (when nonpartisan elections were eliminated) to 1988; and other states, from 1946 to 1988.

10. Interestingly, a minor empirical problem in explaining split control by reference to party competition is that split control has been used to *measure* party competition. See, for example, the original Ranney (1965) index and King's (1989) discussion.

11. In addition to the second, third, and fourth spots held by Colorado, Wyoming, and Idaho, Montana and Utah tie for twelfth on the Democratic-headed divided government list with 41 percent each.

12. So, too, do the citizens of Massachusetts and Rhode Island, which tie for eleventh on the Republican-headed divided government list with 32 percent each.

13. State partisanship is computed from pooled CBS/*New York Times* exit polls conducted between 1976 and 1982 (Erikson, McIver, and Wright 1987). Thirty-eight states showed an excess of Democrats over Republicans, and ten showed the opposite (no data is available for Hawaii and Alaska). I am grateful to Gerry Wright for providing this data.

14. The two parties tied in the House in 1974 and in the Senate in 1948.

15. This is, of course, a common finding in the older literature, when *most* state legislatures were amateur (Hyneman 1938). The definitive texts agree that lawyers and businessmen have long dominated the state legislative scene (Keefe and Ogul 1985, 111–113; Jewell and Patterson 1986, 50).

16. See Fowler and McClure (1989) for a discussion of the attractions of service in the New York state legislature.

17. According to Keefe and Ogul (1985, 112), "The fastest growing occupational group among state legislators is that of educators." Predominantly public sector employees, educators are disproportionately Democratic.

18. Aristotle (von Fritz 1964, 97–98) commented that "Pericles was also the first to introduce payment for service on the law courts. . . . Some people blame him on this account and say that the law courts deteriorated, since after that it was always the common men rather than the better men who were eager to participate in drawing the lot for duty in the law courts." I am indebted to Steven Macedo for this reference.

19. This is calculated from the binomial probability distribution.

20. This abstract logic no doubt would be empirically reinforced by the minority's recognition of it, which would lead that group to concentrate its resources on gubernatorial races.

21. A late summer *Boston Globe* poll reported many striking indicators of public cynicism, among them that 48 percent of respondents volunteered that state government served "the politicians" (5 percent said "nobody"), as opposed to the rich, the poor, or all the people (Lehigh 1990).

22. Dukakis was upset in the 1978 primary following his first term. He served as governor again from 1982–1990.

23. See the poll cited in Note 21. To fully appreciate the mood of the electorate, consider that the following remarks appeared in the *sports* section of the *Boston Globe* (Madden 1990): "I am a lifelong Democrat, a lifelong liberal Democrat, never once voting for a Republican for any office, at any level. My father's words are still clear to me, that my arms would fall off the instant I ever pulled a Republican lever, and I need my arms to type. But I am willing to chance dictating the rest of my stories the rest of my days. . . . In my life I have never been so angry at how the Democratic party has ripped us off, serving only itself and its minions, rotten to its core. And I am a Democrat speaking."

24. Jumping back to the national level again, this argument generalizes Erikson's (1989) delightful thesis that the Democrats deliberately lose the presidency in order to maximize their success in Congress. Equally tongue-in-cheek, my argument implies that, in general, Democrats should lose legislatures if they wish to elect more executives.

25. The model predicts that ticket-splitters vote for the executive candidate of the closer party if the executive is more powerful than the legislature and for the legislative candidate of the closer party if the legislature is more powerful. Thus, either pattern of divided government can occur within the model, the crucial distinction being the power of the executive relative to the legislative branch.

9

LESSONS FROM THE POST–CIVIL WAR ERA

Charles H. Stewart III

For most of the past two decades, the United States has had what amounts to a coalition government at the national level. The Democrats have had an ironclad lock on the House of Representatives since 1955; they have held onto the Senate for most of that same period, interrupted only by the hiatus from 1981 to 1986. At the same time, Republicans have been much more successful in capturing the presidency, winning all but one presidential election from 1968 to 1988.

The persistence of this recent partisan division has produced considerable comment among those concerned about contemporary policymaking difficulties, such as balancing the federal budget and conducting foreign policy (Cutler 1980 and 1989). Only recently have more positively oriented scholars begun to examine the empirical roots of this division and the operation of the Constitution's "checks and balances" in the context of split partisan control (for example, McCubbins 1990b).

In all of this inquiry into the causes and consequences of divided government, we frequently lose sight of the fact that divided government is nothing new: For one-third of U.S. history, control of the federal

TABLE 9.1   Types of Partisan Regimes During Partisan Eras, 1789–1991

Period		Partisan Regime[a]			
Years	Congresses	Unified	President Versus Unified Congress	President Versus Split Congress	Number
1789–1829	1–20	95% (19)	0% (0)	5% (1)	20
1829–1861[b]	21–36	56% (9)	19% (3)	25% (4)	16
1861–1897[b]	37–54	44% (8)	22% (4)	33% (6)	18
1897–1933	55–72	83% (15)	6% (1)	11% (2)	18
1933–1961	73–86	71% (10)	29% (4)	0% (0)	14
1961–1991	87–101	40% (6)	40% (6)	20% (3)	15
Totals		66%	18%	16%	101

[a]Unified = president and both houses of Congress share partisanship; President Versus Unified Congress = president is of one party and both houses of Congress are controlled by the other; President Versus Split Congress = each house of Congress is controlled by a different party.

[b]Presidents John Tyler and Andrew Johnson are classified as Democrats. Classification of Tyler as a Whig would produce the following entries for the 1829–1861 period: Unified, 63% (10); President Versus Unified Congress, 13% (2); President Versus Split Congress, 25% (4). Classification of Johnson as a Republican would produce the following entries for the 1861–1897 period: Unified, 56% (10); President Versus Unified Congress, 11% (2); President Versus Split Congress, 33% (6).

Source: Historical Statistics of the United States, series Y204–210.

government has been split between two parties (Table 9.1). Most episodes of divided government have been temporary and related to the vagaries of midterm congressional elections.[1] Still, two eras stand out for their periods of long-term, chronic partisan division: the middle decades of the nineteenth century (especially after the Civil War) and the middle decades of the twentieth century (especially after 1970).

The purpose of this chapter is to examine some key dynamics of the decades immediately following the Civil War, during what some scholars call the "Third Party System" or the "Civil War alignment" of U.S. politics (see McKitrick 1967; Burnham 1967; Sundquist 1983). This period was characterized not only by chronic partisan division but also by exceptional volatility in partisan control. By examining the dynamics behind this volatility and the strategies that federal politicians adopted in response, we can reach a more general understanding of how separation of powers works in the United States.

The remainder of the chapter is divided into three major sections. In the first, I examine the electoral basis for the partisan division of the period, noting how the regional distribution of partisan preferences throughout the nation was aggregated differently in each branch of the federal government. The constitutionally mandated system of representation thus produced different patterns of party control in the Senate, the House, and the presidency. In the second section, I examine the policy consequences of this pattern of partisan division, concentrating on the history of the protective tariff, one of the most important political issues of the era. In the third section, I discuss how congressional rules changed in response to chronic division, focusing on the mechanism of appropriations oversight in the House.

THE ELECTORAL BASIS OF PARTISAN DIVISION
IN THE MID-NINETEENTH CENTURY

A study of the mid–nineteenth century should give pause to anyone who believes that single party control of the federal government is a given of U.S. politics. Events before the Civil War suggest just how fluid intraparty politics can be,[2] and events following the war suggest just how evenly balanced two parties can be over numerous elections. To provide groundwork for the rest of this chapter, this section reviews the electoral context of the postwar period, outlines the basis of partisan divisions, and sketches the regional distribution of partisanship.

The period following the Civil War was the most volatile in the nation's history from the perspective of the partisan composition of the federal government. Republicans and Democrats frequently shared control of the government following the Civil War (Table 9.2), with the Democrats more successful in the House and the Republicans more successful in the Senate and presidency.

The basis of this volatility has been explored in the literature on partisan realignments in the United States (Chambers and Burnham 1967; Brady 1988), and yet, our understanding of it is still incomplete. Much is known about the dynamics of House elections during this period and about the distribution of presidential support at finely disaggregated levels, but relatively little attention has been paid to how electoral mechanisms filtered this support and produced incumbent politicians. What is clear is that volatility was produced through a combination of factors related to voter preferences and constitutional design.

In terms of preferences, sentiments for the two major parties were about evenly divided nationally following Reconstruction. But different methods of aggregating preferences—directly in the House, through

TABLE 9.2   Partisan Control of the Federal Government, 1861–1931

Years	Congress	President	House	Senate
1861–1863	37	R	R	R
1863–1865	38	R	R	R
1865–1867	39	R	R	R
1867–1869	40	R	R	R
1869–1871	41	R	R	R
1871–1873	42	R	R	R
1873–1875	43	R	R	R
1875–1877	44	R	D	R
1877–1879	45	R	D	D
1879–1881	46	R	D	R
1881–1883	47	R	R	R
1883–1885	48	R	D	R
1885–1887	49	D	D	R
1887–1889	50	D	D	R
1889–1891	51	R	R	R
1891–1893	52	R	D	R
1893–1895	53	D	D	D
1895–1897	54	D	R	R
1897–1899	55	R	R	R
1899–1901	56	R	D	R
1901–1903	57	R	D	R
1903–1905	58	R	R	R
1905–1907	59	R	R	R
1907–1909	60	R	R	R
1909–1911	61	R	R	R
1911–1913	62	R	D	R
1913–1915	63	D	D	D
1915–1917	64	D	D	D
1917–1919	65	D	D	D
1919–1921	66	D	R	R
1921–1923	67	R	R	R
1923–1925	68	R	R	R
1925–1927	69	R	R	R
1927–1929	70	R	R	R
1929–1931	71	R	R	R

R = Republican
D = Democratic

state legislatures in the Senate,[3] and through the electoral college for the presidency—channeled sentiments in different ways, doing little to coordinate policy majorities among the three elected national institutions.

The House

Because the representational mechanism of the House is the most straightforward, I begin with it in discussing national partisan sentiments. The practice of drawing congressional districts was not pristine by any standard. But the constitutional requirement that congressional representation be proportionate to state population and the statutory requirement that congressional districts be nearly equal in population within states allows us to use congressional districts as a good first approximation for gauging the distribution of partisan sentiments in the late nineteenth century.

Between 1860 and 1896, the partisan distribution of the national electorate was profoundly influenced by the questions of slavery (before and during the Civil War) and civil rights (in the postwar period), as well as issues of loyalty that the war itself raised. Patterns of partisan support were tied to region more closely during this period than at any other time in U.S. history.

Although we have no modern, scientific polling evidence on which to base our judgments, electoral outcomes suggest that the patterns of partisan support over time were different among three regions. The northern-most states, stretching from New England through the states bordering on the Great Lakes, were primarily Republican in sentiment. The states of the former Confederacy were primarily Democratic. And what we now term the "border states" were, by and large, up for grabs.[4] Within each of these regions, we can divide the decades from the 1860s to the 1890s into two periods to show how dramatically partisan sentiments shifted with the end of Reconstruction (see Table 9.3; for comparative purposes, this table also shows the patterns of partisan competition for the years 1896–1910).

Not surprisingly, the Civil War/Reconstruction era was a good one for Republicans nationally. No region elected a majority of Democratic representatives from 1860 to 1874 (although Democrats elected a plurality of representatives in the border states) and Republican strength increased as one moved north and west.

Of course, Republican good fortune was, in part, the result of southern secession and military occupation. During the 1850s, 74 percent of the representatives elected from the eleven states of the Confederacy were

TABLE 9.3 Percentage of House Seats Won by the Political Parties by Region, 1860–1910

Region[a]	1860–1874			1876–1894			1896–1910		
	R	D	O[b]	R	D	O	R	D	O
Confederacy	49	40 (15)	11	11	89 (19)	0	6	93 (13)	1
Northeast	73	26 (38)	1	60	38 (31)	2	78	22 (29)	0
Border	24	46 (9)	30	11	87 (11)	1	43	57 (12)	0
Midwest	70	30 (30)	0	52	47 (26)	1	76	24 (27)	0
West	88	13 (8)	0	73	19 (13)	8	84	9 (19)	7
Total	63	31	6	42	56	2	56	43	1

R = Republicans
D = Democrats
O = Other

[a]Regional definitions: Confederacy—Tex., La., Ark., Miss., Ala., Fla., Ga., S.C., N.C., Tenn., Va.; Northeast—Maine, N.H., Vt., Mass., R.I., Conn., N.Y., N.J., Pa.; Border states— Del., Md., W.Va., Ky., Mo.; Midwest—Ohio, Ind., Ill., Mich., Wis.; West—Minn., Iowa, N.Dak., S.Dak., Nebr., Kans., Colo., Wyo., Mont., Idaho, Wash., Oreg., Calif., Nev.

[b]Main cell entries are the percentages of House members elected from the respective regions during the indicated time period. Numbers in parentheses are the percentages of seats held by the relevant regions during the period. For instance, between 1860 and 1874, 40 percent or the House members elected from the states that comprised the Confederacy were Democrats, 49 percent were Republicans, and 11 percent were from other parties. During the period, 15 percent of the individuals elected to the House were from these states. Overall, for the entire period, 31 percent were Democrats, 63 percent were Republicans, and 6 percent were from other parties. For reference, the following numbers of individuals were elected to the House in each period: 1860– 1874, 1,789; 1876–1894, 3,144; and 1896–1910, 3,309.

Source: Martis (1989).

Democrats. Thus, secession cost Democrats about 50 seats in the House or almost half their electoral base, and they did not regain a majority of seats in states of the former Confederacy until the elections of 1874 (the 44th Congress).[5] This radical diminution of Democratic strength in Congress had profound electoral and policy consequences that stretched into the next century.

Republican sentiment was also artificially high in the North during the 1860s because of the Civil War. The war itself generated a short-term surge in the North toward the Republican party, which was seen as the party of union, and caused a short-term surge away from the Democratic party, seen as the party of southern sympathy.

For the period bounded by the elections of 1876 and 1894, partisan sentiments were more evenly balanced nationally, caused, in part, by the South's readmission to national politics and the reestablishment in that region of white political dominance. But, as the data in Table 9.3 suggest, Democrats also experienced a resurgence of support nationally, picking up strength in the border states equal to the strength they had had in the former Confederacy, winning about half the elections in the Great Lakes states from Ohio to Wisconsin, and even gaining two-fifths of the seats in the Northeast (concentrated in New York and Pennsylvania).

The data in Table 9.3 from the 1876–1894 period suggest why partisan majorities in the House might have been precarious after Reconstruction: Approximately two-fifths of the nation was firmly Democratic (the old Confederacy and the border states), another two-fifths was almost as firmly Republican (the states of the Northeast and trans-Mississippi West), and the remaining fifth of the nation was intensely competitive (the Midwest).

For the sake of comparison, Table 9.3 also reports the pattern of partisan competition for the decade after the realignment of 1896. Here, the shape of Republican hegemony following this watershed election is clear: Roughly three-fifths of the nation was now solidly Republican (the Northeast, Midwest, and West), one-fourth was solidly Democratic (the South), and only about one-tenth of the nation was competitive (the border states).

Given that the apportionment of House seats is based on state population, it is not surprising that partisan sentiments reflected at the level of congressional districts were also roughly reflected in partisan control of the House. The Republicans enjoyed uninterrupted control of this chamber from the 1860 election until the election of 1874, and they held it, on average, by comfortable margins. The 1876–1894 period was a different story: Democrats controlled the House for most of this period but usually by narrow margins. (The exceptions were the 1890 and 1892 elections, when the Democrats won 72 percent and 61 percent of the seats, respectively.) The 1896 election ushered in a four-decade period of Republican domination of the House, interrupted only by four congresses in the second decade of the twentieth century.

The Presidency

The method that governs presidential elections filters popular support through a "winner-take-all" electoral college. Thus, to a greater extent than in the House, the party controlling the presidency during and after the Civil War was determined not only by popular sentiments

TABLE 9.4   Popular and Electoral Votes Received by Presidential Candidates by Region, 1860–1908[a]

Region	1860–1872			1876–1892			1896–1908		
	R	D	O	R	D	O	R	D	O
POPULAR VOTE									
Confederacy	38	51	11	36	59	5	36	60	4
		(15)			(19)			(13)	
Northeast	46	44	1	51	47	3	60	36	4
		(38)			(31)			(29)	
Border	37	53	9	43	53	4	49	48	2
		(9)			(11)			(12)	
Midwest	55	45	0	49	46	4	56	40	4
		(30)			(26)			(27)	
West	58	41	1	53	36	12	54	40	6
		(8)			(13)			(19)	
Total	51	46	3	47	48	5	53	43	4
ELECTORAL VOTE									
Confederacy	41	47	12	4	96	0	0	100	0
		(19)			(26)			(25)	
Northeast	89	11	0	69	31	0	100	0	0
		(37)			(29)			(26)	
Border	32	60	8	0	100	0	55	45	0
		(13)			(11)			(10)	
Midwest	98	2	0	79	21	0	100	0	0
		(23)			(21)			(19)	
West	97	3	0	85	7	8	77	23	0
		(9)			(13)			(19)	
Total	75	21	3	48	51	1	66	34	0

R = Republicans
D = Democrats
O = Other

[a]See note to Table 9.3.

Source: Congressional Quarterly (1975).

toward the parties but also by the regional distribution of those sentiments (see Paullin 1932). As with the House, to adequately understand the relationship between popular sentiments and electoral outcomes, we must consider the periods before and after 1876 separately (Table 9.4).

First, Table 9.4 clearly shows that, regardless of eras, the method of aggregating popular sentiments through the electoral college tended to exaggerate partisan strength within regions. For instance, after Reconstruction, Republican presidential candidates were competitive in garnering popular votes in the border states, yet they never gained a single electoral vote in the region over a period of five elections.

Second, Republicans held a healthy national majority of popular votes in presidential elections during the Civil War and Reconstruction. Thus, it is not surprising that they dominated control of the electoral college—and thus the presidency—from 1860 to 1872. After that, however, popular sentiments changed nationally in favor of the Democrats, but Republican candidates were still able to win the electoral vote.

The reason for this continued domination of the presidency by the Republicans is that the electoral college served to discount popular Democratic support and aid Republican candidates beginning in 1876.[6] Democratic presidential candidates had substantial popular support, but, unfortunately for them, their overwhelming support in the un-competitive South could not be transferred northward, where it was needed. Not surprisingly, given the need to increase that party's strength in the North, the most successful Democratic presidential candidate of this period was Grover Cleveland, former governor of New York—the most important competitive state in the union.

One final consequence of the difficulties that Democratic presidential candidates faced is that in the five elections between 1876 and 1892, they won the popular vote four times but won the presidency just twice. In the only election in which the Republican candidate won the popular vote (1880), James Garfield's plurality over Winfield Hancock was less than 2,000 votes out of 9 million cast.

The Senate

Senate elections are much more difficult to approach. The history of Senate elections has rarely been studied, so we have a relatively weak base of prior research on which to build. Furthermore, as a consequence, we have very little direct evidence about popular sentiments toward Senate candidates during this period. Thus, understanding the chain of causation that extended from popular sentiments through election outcomes and ultimately to partisan control of the Senate is more challenging.

It is not impossible, however. By making some reasonable assumptions, we can gain an initial understanding about how the Senate's electoral mechanism produced election outcomes out of popular preferences. This, in turn, will clarify the Senate's role in producing divided government during the Third Party System.

The most important assumption I will make is this: The underlying (and unobserved) popular support for Senate candidates can be adequately approximated by the popular votes given to House candidates.

TABLE 9.5 Percentage of Senate Seats Held by the Political Parties by Region, 1860–1910[a]

Region	1860–1874			1876–1894			1896–1910		
	R	D	O	R	D	O	R	D	O
Confederacy	66	30	4	10	89	1	2	97	1
		(22)			(28)			(24)	
Northeast	92	8	0	84	16	0	96	4	0
		(28)			(23)			(20)	
Border	20	66	14	3	97	0	54	46	0
		(15)			(13)			(11)	
Midwest	84	16	0	61	30	9	88	11	1
		(16)			(13)			(12)	
West	81	19	0	88	9	3	77	15	8
		(20)			(25)			(33)	
Total	72	25	3	52	46	2	61	36	3

R = Republicans
D = Democrats
O = Other

[a]See note to Table 9.3. For reference, the numbers of Senate seats held during each period were: 1860–1874, 512; 1876–1894, 795; 1896–1910, 807.

Source: Martis (1989).

That is, I assume that had voters been given the opportunity to vote directly for Senate candidates before 1874, Republicans would have dominated Senate elections throughout the country during the Civil War and Reconstruction, with the only real competition coming in the border states. I further assume that Democratic candidates would have been the most competitive in the South, in the border states, and in the Midwest from 1876 to 1894 and that Republican candidates would always have done better as they moved north and west.

If this is a reasonable first approximation, then Table 9.5 suggests that the distribution of two senators per state tended to exaggerate the strength of the dominant party in each region as represented in Senate delegations. Most striking is the success of Democratic senators in the border states during the Civil War and Reconstruction: 66 percent of border state senators were Democrats, compared to only 46 percent of House members.

A close reading of Tables 9.3 and 9.5 together reveals an interesting pattern that helps us understand why the Republicans were so much more successful in the Senate than in the House from the 1870s to the 1890s: There were many more Republican *states*, although there were more Democratic *districts*. The result was frequent Democratic majorities in the House and Republican majorities in the Senate during the second half of the Third Party System.

One very interesting question arises from this history of Democratic advantage in districts versus Republican advantage in states. Because the period was one of relentless westward expansion, including the admission of several new states to the Union, was the admission of such states related to the Republican advantage in the Senate?

The answer is yes. The distribution of House seats can be seen as mostly exogenous for our purposes. But the distribution of Senate seats—especially the relative Republican advantage from the 1870s to the 1890s—cannot.[7] Some of the growth in Republican fortunes in the Senate must be attributed to the decisions to admit new states, beginning with Minnesota in 1858.[8] Of the thirteen states admitted in the nineteenth century from that date forward, only one (West Virginia) regularly elected two Democrats to the Senate, and only two (California and Nevada) regularly split their delegations.

In the 1890 census, Minnesota and the states admitted after it accounted for 30 percent of the Senate seats but only 6 percent of the House seats. In the 1890 election, which produced one of the largest House Democratic majorities in U.S. history (238 of 332 seats, or 72 percent), Democrats won exactly half (14 of 28) of the Senate seats up for election. Further, the "new" (that is, post-Minnesota) states accounted for 19 percent of the Republican members of the House elected in 1890 and exactly half of the Republicans elected to the Senate that year. On the other hand, these same states accounted for 5 percent of the Democratic strength in the House, and they elected no Democratic senators.

Nor is this pattern simply a product of one election, as Figure 9.1 demonstrates. This figure graphs the Democratic proportion of the House and Senate, calculated in two ways: the actual proportion of Democrats serving in these chambers for each year between 1857 and 1911 and the proportion of Democrats serving in these chambers excluding those from the "new" states (those admitted from Minnesota onward).

Because the newly admitted states had such small populations, neither calculation significantly affects the partisan composition of the House. In particular, except for the 51st Congress (1889–1891), the Houses that were controlled by Republicans still had Republican majorities without even considering the states that were admitted in the second half of the nineteenth century. On the other hand, because these newly admitted, Republican states received equal representation in the Senate despite their meager populations, their admission significantly affected partisan control of the Senate for several congresses. This is especially

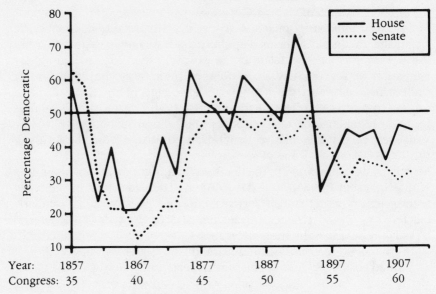

a. Actual Percentages

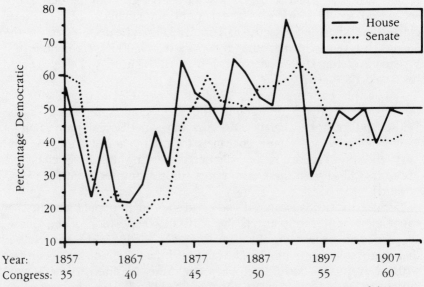

b. Hypothetical Percentages

FIGURE 9.1 Actual and Hypothetical Democratic Percentage Composition of the House and Senate, 35th–61st Congresses. (Hypothetical percentages calculated by excluding Minnesota and states admitted between 1858 and 1907)

true for the 47th through 54th congresses (1881–1897). The Republicans controlled seven of these eight Senates, but without the "new" state senators they would have controlled none.

Thus, in the final decades of the nineteenth century, the Republican party was successful in buffering the Senate against changes in partisan tides in the electorate, ensuring the existence of a Republican enclave in the federal government that would be constitutionally capable of vetoing Democratic proposals when the Democrats captured the presidency and the House. Although the Senate was, indeed, designed to provide some cushion against wild swings of popular sentiment, the degree of buffering during this period was extreme.

Throughout U.S. history, the partisan composition of each entering Senate class has, on average, matched that of the contemporaneously elected House. The one exception occurred in the second half of the Third Party System, when there was practically no such relationship.

Thus, we have an explanation for why the Senate was regularly controlled by Republicans following Reconstruction despite the fact that the partisan balance of the nation was razor-thin. And we therefore have a better sense of how split partisanship came about. Had Oregon, Kansas, Nevada, Nebraska, and Colorado been admitted after 1884 rather than before, Cleveland's first administration could have been quite different. Without the senators from these five states, the Republicans could not have organized the Senate, and Democrats would have controlled the entire federal government. We will never know precisely what difference this would have made because Cleveland and Congress were not notorious for working together when the Democrats finally controlled the federal government in the first half of his second administration. But it is possible that policy areas such as the tariff, currency, and civil service reform would have followed entirely different trajectories.

Thus, the Civil War and Reconstruction played important roles in postwar congressional politics that are frequently overlooked. Large Republican congressional majorities facilitated the addition of five new states during that era (Kansas, West Virginia, Nevada, Nebraska, and Colorado), four of which were undoubtedly Republican in character.[9] In the two decades that followed, slimmer Republican majorities were able to add another half-dozen Republican states, swelling their ranks in the Senate even as Democrats triumphed in House elections. Thus, divided control of Congress during the latter half of the Third Party System stemmed, in part, from conscious decisions by Republicans to enhance their strength in the Senate by admitting new states.[10]

Summary

The spate of divided government that characterized the decades at the end of the nineteenth century had its genesis in a combination of partisan preferences expressed by citizens and the rules that aggregated these preferences into electoral outcomes. In the arena designed to reflect popular sentiments most faithfully—the House—control was most likely to vacillate, although the Democrats ended up holding the House more often than not in the second half of the Third Party System. In the two bodies where responsiveness is designed to be more muted, Republicans were able to virtually shut out the Democrats. In the Senate, part of this shutout was intentional, through the admission to the union of new, Republican states.

Republican ascendancy in the presidency was less a conscious design than a matter of the distribution of Democratic support.[11] The problem this posed for the Democrats was the classic one of "having it where you don't need it": Overwhelming majorities in southern states could not be transferred to northern states with close races.

Table 9.6 summarizes the institutional bottom line of these various patterns of electoral support. Bracketed by periods of Republican hegemony at the national level, the latter half of the Third Party System witnessed intense competition for control of the House, while the typical state of affairs was for the Republicans to control the Senate and presidency.

The last quarter of the nineteenth century, therefore, is an interesting case study in the workings of U.S. bicameralism, the separation of powers, and the accompanying unique electoral schemes for each elected national institution. Contrasting that era with the current period of partisan division, we can see that the first important difference lies in the volatility of partisan regimes: Partisan "swing" was more pronounced in all institutions at that time, lending an unpredictability to national politics. The second important difference is that after 1876, one party was firmly ensconced in two branches (the Republicans in the Senate and White House), and competition was primarily focused on the House. Today, each party has a claim on a different branch (Democrats hold the House, and Republicans hold the White House), and competition centers on the Senate. This difference is especially important because the president and Senate can act together in certain executive areas without direct House assent. Thus, lower-chamber Democrats in the late nineteenth century were faced with challenging a Republican administrative state that was fortified through the presidential-senatorial axis on appointments (White 1958), but in the contemporary period, no such constitutional cartel is so easily established. Republican pres-

TABLE 9.6 Measures of Partisan Control of National Political Institutions, 1860–1930

	1860–1874	1876–1894	1896–1908
Percentage of elections in which the Republican party gained control of national institutions.			
House	88	30	88
	(8)[a]	(10)	(8)
Senate (total)[b]	100	75[c]	100
	(8)	(10)	(8)
Senate (class)[d]	88	60	94[e]
	(8)	(10)	(8)
Presidency	100	60	100
	(4)	(5)	(4)
Average percentage of seats held by Republicans in the Senate and House, along with the average popular and electoral vote received by Republican presidential candidates.			
House	61	46	54
Senate (total)[b]	71	51	60
Senate (class)[c]	70	49	59
President (popular)	50	48	53
President (electoral)	75	49	66

[a]Entries are in percentages; numbers in parentheses are the number of cases.
[b]Based on all seats in the Senate.
[c]Republicans and Democrats contested control of the 47th Congress; thus, each party is credited with controlling half of that Congress.
[d]Restricted to the seats up for replacement in a particular election.
[e]Republicans and Democrats elected an equal number of senators to begin service in the class of 1911; thus, each is credited with controlling half of the class.

Source: Martis (1989); U.S. Department of Commerce, Census Bureau (1975).

idents must now frequently deal with Democratic senates in identifying who will run the executive branch and sit as judges.

The structure of the earlier electoral environment induced ongoing fights over the control of federal policymaking for three decades in the late nineteenth century. It is to those fights that I now turn.

DIVIDED GOVERNMENT AND PUBLIC POLICY: THE CASE OF TAXING AND SPENDING

The persistence of divided government following Reconstruction had a lasting impact on policymaking at the federal level. This section examines how that affected federal taxing and spending decisions in the late nineteenth century—two issues that cut to the core of the differences between the major parties.

The origins of the two major parties, along with the legacy of the Civil War, led to sharp partisan divisions about federal spending and taxation. The Republican party stood for the protective tariff and had an expansive vision of federal power. The Democrats were primarily the "free trade" party and distrusted an expansive federal government that was symbolized by the army, navy, veterans pensions, and internal improvements.

These differences over taxing and spending policies were rooted in the different constituency bases of the two parties. On the tariff side, the Democratic party's constituency base included farmers who produced crops (especially cotton) that could be exported to compete in international markets. They thus favored lower tariffs for fear of retaliation against their products in those markets. Republicans were more likely to represent districts with "infant industries," and they claimed that tariff barriers against lower-cost imports were necessary so that indigenous U.S. industries could grow and prosper.

On the spending side, Democrats had inherited the mantle of Thomas Jefferson, who urged distrust of centralized, national political power. A large national government was seen as a temptation to "corruption," and revenues acquired through a tariff only encouraged the creation of a large national government. The Republicans, on the other hand, inherited the ideology of the Whigs (and Alexander Hamilton before them) and especially Henry Clay's "American system," which envisioned an active role for the national government in developing the nation's industrial infrastructure. They therefore believed that a tariff could not only protect infant industries but provide revenue for large-scale public works as well.

The course of the Civil War further divided the parties on issues of the size of the national government and government spending. And the two largest components of federal spending—the army and military pensions—were bound to cause partisan animosities, given the undying affiliation of southern whites with the Democratic party.

The particulars of U.S. politics sometimes served to blur the distinctions between the parties: Pennsylvania Democrats acquired a taste for protective tariffs, and border-state Democrats frequently represented districts with numerous Union veterans and thus supported generous pensions. But the central tendencies of the two parties in the years following the war and Reconstruction were as clear then as the differences between the two parties are today. (Of course, those tendencies have now been largely reversed.)

These differences were nicely illustrated in the respective party platforms for the 1888 election, which was held in the context of the late-nineteenth-century protective system. This system was characterized by high tariffs on protected goods, and it resulted in high federal revenues and frequent surpluses. (Throughout the 1880s, the federal government spent, on average, only 96 percent of the revenues collected in each fiscal year.) These surpluses proved electorally troublesome for the Republicans for they undercut support for protection. As a result, they sought ways to spend the surpluses, while the Democrats increasingly advocated frugality and a "tariff for revenue only."

In their 1888 party platform, the Democrats consequently attacked the system of protective tariffs, accusing the Republican party of trying "to meet and exhaust by extravagant appropriations and expenses" the surplus that protection had yielded. They pledged both to "enforce frugality in public expense" and to "abolish unnecessary taxation" by reforming the tariff. Meanwhile, the Republicans actually had few quarrels with the Democrats' characterizations of their fiscal program. Their platform defended the tariff system and even called for further barriers. And, in contrast to the Democrats' call for extraordinary frugality in public spending, the Republican party demanded "appropriations for the early rebuilding of our navy, for the construction of coast fortifications . . . for the payment of just pensions to our soldiers, for necessary work of national importance in the improvement of harbors and the channels of internal, coastwise, and foreign commerce, for the encouragement of the shipping interests" (Noyes 1909, 128–129).

Given the contrasting preferences of the parties and the persistence of divided government, it is important to ask whether the parties could actually accomplish the goals they professed—whether Republicans could maintain protection and high levels of spending, whether Democrats could attack protection and retrench spending, and whether either could effect a balanced budget.[12]

To answer these questions, we must consider the tariff and spending separately because, then as now, these issues were considered under two entirely different sets of rules. In barest terms, the important point is that tariff rates were permanently set in statute, but appropriations were passed (and expired) annually. The difference this makes is illustrated through two simple spatial models discussed in the appendix. Simply put, because tariff rates were written into statute, the system of protection could be altered only through the passage of new laws. This gave Republicans a distinct advantage after the Civil War and Reconstruction in legislative battles over protection for they almost always controlled at least one of the three institutions involved in legislating—there was always a veto point somewhere.

On the other hand, spending was determined through annual appropriations bills. Failure to enact such a bill would bring government activity in that area to a halt. During periods of division, if the Republicans demanded spending that the Democrats regarded as too high, the Democrats could plausibly threaten to delay passage of the

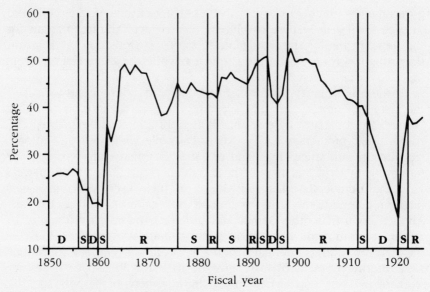

D = Democrats control government
S = Split control of government
R = Republicans control government

FIGURE 9.2 Yield from Import Duties as a Percentage of the Value of All Imports Subject to Duty

annual bill past the fiscal year, as nearly happened with the 1880 army appropriations bill. The Democratic party, which preferred lower spending, was thus advantaged in bargaining over appropriations whenever the government was divided. Finally, during periods of partisan division, the combined effect of the Republican advantage in keeping tariff revenues up and the Democratic advantage in keeping spending down could be expected to produce surpluses in those fiscal years.

Two key empirical questions are posed by this discussion: First, were the Republicans in fact able to perpetuate high tariff levels during periods of split control? And second, were the Democrats in fact able to bring spending down during those same periods?

The Tariff

To aid the discussion of tariff history in the late nineteenth century, Figure 9.2 graphs the standard measure of the level of protection—the yield from import duties as a proportion of all imports subject to duty. Immediately preceding the Civil War, tariff rates had reached the lowest level since 1821—the first year for which we have reliable data (U.S.

TABLE 9.7 Composition of Federal Revenues, 1860–1880 (millions of nominal dollars)

	1860	1865	1870	1875	1880
Customs	53.2	84.9	194.5	157.2	186.5
Income tax	0.0	61.0	37.8	0.0	0.0
Excises	0.0	148.5	143.3	109.6	123.6
Miscellaneous	1.1	38.3	32.3	19.8	22.4
(Total domestic)	(1.1)	(247.8)	(213.4)	(129.4)	(146.0)
Public lands	1.8	1.0	3.4	1.4	1.0
Total	56.1	333.7	411.3	288.0	333.5

Source: U.S. Department of Commerce, Census Bureau, 1975, Series Y352–356.

Department of the Treasury 1892, 15). These relatively low levels of protection were a result of Democratic rate cuts in 1846 and in 1857.

When the Republicans gained de facto control of Congress in the months immediately preceding the Civil War, they managed to pass the first of a series of protective measures—the Morrill Tariff of 1861. The level of protection skyrocketed during the course of fighting and financing the Civil War, with both the number of items subject to duties and the ad valorem rates themselves rising under two acts—the Tax and Tariff Act of 1862 and the Tariff Act of 1864.

Of course, these acts had purposes paramount to protection—financing the war effort. This was a fiscal enterprise previously unparalleled in U.S. history, with federal spending increasing six-fold in just one year and eighteen-fold over the four-year course of the war. Although the war was financed primarily through loans and the issuance of paper money, an increase in taxation (including an increase in tariffs), a dramatic increase in excises, and the institution of an individual income tax were also used.

Once the war had ended, these taxes were naturally reduced. But once they were lowered in the early 1870s to what could be characterized as an equilibrium (Table 9.7), it is interesting that total domestic taxes (especially the income tax) declined dramatically while the system of high tariffs, which had been instituted as an emergency financing scheme, remained, overtly as a system of protection (Studenski and Krooss 1963).

Republican majorities in Congress joined Republican presidents in ratifying tariff reductions in 1870 and 1872, but a downturn in revenues due to the Panic of 1873 led to a repeal of the 1872 reductions in 1875. Further spurred on by continuing surpluses, President Chester Arthur appointed a commission to study how the tariff rates could be reduced sufficiently to bring the budget into balance. Congress members largely ignored the commission's recommendation to reduce tariffs by an estimated 25 percent. Instead, they adopted the Tariff Act of 1883, which basically reshuffled rates on particular items (Taussig 1931b, 249–250).

Major changes occurred five times in the next forty years. The Tariff of 1890 (the "McKinley Tariff") produced "a radical extension of the protective system. . . . The question of principle never was so squarely presented" (Taussig 1931b, 283). The Tariff of 1894, the only major tariff act passed in the late nineteenth century with a Democratic majority in Congress and a Democratic president, effected a sharp cut in dutiable rates (see Figure 9.2). But even here, the armor of protection was only dented because rates on dutiable goods failed to approach prewar levels and Democrats failed to effect further reductions in the most dramatic and publicized areas, such as rates on sugar. In any event, whatever Democratic character had been instilled in tariff policy due to the 1894 act was quickly repealed with the passage of the 1897 tariff, coming as it did on the heels of the realigning 1896 election.

Upon taking control of the federal government with the 1912 election, Democrats passed the Tariff Act of 1913 (the "Underwood Tariff"). As Figure 9.2 shows, average ad valorem rates were cut almost in half, and other measures favored by many free-trade advocates, such as the repeal of reciprocity, were enacted. The return of Republicans to control of the federal government following the 1920 election undid these changes, and the 1922 Tariff Act (the "Fordney-McCumber Tariff") returned rates to pre-Underwood levels.

Histories of tariff politics in the years between the Civil War and the Great Depression thus emphasize the positive action of Republicans and the defensive action of Democrats. The Republicans were able to use their uncontested majorities in the 1860s to develop a new system of protection. Faced with the fiscal problems of either embarrassing surpluses (in 1870, 1872, and 1883) or troubling deficits (in 1875), they were able to fine-tune this system. And blessed with huge majorities after the election of 1896, they were able to refine it even further.

Because they controlled the entire federal government for only two years between 1860 and 1910, the Democrats were grossly ineffective in their efforts to modify protection. In both 1884, when Democrats controlled only the House, and 1886, when they controlled the House and the presidency, Democratic leaders tried to push through tariff reform. The 1884 effort failed in the House, where a small number of Democrats joined a united Republican minority to strike the bill's enacting clause (see Perry 1887). In 1886, Democrats were successful in getting a bill through the House to roll back protection, but the ensuing Senate bill was a "counter manifesto" (Taussig 1931b, 254) that proposed to extend protection even further. Not surprisingly, the two chambers never resolved their differences, and the protective system was protected.

In sum, protection was established through the Republican majorities of the 1860s. And throughout the 1870s, 1880s, and 1890s, the GOP was able to shield the centerpiece of its platform from pro-Democratic surges in the electorate, relying on both the deliberately created Republican lock on the Senate and the Republican hold on the presidency.

Spending

Were Democrats able to exert a leverage over spending that was denied them in terms of the tariff? The answer here is yes, although historians of public finance have rarely examined this issue with the same zeal as they have examined tariffs. But the results here are more ambiguous. In the appendix, I examine this question using econometric techniques that may be unfamiliar to many readers. I will therefore briefly summarize those findings here and refer those who are curious about the details to the appendix and to Stewart (1989, Chapter 4).

To explore whether Democrats were able to force spending downward whenever control of the federal government was split, I examined spending patterns of eleven annual appropriations bills that were passed between 1871 and 1916. In addition to examining partisan-based differences in the spending patterns, I also included measures of the fiscal surplus, past spending levels, and a control for the effects of the Spanish-American War.

First, to establish that Democrats preferred lower spending than Republicans, I compared spending levels during years when the Democrats controlled the federal government with levels during Republican years. In every case but three, spending was lower in Democratic years, according to the coefficients that I estimated econometrically. Unfortunately, because there were so few years of Democratic control between 1871 and 1916, these coefficients are statistically imprecise; therefore, we cannot say, in a statistical sense, that Democratic spending was lower than Republican spending.

There were many more years of split control, so the comparison between Republican and split years yields more precise estimates that confirm my expectations. Eight of the eleven annual bills experienced slower spending growth during years of split partisan control than during years of Republican control. These differences are confirmed at traditional levels of statistical significance. Of the remaining three bills, the difference is in the expected direction but not statistically significant in two cases; there is no difference in one bill (pensions). The bills taking the strongest beating in split years were those associated with the military (especially fortifications, the military academy, and naval affairs) and with the Far West (Indian affairs). The bills escaping cuts during years of split control were those providing for agriculture, the diplomatic service, and pensions.

Summary

Clearly, the policy effects of split control of the federal government were significant in the late nineteenth century. In one of the most crucial policy areas of the time, the protective tariff, years of split control helped entrench protection as a national policy. In those same years, however, Democrats were able to use their bargaining leverage to reduce federal spending. Thus, one consequence of divided control during this period turns more modern outcomes on their heads: Late in the nineteenth century, divided government was associated with budget *surpluses,* unlike the current period when divided government is associated with *deficits* (see Alt and Stewart 1990; McCubbins 1990b).

DIVIDED GOVERNMENT AND HOUSE RULES: THE CASE OF APPROPRIATIONS OVERSIGHT

A little-understood dimension of divided government is how institutions change as a consequence of division. For instance, consider the situation of House Democrats after Reconstruction. They knew that gaining a majority in the Senate and winning the presidency would be an uphill struggle. The best they could hope for would be to use their beachhead in the House to influence the behavior of Republican presidents and a Republican Senate. How might they have done this?

One way would have been to strengthen the ability of the House to oversee the operation of the Republican administrative state. Although House Democrats could not have directly influenced the bureaucracy through appointments, they could have exerted influence over bureaucratic behavior through the annual appropriations process. Another source of influence derived from the fact that appropriations bills were passed annually. The yearly traffic of agency officials en route to Capitol Hill to justify their appropriations requests gave Democratic House members the opportunity to closely scrutinize the activities of those agencies. At an extreme, provisos to appropriations bills could be used to constrain the behavior of the executive.

During the 1870s, Democrats in the House developed a particular mechanism within the House Rules with which to constrain federal agencies: the "Holman Rule," passed in 1876 and named for its most staunch supporter, John Holman (D–Ind).[13] This rule allowed substantive riders to appropriations bills as long as they purported to retrench spending. Though modern budgetary scholars have focused on the *retrenching* side of the rule (for example, Fisher 1975; Schick 1984) and suggested that its purpose was policy-neutral frugality, taking into account the Democrats' political plight helps us see how this rule could have been a partisan vehicle.

Between 1837 and 1876, House Rule 120 governed the consideration of floor amendments to appropriations bills. A literal reading of the rule seemed to prohibit appropriations for items not yet authorized by law. But Barclay's (1874) *Digest* reported that the rule was actually framed for the purpose of increasing expenditures, especially salaries; it had been used frequently by Republicans after the Civil War to quietly raise salaries of patronage appointees even beyond levels allowed by law.

The Holman Rule, as it passed the 44th House (1875–1877), read as follows: "Nor shall any provision in any such [appropriations] bill or amendment thereto, changing existing law, be in order except such as, being germane to the subject-matter of the bill, shall retrench expenditures" (Stewart 1989, 85).

In the debate that preceded the passage of the Holman Rule, Democrats and Republicans struck the partisan themes that would resound virtually every time the rule was broached over the next fifty years. Democrats emphasized the retrenching aspects of the rule. Republicans interpreted it as an attempt by Democrats to add legislative provisions (riders) to appropriations bills and thereby centralize policymaking within the House Appropriations Committee (HAC). By implication, this strengthening of the Appropriations Committee would loosen the controls that the legislative committee had on federal agencies.[14]

Nor were Republican fears implausible. Shut out of the federal government for fifteen years and laboring against a Republican Senate and presidency, Democrats could be expected to grasp for any hook on the policy process that they could find. The best hope they had of influencing issues such as army regulation, the status of the South, and administrative reform was through adding substantive legislation to appropriations bills. The partisanship of this measure was revealed on the vote to pass the rule in 1876: Democrats favored it by a vote of 151 to 6; Republicans opposed it 4 to 94.

In subsequent years, the presence of the Holman Rule was strongly correlated with Democratic houses facing Republican presidents: The Democratic House repealed it when Cleveland took office in 1885, the long stream of Republican houses from 1895 to 1911 never instituted it, and when the Democrats once again regained control of the House in the 1910 election (against the Republican President William Howard Taft), the first rules change they made reinstated the Holman Rule over Republican objections.

The classic example of the Democrats' use of legislation on appropriations bills was the suspended enforcement of Civil War and Reconstruction era acts that authorized federal marshals and troops to supervise elections and "ensure the peace" at polls in the South. Especially in the aftermath of the disputed 1876 election, in which the role of federal forces in southern states was caught in the confusion about those states' electoral outcomes, Democrats viewed this use of the army as yet another instrument through which Republicans denied Democrats their legitimate place in national politics. Democrats were barred from repealing this legislation outright in the 45th Congress (1877–1879) because Republicans controlled both the Senate and the White House. Democrats controlled both chambers in the 46th Congress, but the Republican Rutherford B. Hayes was still president, and he stood ready to veto any bill that would restrict the power of the army or federal marshals in the South.

Achieving this result was tortuous and spanned the 45th and 46th congresses. The 45th adjourned without passing either the army or the legislative, executive, and judicial appropriations bill. In the 46th Congress (1879–1881), with a Democratic House and Senate aligned against a Republican president, the army was finally restricted from activity at the polls through a rider to the army bill. Marshals were restrained from policing the polls when the appropriation for their salaries and activities was removed from the legislative, executive, and judicial bill. A separate appropriation for the marshals, with language restricting their activity, passed Congress, was vetoed by Hayes, and then failed in an override attempt. Congress then adjourned without funding the marshals at all.[15]

Another institutional change, not frequently thought of in terms of partisan control, was the series of decisions between 1877 and 1885 to give legislative committees oversight on nine of the fourteen appropriations bills (Stewart 1989). Many have attributed the denouement in 1885, when seven bills were taken from the HAC and given to the appropriate legislative committees, to a personal vendetta against the HAC's chair, Samuel Randall. And many others have associated this devolution with a rise in federal spending late in the nineteenth century (Brady and Morgan 1987; Cogan 1988).

On closer examination it appears that neither set of explanations is entirely compelling: Randall's prior infidelity to his Democratic followers and his collaboration with Republicans on the tariff issue may have demanded some sort of sanction from the Democratic caucus, but sanctioning Randall by emasculating the HAC was like killing a mosquito with a bazooka. Further, much of the spending escalation after 1885 can be attributed to factors other than the "devolution of 1885" (see Stewart 1989, Chapter 4). One interesting pattern stands out, however, across the decade during which the House dispersed the authority of its Appropriations Committee: Every effort, successful or not, to diminish the scope of the HAC's authority occurred in years when Democrats controlled the House, and every assault against the HAC was led by a Democrat.

Why would Democrats be more interested in decentralizing appropriations authority in the House, especially if the Democrats were the party of "small government"? One possible answer is that congressional Democrats were using the strategy of appropriations devolution to strengthen their hand against the executive branch, which was inevitably headed by a Republican and whose subordinate officials were appointed by the Republican president and confirmed by the Republican Senate.

Dispersion of appropriations authority among eight standing committees in addition to the HAC (the Military Affairs Committee oversaw two bills) multiplied the "eyes on the executive branch" eight-fold. It transferred the opportunity to scrutinize controversial agencies to those legislators who were most likely to have information about such agencies. And for the HAC, which still oversaw half the budget, its ability to closely review the bills it retained must have been enhanced even further.

Thus, although it is tempting to interpret the devolution of 1885 as a devolution of *authority* from the center to the periphery, it can also plausibly be interpreted as a form of strategic division of labor, intended to give Democrats greater opportunities to influence the behavior of federal bureaucrats. Using this, together with the Holman Rule that also enhanced the influence of legislative committees over agencies, Democrats crafted a set of potentially powerful tools out of the appropriations process.

CONCLUSION

A literal reading of the Constitution and a cursory review of U.S. history proves that nothing guarantees that the federal government will be controlled by one party. Confronting this fact, one can protest that divided government encourages impasse at too high a cost to the commonweal, or one can try to understand how politicians attempt to pursue their ends in the face of the obstacles that division brings. Believing that we will stand in better stead by understanding how politicians actually cope with such problems, my purpose in this essay has been to examine the origins and some of the institutional and policy consequences of the divided governments of the last century.

In certain respects, the division of the last century and that of the Second half of the twentieth century spring from different causes and will likely have different consequences. The jury is still out in terms of explaining the locus of divided government in the post–World War II period. But the lion's share of the explanation probably derives from the decline of party in the U.S. electorate, which has, in turn, encouraged phenomena such as split-ticket voting and the related rise of incumbency as a voting cue. At the other end of the spectrum, if we know anything about the locus of division in the last century, we know it was not due to a weakness of political parties; indeed, it may have arisen from their strength.

In particular, divided government a century ago was deeply rooted in the geographic and constitutional structure of representation at the national level. Once national politics had returned to its uneasy equilibrium with the passing of Reconstruction (and the unfortunate political failure of the "seven mystic years" in the South), partisan sentiments were closely matched in the nation as a whole. This may have been enough to ensure volatility in the composition of the federal government, but it was insufficient to ensure the type of chronic division that ensued. That is, an electorate closely balanced in allegiance between the two major parties may have swung from one party to the other in presidential years, electing majorities of one party to the presidency, House, and Senate on one occasion and majorities of the other party on the next. Division might have occurred frequently in the off years (and might have persisted in the presidential years because of the system of classes in the Senate), but the pull of coattails was strong enough in the late nineteenth century that a close partisan division in the electorate was more likely to produce volatility (depending on which party was luckier in a particular year) than division.

Thus, the geographic distribution of partisan preferences and the peculiar place of the Senate become important in understanding why party composition of the federal government was both volatile *and* chronically divided. On the presidential side, the Republicans were aided by having more dispersed support around the country while the Democrats' support was concentrated in the South. On the Senate side, the Republicans were aided by the healthy Republican tendencies of the newly admitted states, whose admission was not entirely exogenous to Republican designs on the federal government.

The result may be termed policy stalemate, but it was not uniform stalemate, and national politicians proved remarkably skilled at adapting.

In areas that required the ongoing cooperation of the branches, such as appropriations or appointments (see White 1958), decisions were, indeed, made, and the federal government did not grind to a halt. The requirements that such mundane items be constantly renewed gave both parties, but especially the Democrats, opportunities to influence the course of politics that they might not have had otherwise. On the other hand, the system of protection, which was the policy status quo inherited by this era of partisan division, was quite resilient *because of* the division.

Were policy results "good" or "bad" because of the partisan divisions of the Third Party System? The answer depends on the criteria one uses. But in any case, the answer may not be straightforward. Consider the most classic criteria, those of the Founding Fathers: To ensure that major national policies such as the tariff would remain essentially unchanged in the absence of a clear consensus among the citizenry to alter policy was precisely the point of the separation of powers. But on the other side of the ledger, the perversities of the electoral system that were continually revealed, especially those concerning the Senate, must have left the Founding Fathers spinning in their graves.

APPENDIX

Covariation in Partisan Composition of the House and Senate

In this chapter, I argue that there was no relationship between the partisan composition of entering Senate classes and the composition of the House following Reconstruction. Further, I suggest that this lack of a relationship is unique in U.S. history, at least in the period during which Democrats and Republicans have contended nationally. I base these assertions on the following analysis.

Let Y_t = the percentage of seats held by the Democrats in the Senate class chosen in year t, and let X_t = the percentage of seats held by the Democrats in the House following the election in year t. I first regressed Y on X for the period 1856–1986, yielding the following results:

$$Y_t = -0.01 + 1.01X_t$$
$$\quad\quad (0.05) \quad (0.10)$$
$$N = 66$$
$$\text{std. err. reg.} = .10$$

sum sqr. resid. = 0.6443
r^2 = .64

These findings are just what we would expect if the two variables were, on average, the same because the intercept is effectively 0 and the slope is effectively 1.

The next step is to see whether these coefficients are stable across time periods; in other words, do the data "pool"? To test whether they do, I subdivided the data set into the following two time periods: (1) the 10 elections from 1876–1894 and (2) the remaining 56 elections before and after 1876–1894. I then reran the regression above, obtaining the relevant coefficients for each time period:

Period	Intercept (standard error)	Slope (standard error)	N	Standard error of regression	Sum of squared residuals	r^2
1856–1874 } 1896–1986	−0.06 (0.05)	1.09 (0.10)	56	0.10	0.5535	.68
1876–1894	0.28 (0.08)	0.40 (0.16)	10	0.06	0.0280	.43

By breaking the past century and a quarter into two periods and estimating separate equations for each, we do a better job of fitting the model to the data: The sum of squared residuals (SSR) for the first regression was 0.6443, and the SSR for the second set of two regressions taken together is 0.5815. The question is whether this difference is statistically significant. The appropriate test (a "Chow Test") is explained in Pindyck and Rubinfeld (1981, 118). Using that test, we obtain the following test statistic: $F_{2,62}$ = 3.29, which is significant at the 95 percent confidence level. Thus, we conclude that the slopes probably really do differ during the 1876–1894 period and that changes in the Democratic proportion of the Senate were not very responsive to changes in the Democratic proportion of the House. (Experimentation with alternate subdivisions of the time period revealed similar results.)

Spatial Model of Taxing and Spending Decisions

I also argue that Republicans were able to defend the protective tariff and Democrats were able to reduce spending during periods of divided government. The ability to do this was rooted in the different mechanisms through which taxing and spending policy were determined. Why the different mechanisms for determining spending and taxing

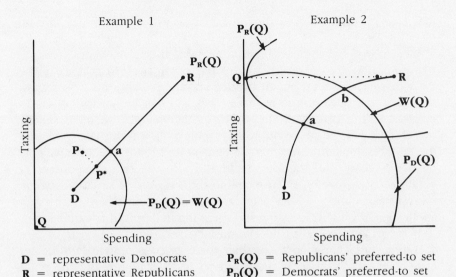

FIGURE 9.3   Fiscal Decisionmaking Under Different Reversion Rules

make a difference is shown through a simple spatial model, illustrated with two examples in Figure 9.3.

Figure 9.3 illustrates a stylized world in which Republicans prefer high spending and taxing and Democrats prefer low levels of each. In both examples in this figure, I have plotted representations of ideal points for representative Democrats (labeled *D*) and Republicans (labeled *R*). (The examples are drawn so that ideal spending equals ideal taxing for both Democrats and Republicans, indicating that each would prefer a balanced budget with either a "big government" [Republicans] or a "small government" [Democrats].)

In keeping with the stylization, I assume that the presidency, the Senate, and the House are each composed of a single individual, who is either a Democrat or a Republican, and that to enact legislation, all three institutions (individuals) in power must agree to change the status quo.

In the first example, imagine that Republicans have control of the entire federal government, as they did in the 1860s. Thus, preferences represented in each of the three institutions lie precisely at point *R*. Regardless of the reversion rule for taxing and spending and regardless of whether taxing and spending are considered together or separately, policy will continue to be characterized by point *R* as long as Republicans control all three institutions. If the Democrats should take control of the entire government, then the same analysis would have policy shifting to point *D*—low taxes and low spending with a balanced budget.

What if one of the three institutions falls under Democratic control, while Republicans retain control of the other two? In that case, the Democrat who controls one institution and the Republicans who control the other two must mutually agree to changes in budgetary policy. To understand the details of the policies that emerge, we must specify two things: (1) the reversion point of policy should the Democrat and the Republicans fail to reach an agreement and (2) the relative weights the Republicans and the Democrat assign to the two components of fiscal policy. In example 1, I examine the simplest of situations where the reversion point is 0 for taxes and spending and where each party applies equal weights to taxing and spending in their utility calculations.

If taxing and spending levels must be set anew each year or else spending and taxing go to 0, then there is considerable latitude for agreement. In Example 1, the reversion level is represented by point *Q*, which is at the origin. With each party equally weighing taxing and spending, the circles in each example represent the taxing/spending mixes that each party would find equally attractive compared to the reversion level; the regions within the circles define proposals that they would find more attractive. The single circle drawn in Example 1 encompasses the set of all points (that is, the mixes of taxing and spending) that the Democrat would prefer, compared to having no taxing and no spending. This is termed the Democrat's "preferred-to set" against *Q*, written as $P_D(Q)$. A similar set could be drawn for the Republicans, but it would be so large (given the way in which the example is constructed) that it would take up the entire diagram. Thus, we can consider the entire graph to constitute the Republicans' preferred-to set, $P_R(Q)$. The intersection of these two sets, termed the "win set"—labeled $W(Q)$—is the region where the Republicans and the Democrat can all agree to move spending and taxing in the next fiscal year. Because of the example's construction, $P_D(Q) = W(Q)$.

The line segment connecting *D* and *R*, the "contract curve," represents the set of likely outcomes to any bargain that will be struck between the Democrat and the Republicans. If there is a preliminary agreement to set spending and taxing levels off the line, at point *P*, for example, there is at least one point on the line, such as *P**, that both *D* and *R* would prefer simultaneously. Thus, any agreement off the contract curve is inherently unstable. Once a deal is struck that places policy on the contract curve, such as at *P**, then deviations from that policy must make either the Democrat or the Republicans worse off. Therefore, any point on the contract curve is a retentive equilibrium.

Thus, we can assume that policy will reside somewhere on the part of line segment *DR* that lies within the win set, and thus policy will lie somewhere along the line segment *Da*. But, without specifying other institutional details (such as who has proposal power), we cannot specify precisely where policy will emerge. What we can conclude, however, is that if the reversion level for taxing and spending were 0 in the absence of an explicit agreement between the two parties to move away from the reversion level and if taxing and spending were equally important to each party, then it would be possible for the Democrat to force a reduction in taxes and spending (compared to the Republican ideal) and for balanced budgets to emerge under a split partisan regime.

However, the world we are trying to understand differs in two important respects from that presumed in Example 1. First, the reversion levels are not the same for taxing and spending. If the Democrat and the Republicans cannot agree on levels of taxation, then the previous period's tax level is retained; if they cannot agree to setting spending levels, then spending reverts to zero. Second, the Democrat and the Republicans do not give equal weight to taxing and spending. During the historical period considered here, it is reasonable to assume that the Republicans cared much more about tariff policy relative to spending policy than did the Democrat. For the Republicans, interest in a large government was, in part, induced by the desire to disperse tariff revenues back into the economy and minimize the political target that surpluses could have presented to the Democrat. So, protection was the Republicans' watchword, with all else flowing from that. For the Democrat, protection and a large, activist government were one and the same; thus, they were more likely to weigh both parts of fiscal policy more equally.[16]

A more relevant illustration is given in Example 2 of Figure 9.3. Here, the ideal points are the same as in Example 1, but two things have been changed: (1) the reversion level (this point is also labeled *Q*) and (2) the shape of the Republican indifference curve. The relevant preferred-to sets, win set, and contract curve have been drawn to complete the figure.

Notice that in this more realistic example, the contract curve between the Republican and Democratic positions bows outward, away from the contract curve drawn in Example 1.[17] This bowing is caused by the redefinition of the Republican indifference curve. Also notice that the win set is now a relatively small region of the entire graph. In Example 2, it is impossible under any bargaining details to reach the Democratic ideal point. Consequently, the portion of the contract curve open to negotiation is quite limited. What these changes represent substantively is that the Republicans are willing to relinquish only a small amount of protection in return for the ability to pass appropriations. Similarly, the Democrat is able to effect a substantial cut in appropriations, but because the Republicans are so adamant about protection, the Democrat is able to bargain down protection only slightly.

Unlike Example 1, where the budget is balanced in the resulting policy deal, in Example 2, the budget runs a surplus because the contract curve traces out policy options in which tax levels always exceed spending. This combination of reversion points, salience weights, and bargaining rules would make it difficult for the Democrats to make a dent in the system of protection, but they would be more successful in reducing spending. One important consequence of this asymmetrical power to influence spending and taxing levels would be large budget surpluses when the two parties shared control of the government.

Spending Under Split Partisan Regimes

In the text, I describe an econometric analysis to ascertain whether federal spending was lower during periods of divided partisan control of the federal government. In the following paragraphs, I offer more detail on that analysis.

Using data gathered for another project (Stewart 1989), I explored the total amount of money contained in eleven annual appropriations bills during each fiscal year between 1872 and 1916. For each bill, I estimated the following regression equation:

$$ln(B_t) = a_1 ln(B_{t-1}) + a_2 U_{t-1} + a_3 W_t + a_4 D_t + a_5 R_t + a_6 S_t + e_t,$$

where B_t = amount contained in the bill as finally passed; U = a measure of the federal budgetary surplus;[18] W = a dummy variable indicating the years of the Spanish-American War; D, R, and S = dummy variables indicating years when the bill was passed under a Democratic, Republican, or split partisan regime; and e = a stochastic error term.[19] Therefore, the dummy variables D, R, and S are intercepts that measure the average level of spending growth under each type of partisan regime.

Given partisan inclinations, we should expect that, for each bill, $a_4 < a_5$, meaning that spending grew more slowly under Democrats than under Republicans. If the model outlined in Figure 9.3 is true, then we should expect $a_4 \leq a_6 < a_5$, meaning that when Republicans and Democrats shared control of the federal government, growth was either intermediate between Republican and Democratic growth rates or it was equal to Democratic rates.

The results in Table 9.8 bear out these predictions, although the results are not statistically very strong due to the paucity of Democratically controlled fiscal years (six, compared to twenty-three Repub-

TABLE 9.8 Spending in Eleven Annual Appropriations Bills, FY 1872–1916[a]

Bill	Intercepts			t-tests for	
	Democratic	Republican	Split	Democratic < Republican	Split < Republican
Army	1.22[b]	1.32[b]	1.23	1.65	-1.78[c]
Consular and diplomatic	0.88[c]	0.90[b]	0.85[c]	0.45	-1.35
Indian affairs	5.04[b]	5.10[b]	4.99[b]	0.77	-1.73[c]
Military academy	0.85	1.15	0.90	1.87	-1.92[c]
Naval affairs	0.45	0.53	0.38	1.57	-3.46[c]
Post office	0.27	0.29	0.25	1.18	-2.69[b]
Agriculture	-2.13[b]	-2.14[b]	-2.17[b]	-0.20	-0.60
Fortifications	-0.97	-0.60	-1.17	1.95[c]	-3.95[b]
Legislative, executive, and judicial	1.71[b]	1.71[b]	1.67[b]	0.07	-2.08[b]
Pensions	0.98[c]	0.97[c]	0.97[c]	-0.21	0.01
Sundry civil	2.85[b]	3.00[b]	2.81[b]	1.60	-2.46[b]

Note: Seemingly unrelated regression; only partisan regime coefficients reported, to save space.

[a]Tests of whether the partisan regime intercepts are different from 0 were conducted with two-tailed tests. Tests of inequalities of intercepts were conducted using one-tailed tests.

[b]$p < .01$

[c]$p < .05$

lican years and sixteen split-years). To save space, I have reported only the partisan regime intercepts and the results of the relevant t-tests in Table 9.8.

NOTES

The original draft of this chapter was presented at the Conference on the Causes and Consequences of Divided Government, University of California at San Diego, June 29–July 1, 1990.

1. There have been eighteen transitions from unified to split control of the federal government. Ten of these transitions (56 percent) were followed in the next election by the reestablishment of a unified regime. Nine of these ten one-time-only transitions occurred during a midterm congressional election.

2. The 1850s and early 1860s witnessed the extinction of the dominant opposition party (the Whigs) and the rise of a new party, from creation to national dominance (the Republicans). As reported by Martis (1989), 15 percent of all members of the House and 9 percent of senators elected in the 1850s and 1860s were from "third parties" (that is, not Democrats, Republicans, or Whigs).

3. The election of senators by state legislators was much more complicated than one might suppose, given the constitutional mechanism. For more details on senatorial elections in the nineteenth century, see Riker (1955) and Stewart (forthcoming).

4. It should also be noted that the southern reaches of the northern states, such as southern Pennsylvania and the Ohio Valley districts of Ohio, Indiana, and Illinois, were much like the border states in their vacillation between parties.

5. Of course, this discussion suffers from the difficulties of taking into account the preferences of newly emancipated slaves. They represented a large portion of the Republican electoral strength in the late 1860s and early 1870s, and their effective disenfranchisement with "redemption" certainly depressed the natural sentiment for the Republican party in that region. Speculating about what the electoral balance would have been in the South had blacks not been effectively disenfranchised following Reconstruction is well beyond the scope of this chapter, but it is a question that should always be kept in mind in discussions of southern partisan strength during this period.

6. One measure of this discounting is the "bias" of the electoral college, measured according to Tufte's (1973) technique; the measure of the responsiveness of electoral votes to changes in the popular vote is the "swing ratio" of the electoral college. Using Tufte's technique, we find a 9 percent bias toward the Republican party in the electoral college between 1860 and 1900, with a swing ratio of 1.13.

7. The distribution of House seats cannot be described as entirely exogenous because some western settlement was carried out precisely to influence the political complexion of the territories and new states.

8. When Minnesota was first admitted to the union, it selected two Democrats to represent it in the Senate, along with two Democratic representatives in the House. By 1859, both representatives were Republicans; by 1861, so, too, were both senators. Thus, although Minnesota was admitted as a "Democratic" state, it quickly became Republican. Every newly admitted state in the nineteenth century from Nevada on (excepting West Virginia, which had a very peculiar partisan configuration surrounding its admission) elected two Republican senators upon admission, and all House members elected immediately after admission were Republicans. To the extent that these states deviated from the Republican fold in later elections, it was frequently toward Populist and "Silver" candidates, not Democratic ones.

9. Nevada was the classic rotten borough: At the time of its admission in 1864, it had only a few thousand residents, and it was widely acknowledged that its admission was primarily a consequence of Abraham Lincoln's desire for another two Republican votes in the Senate. Nevada's population did not even approach the size of an average congressional district (a common criterion for admission) until the 1970 census.

10. I am not arguing that decisions to admit states after 1860 were made solely on partisan grounds. Clearly, with the inexorable march of western expansion, it was only a matter of time before these territories were admitted as states, regardless of their partisanship. Still, the political importance of western expansion for understanding the growth of the federal government after Reconstruction has not been fully appreciated in the literature on U.S. political development.

11. The admission of approximately one dozen Republican states in the second half of the nineteenth century probably does not account for much of the Republican lock on the presidency. Because electoral votes are allocated according to population (after the initial endowment of 3 votes to all states) and because these states were small, they did not figure very prominently in the presidential equation. Further complicating matters, of course, is the fact that these states were the most likely to give their support to third party candidates, especially those of the Greenback and Populist parties. For instance, they cast many of their electoral votes for William Jennings Bryan (who had the Populist endorsement) in 1896.

12. On the ideology of a balanced budget throughout U.S. history, see Savage (1988).

13. Much of this account is taken from Stewart (1989, 84–89, 182–184).

14. A question frequently arises at this point: If the Holman Rule applied to *amendments* to appropriations bills, why was there concern that the rule would enhance the power of the *committee,* given the fact that amendments are typically made to committee-reported bills? The answer is that the Holman Rule was seen as legitimating riders from any source and that substantive provisos originating in committee would be allowed under the rule.

15. A full accounting of the perils of the army bill and the legislative, executive, and judicial bill may be found in Appleton's *Cyclopedia* for 1879 and 1880. My interpretation of these events diverges significantly from Leonard

White's; he termed the outcome of this episode "a clean-cut victory for the President and a powerful precedent against congressional encroachment on the executive power by means of appropriation riders" (1958, 38). Given that the appropriation for marshals reverted to zero in FY 1880 and that a rider prohibiting the army from being present at southern polls was attached to the FY 1880 army bill that Hayes finally signed, this hardly represents a clean-cut victory for the president or a precedent for executive dominance of Congress.

16. It may be that Democrats despised protection more than the federal spending that flowed from it, but what is important is that they regarded the two issues of spending and taxing as relatively more equal in importance than did the Republicans.

17. The contract curve is constructed by a straightforward but tedious application of elementary calculus and algebra. I will provide the details upon request.

18. In particular, $U_t = 1n(R_t/E_t)$, where R_t = total revenues for fiscal year t and E_t = total expenditures.

19. This setup has the discomforting characteristic of having a lagged endogenous variable. If there is serial correlation in the model, then the estimated coefficients will be biased and inconsistent (Pindyck and Rubinfeld 1981, 193). To test for the presence of serial correlation, I used Durbin's test for serial correlation in the presence of a lagged endogenous variable. In two cases—the army and sundry civil bills—I had to reject the null hypothesis of no serial correlation, but in the remaining nine cases, the level of serial correlation was statistically insignificant.

⚡ 10

CONCLUSION

Gary W. Cox and Samuel Kernell

The obstruction of the constitutional mechanism must be overcome, and it is the party that casts a web, at times weak, at times strong, over the dispersed organs of government and gives them a semblance of unity.
—V. O. Key, Jr.[1]

One of the first things that the beginning student learns about U.S. political parties is that they serve various important "functions" in the larger political system. Prominent among these functions is that of providing "a force for unification in the divided American political system" (Sorauf and Beck 1988, 16). In addition to connecting state and federal politics, U.S. political parties are looked to as vehicles to link the constitutionally separated powers exercised by the president, House, and Senate—harnessing them all to an overall national purpose. In this way, the governmental paralysis that might ensue if the branches could not agree or the working at cross-purposes that might result if they pursued different aims can be avoided.

Although modern textbooks still mention the need to unify what the constitution has put asunder, they are apt nowadays to note that political parties have not always been up to the task in recent decades. Governmental paralysis, such as that evidenced in the 1990 budget standoff, has been a frequent complaint. And U.S. foreign policy has been decidedly at cross-purposes on occasion: While the Reagan administration pursued a hard-line policy toward the Sandinista regime in Nicaragua—elements of which had been specifically forbidden by Congress and were thus carried on in secret—Speaker James Wright and the Democrats in the House of Representatives pursued their own quite different policy, independently of White House control.[2]

Stalemate and conflicting actions, rather than vigor and complementary actions, are to be expected given that no single party has controlled all branches of government in recent years. A party can unify government if it wins control of both the executive and the legislative branches; but if no party wins such a broad electoral mandate, then to the institutional separation of power contrived by the Founding Fathers must be added a partisan separation of purpose.

The question—whether parties act out their textbook role, promoting vigorous government by unifying constitutionally separate powers or, in contrast, exacerbate the divisions in U.S. government by entrenching themselves in distinctive institutional bastions—then becomes one of frequency. If the electoral system is structured in a way that promotes party sweeps of all branches of government or if mass behavior by itself produces sweeps, then parties can perhaps perform their unifying function and overcome the institutional separation of powers.[3] But if the electoral system regularly produces divided control, then partisan differences will magnify, rather than diminish, the importance of the institutional separation of powers.

Moreover, the direction of causality may be the opposite of that suggested in the textbooks. Rather than clean party sweeps in the electoral system unifying separate institutions, the institutional separation of powers may actually disunify electoral competition. The notion that parties are characterized by electoral *nuclei,* with each nucleus specializing in the task of winning control of a particular office or institution, is a well-known one in the literature on party organization (Burns 1963; Schlesinger 1965; Schlesinger and Schlesinger 1990). What we may have been seeing since about the mid-1950s is an increase in the degree to which the party nuclei clustering around the Senate, House, and presidency are separate organizations with separate electoral imperatives.

Several of the essays in this volume can be read as contributions to this theme: that the separation of powers induces a natural specialization of function within the parties, which carries with it the possibility of divided control when some nuclei of the major parties are more successful than others. Several other essays here contribute to a second and related theme: that the separation of powers may be especially consequential when different parties control different powers.

THE CAUSES OF DIVIDED GOVERNMENT

The first theme appears most prominently in the essays by Jacobson and Petrocik. Both emphasize that different issues matter in presidential and congressional elections and that the parties (or their appropriate nuclei) seem to have established advantages on different sets of issues (the Republicans on "presidential" issues, the Democrats on "congressional" issues).[4] Thus, for example, Jacobson uses survey data to demonstrate both a Republican advantage on such "national" issues as the budget deficit, foreign affairs, and defense policy and a Democratic advantage on the more district-specific issues entailed in domestic policy.

There is even an explanation for why different parties might acquire advantage in different institutionally defined issue areas. To put it more baldly than its many proponents would, this explanation is that voters want aggressive benefit-seekers (that is, Democrats) for their own districts, coupled with tightfisted (that is, Republican) presidents to keep overall spending and taxes to a reasonable level. As long as voters act as if they think this way, there will be a tendency toward divided control; whichever party gains the advantage as the "provider of benefits" automatically loses a step as the "controller of spending and taxes."

Petrocik complements this institutionally focused explanation with one that looks more to the nature of the electoral coalitions to which the two parties cater. Executive elections tend to be difficult for the party with the larger and more heterogeneous coalition—the Democrats. Their very success in adapting to all the varied electoral niches in the legislative arena is a handicap when it comes to waging a unified campaign for the presidency.

Wattenberg adds another dimension to the argument by noting the structural advantages that the Republicans have acquired in the presidential nomination process. The Democrats have unintentionally developed a nomination process that exacerbates intraparty squabbling, with consequent damage to their general election prospects (Polsby 1983; Shafer 1983).

Both of these explanations for the prevalence of divided government at the federal level—one focusing on the parties' differential successes at establishing credible and attractive positions on different sets of issues, the other on the parties' different nomination procedures—are brought into question by the high incidence of divided partisan control in the states. Fiorina and Petrocik, too, suggest that the forces producing divided government may be at work throughout the federal structure. If so, previous explanations based exclusively on national politics may be too "level specific."

Fiorina argues that our current electoral system makes change in partisan control of a legislative body unlikely, relative to change in partisan control of an executive office. This leads to a recurrent pattern wherein the electorate punishes the dominant party by electing a governor (or president) of the opposite party. In some ways, this line of thought stands the old notion of a referendum vote on its head. Instead of the legislative vote being a referendum on the executive, the executive vote is a referendum on the party controlling the legislature; whenever things are going badly, the verdict is negative, and divided government results.

THE CONSEQUENCES OF DIVIDED GOVERNMENT

The extent to which different party nuclei now face different electoral contexts (different issues, different rules of the game, or different electoral exposures) is the primary explanation given here for the recent frequency of divided government. The consequences of this division in control at the federal level are dealt with in the essays by Kernell, Cox and McCubbins, McCubbins, and Stewart.

One important consequence of divided government, with which the essays by Kernell and Stewart deal, is institutional conflict. Even after more than two hundred years of accumulated practice and precedent, there remains considerable ambiguity in the Constitution's prescriptions. As a result, both parties aggressively—and strategically—assert the prerogatives and powers of whatever branches of government they happen to control.

Another important consequence of divided government, taken more or less as a given in all these essays, is that all major policy decisions are now the result of an institutionally structured bargaining process, with each party possessing a veto. Knowing little more than this about U.S. politics, coupled with a bit of bargaining theory, one can account for some of the prominent features of our recent governmental experience.

Note first that the parties have three broad bargaining options. They can bargain "within the beltway," accepting the cards that the electoral and constitutional systems have dealt them. They can attempt to expand the context within which bargaining occurs by appealing beyond the beltway to public opinion (Kernell 1986). Or they can seek to prosecute policy without the assent of the other party. Let us consider each of these options in reverse order.

The last option is largely a decision not to bargain and instead to pursue policy goals with the resources available to whatever branches of government one controls. One of the most dramatic examples is the pursuit of separate foreign policies by the Reagan administration and the Wright speakership regarding Nicaragua. Such attempts by one or the other branch to "go it alone" must eventually come into conflict with the regular policymaking process, as Colonel Oliver North and Admiral John Poindexter found out. As long as each branch is willing to defend its constitutionally mandated role, in other words, unilateral pursuit of policy can only be a temporary strategy—a postponement of bargaining, rather than a total avoidance of it. Nonetheless, the ability to pursue a policy unilaterally can present the other branch with a fait accompli that it is difficult or impolitic to overturn. The president's use of his warmaking powers under the War Powers Act—illustrated by President Bush's handling of the 1991 Gulf war—is a case in point.

In addition to the "go it alone" option, there is also the option of "going public" (Kernell 1986). The most prominent is a bridge-burning tactic: making public commitments to particular positions in order to raise the costs of reneging and thereby strengthen one's bargaining position (Schelling 1960). This was exemplified by George Bush's "read my lips" pronouncement, before he changed it to "read my hips."

The third option is bargaining within the beltway, on the terms established by electoral outcomes and constitutional prescriptions. Such bargaining is typically characterized by delay and brinksmanship, careful attention to reversion points, and the selling out of junior partners. We shall say a few words about each of these by way of illustration.

Delay is one of the primary techniques in *any* bargaining game in which the assent of all parties is necessary to an agreement; moreover, it is virtually the only credible "within the beltway" method that the parties have to demonstrate toughness and determination. Thus, when the parties are far from agreement yet some agreement must be reached (as has notoriously been true in budget politics of the Reagan and Bush administrations), one finds that the early stages of negotiation seem to go nowhere. Agreements are reached only at the eleventh hour or after, as the pressures of budgetary chaos mount and extort compromises from the opposing sides.

The game that the parties play is something like the game of chicken: The worst outcome for both is no agreement, but neither wants to be the one to back down first. As the fiscal year deadline nears, the risk of the "no-agreement" outcome increases, and the side that fears this outcome more backs down. Willingness to delay—and thereby increase the risk of the "no-agreement" outcome—is the primary mechanism for demonstrating toughness (and for bluffing).

There seems to be some doubt about this line of analysis in the journalistic world. For example, an analysis of the 1990 budget crisis referred to divided government as the "snap" explanation for the recurring budgetary paralysis, of which 1990 was the latest and greatest example. The analysis went on to argue that "it is not clear whether the government would act more decisively if the same party controlled Capitol Hill and the White House. Democrat Jimmy Carter's rocky relations with a Democratic-controlled Congress provide a sobering counterexample" (Hook 1990). Yet, if one looks at the record, one finds that the delay in appropriations bills during Reagan's first six years was, at least when measured by how much of the federal government was financed in omnibus continuing resolutions, significantly greater than the delay under Carter. In Carter's four years (FY 1978 to FY 1981), an average of $55 billion in appropriations was effected through omnibus continuing resolutions. The corresponding figure for Reagan's first six years (FY 1982 to FY 1987), when the Republicans also held the Senate, was over five times as large.

A second important feature of the bargaining context, not so obvious as budgetary brinksmanship, is that vetoes mean different things in different policy areas. The key consideration is the "reversion point"— the policy that will stand in force if no agreement is reached. In some policy arenas, such as taxation, failure to reach an agreement means that the status quo is perpetuated. In others, such as appropriations, failure to reach an agreement means that substantial cuts in spending will ensue. Which kind of reversion point a given policy arena has affects the bargaining outcome in sometimes nonobvious ways, as is illustrated amply in the essays by Kernell, Cox and McCubbins, McCubbins, and Stewart.

Finally, in politics one generally bargains with those who can deliver the votes. This simple maxim means that Republican presidents ultimately have to deal with the Democrats, who control Congress, rather than with their Republican colleagues, who do not. The consequence has been frequent strains in the relationship between congressional Republicans and their presidents—as we saw in the dramatic disagreement over the 1990 budget.

A strong indication of the frequency of these interinstitutional strains within the Republican party is the lowered party cohesion among House Republicans when their party controls the White House. A straightforward regression analysis of Republican unity on roll call votes from the 73d to 100th congresses shows two things: First, party cohesion among House Republicans has steadily eroded over this time period; second, House Republicans have been significantly less cohesive when their man is in the White House.[5]

A similar regression analysis of Democratic unity on roll calls shows that the House Democrats have not suffered nearly as much of a decline in party cohesion over the same period and—more important for present purposes—that they do not experience a significant decline in cohesion when there is a Democratic president.[6] This latter finding makes some sense when one recognizes that Democratic presidents since Woodrow Wilson (except Harry Truman during the 80th Congress) have always bargained directly with the legislative leaders of their *own* party. Just like Republican presidents, they often seek the bulk of votes needed to pass legislation from the majority party. This, together with the natural desire of legislative leaders to maintain the majority status of their party and hence to please the party's constituencies, leads to legislation that the Democratic party can support. It is instructive to recall that during the 80th Congress (the one instance in which a Democratic president faced a Republican Congress), Democratic legislators complained about the president's lack of consultation with them. For example, when Truman introduced his tax proposals in that Congress, the ranking member of the Ways and Means Committee complained: "We Democrats were not called into consultation when the bill was being prepared" (Hartman 1971, 133).

A CASE IN POINT: THE BUDGET CRISIS OF 1990

The general points just made about the consequences of divided government for bargaining within the beltway are all nicely illustrated in the budget crisis of 1990. Long before there was a crisis, it was recognized that both the Republican president and the Democratic Congress would have to agree to the major outlines of the budget—after all, both had a veto.[7] In light of this fact, the two sides set up a working group composed of a large number of key congressional and White House players, charged with developing a workable compromise. Many months later, this working group had produced nothing but an occasional headline about whose intransigence was preventing progress.

This might have been anticipated. Delay meant an increased chance that no budget would pass and hence that either the government would be forced to close, the automatic cuts of the Gramm-Rudman Act would be invoked, or both. Willingness to incur these fearsome reversionary outcomes was the primary method by which each negotiator could demonstrate the depth of his or her commitment to whatever point was at issue. Thus, the interminable wrangling that characterized the initial attempts at making a budget, though far from inevitable, was not surprising.

In the next stage of the negotiations, the group assigned to come up with a proposal was pared down to just the majority and minority party leadership of the House and Senate and the top White House negotiators. Brinksmanship continued, but finally, at the last moment, a deal was cut.

The fatal flaw in this deal can be diagnosed as a premature selling out of the junior partners. The congressional Democrats had insisted that any budget compromise receive not only a public endorsement from the president but also the votes of a majority of House and Senate Republicans. In this way, the Democrats insured themselves against being blamed in the upcoming election for any new taxes or other unpopular features of the package. But by the same token, the Democrats' insistence on Republican support in Congress empowered a group that was rarely so empowered: If a majority of Republicans chose to vote against the budget, they could kill it.[8]

Partly for this reason, the initial large group of negotiators and the final smaller group had both included Republicans. And it is likely that their input was taken more seriously than in other White House–congressional negotiations in which the Democrats had not insisted on Republican support in Congress. But neither the leaders nor the followers in the House Republican party were united in their view of their president or the budget package to which he agreed. Indeed, many of them were utterly dismayed by Bush's renunciation of his "no new taxes" pledge—this very pledge formed an important part of both their personal ideology and their campaign strategy. But from the president's perspective, it was the price he had to pay to get the Democrats to agree on a budget. What did he get in return? Primarily, it seemed to have been avoidance of the reversionary outcome—implementation of the Gramm-Rudman Act's across-the-board budget cuts—and avoidance of the blame for this outcome.

The outcome itself was terrible for both sides: the Democrats particularly feared the damage to their domestic programs, and Bush especially loathed the cuts in defense spending. In the game of budgetary chicken, Bush's position was perhaps less strong—given his engagement in the Middle East with Saddam Hussein—and he blinked first (by renouncing his pledge on taxes). But Bush may also have recognized that the final stage of the game before implementation of the Gramm-Rudman cuts was a final, take-it-or-leave-it offer from the Democrats in Congress. Such an offer was unlikely to be much better than a compromise arrived at earlier, and, if the president vetoed it, the Democrats were in a good position to lay most of the blame for the resulting broad cuts at the door of the White House.

The important thing to note about what the president apparently got out of his recantation on taxes is that it benefited him, not congressional Republicans. Many congressional Republicans, especially in the House, would have preferred a hard-line maintenance of the "no new taxes" pledge. But Bush, given a choice between what looked best for the next presidential election and what some firebrands in the House thought best for the impending midterm elections, chose predictably.[9]

In other words, to deal with the party that controlled Congress, the president followed the path of many of his predecessors and sold out his junior partners in Congress. Given the rare opportunity to retaliate effectively, these junior partners—led by Minority Whip Newt Gingrich— did so. Despite the fact that the president had made a nationally televised appeal for passage of the budget compromise, it became obvious well before the end of the vote in the House that the Republicans would not come up with their required majority. This freed a great many Democrats who had been holding back from a hard decision, and the bill went down to a resounding defeat.

One might wonder about the strategic reasoning of the Republicans who voted against the budget compromise. After all, in the next round of negotiations between the White House and Congress, their interests were even less well represented because both sides knew that it would have to be mostly Democratic votes that passed any agreement. And the budget that passed was clearly worse from the perspective of those Republicans who voted against the initial proposal. As *The Economist* put it in a brief budget postmortem: "The five-year package eventually passed stuck closely to the budget-summit deal rejected by the House in early October. . . . The main changes were a smaller rise in petrol taxes, an increase in the top income-tax rate from 28% to 31% and a smaller bite out of Medicare" ("At Last, Quite a Lot" 1990, 24). If one asks who benefited from these changes, the answer seems to be oil-state Democrats (via smaller petrol taxes) and liberal Democrats (via an increased top income tax rate and a smaller bite out of Medicare).

But it was probably more an electoral than a policy calculation that led these Republicans to vote in the way that they did, and they may have held out some hope that Bush would once again hang tough on taxes—all the way to the election. In any event, the kind of divisions among House Republicans that the vote on the initial budget proposal revealed were not unusual or unprecedented, as indicated by the regression results on Republican voting cohesion presented earlier.

NOTES

1. Quoted in James L. Sundquist (1982, 43).

2. To these recent instances of interbranch rivalry in the conduct of foreign affairs might be added a whole series dating from the Nixon and Ford administrations: "When Gerald Ford succeeded Nixon, Congress refused to

acknowledge the secret commitments Nixon had made to President Thieu of South Vietnam and tried to set its own course in foreign affairs in defiance of the President and Secretary of State Henry Kissinger—destroying Ford's trade agreement with the Soviet Union, casting its lot with Greece against Turkey in the Cyprus dispute, refusing to let the President intervene in Angola, and rejecting his proposed last-ditch aid to South Vietnam" (Sundquist 1982, 53–54).

3. The electoral system can promote party sweeps by, for example, promoting straight-ticket voting through the use of party strip ballots.

4. A similar theme is struck by Byron Shafer (1989).

5. The regression used the *Congressional Quarterly*'s party unity score (equal to the average Rice coefficient of cohesion across all votes in which a majority of Republicans opposed a majority of Democrats) for the House Republicans as the dependent variable and a constant term, a time trend, and a dummy variable tapping Republican control of the presidency (equal to 1 if there is a Republican president and Democratic House, equal to 0 otherwise) as independent variables. The coefficient on the divided control dummy variable was −3.60 (with a t-statistic of −2.79).

6. On the first point, see Cox and McCubbins (forthcoming).

7. The president's veto can, of course, be overridden.

8. Actually, the Democratic strategy of insisting on a majority of Republican votes on tax hikes and other unpopular measures is a long-standing (dating at least to John Garner's speakership) and not particularly rare one. But, considering the entire array of issues on which Congress votes, the House Republicans are rarely so empowered.

9. Another item in the file on Republican presidents sacrificing the midterm interests of their congressional partymates is the regularity with which Republican presidents have presided over recessions at midterm—on which, see Alesina and Rosenthal (1989).

REFERENCES

Aberbach, Joel. 1990. *Keeping a Watchful Eye.* Washington, D.C.: Brookings Institution.

Alesina, Alberta, and Howard Rosenthal. 1989. "Partisan Cycles in Congressional Elections and the Macroeconomy." *American Political Science Review* 83:373–398.

Alford, John, and David W. Brady. 1988. "Partisan and Incumbent Advantage in U.S. House Elections, 1846–1986." Working Paper No. 11, Center for the Study of Institutions and Values, Rice University, Houston, Tex.

Alston, Chuck. 1990. "Bush Crusades on Many Fronts to Retake President's Turf." *Congressional Quarterly Weekly Report* 48:291–295.

Alston, Chuck, and Glen Craney. 1989. "Bush Campaign-Reform Plan Takes Aim at Incumbents." *Congressional Quarterly Weekly Report* 47:1648–1659.

Alt, James E., and Charles Stewart. 1990. "Parties and the Deficit: Some Historical Evidence." (Paper prepared for the Conference on Political Economics, National Bureau of Economic Research, Cambridge, Mass., February 2–3, 1990.)

Ansolabehere, Steven, David W. Brady, and Morris P. Fiorina. 1988. "The Marginals Never Vanished?" Domestic Studies Program, Working Papers in Political Science P–88–1, Hoover Institution, Stanford University, Stanford, Calif.

Appleton's Annual Cyclopaedia and Register of Important Events of the Year. 1878. New series vol. 3. New York: D. Appleton.

Aranson, Peter, and Peter Ordeshook. 1972. "Spatial Strategies for Sequential Elections." In Richard Niemi and Herbert Weisberg, eds., *Probability Models of Collective Decision-Making.* Columbus, Ohio: Charles E. Merrill.

Asher, Herbert B. 1978. "The Unintended Consequences of Legislative Professionalism." (Paper delivered at the 1978 annual meeting of the American Political Science Association, New York, August 31–September 3.)

"At Last, Quite a Lot." 1990. *The Economist,* November 3.

Baker, Russell. 1956. "Stevenson, Kefauver Find Agreement in TV Debate." *New York Times,* May 22.

Barkley, John. 1874. *Digest of Rules of the House of Representatives of the United States and the Joint Rules of the Two Houses.* 43d Congress, 2d Session. Washington, D.C.: Government Printing Office.

Barnes, James. 1931. *John G. Carlisle: Financial Statesman.* New York: Dodd, Mead.

Barro, Robert J. 1979. "On the Determination of the Public Debt." *Journal of Political Economy* 87:940–971.

Bartels, Larry M. 1988. *Presidential Primaries and the Dynamics of Public Choice.* Princeton, N.J.: Princeton University Press.

Beck, Nathaniel. 1982a. "Does There Exist a Political Business Cycle: A Box-Tiao Analysis." *Public Choice* 38:205–209.

————. 1982b. "Parties, Administrations and American Macroeconomic Outcomes." *American Political Science Review* 76:83–93.

Bettinger, Stephen. 1986. "Spending Panels Confront Life After Gramm-Rudman." *Congressional Quarterly Weekly Report* 44:1258–1261.

Binkley, Wilfred. 1962. *President and Congress.* 3d ed. New York: Vintage Books.

Brady, David. 1988. *Critical Elections and Congressional Policy Making.* Stanford, Calif.: Stanford University Press.

Brady, David, and Mark Morgan. 1987. "Reforming the Structure of the House Appropriations Process: The Effects of the 1885 and 1919–20 Reforms on Money Decisions." In Mathew D. McCubbins and Terry Sullivan, eds., *Congress: Structure and Policy.* New York: Cambridge University Press.

Brams, Steven J., and Morton D. Davis. 1974. "The 3/2's Rule in Presidential Campaigning." *American Political Science Review* 68:113.

Braybrooke, David, and Charles E. Lindblom. 1967. *A Strategy of Decision.* New York: Free Press.

Browning, Robert X. 1986. *Politics and Social Welfare Policy in the United States.* Knoxville: University of Tennessee Press.

Bryce, James. 1924. *The American Commonwealth.* New York: Macmillan.

Budge, Ian, and Dennis J. Farlie. 1983. *Explaining and Predicting Elections.* Boston: Allen and Unwin.

"Budget Office Evolves into Key Policy Maker." 1985. *Congressional Quarterly Weekly Report* 43:1815.

Buell, Emmett H., Jr. 1986. "Divisive Primaries and Participation in Fall Presidential Campaigns: A Study of 1984 New Hampshire Primary Activists." *American Politics Quarterly* 14:376–390.

Burnham, Walter Dean. 1955. *Presidential Ballots, 1836–1892.* Baltimore, Md.: Johns Hopkins University Press.

————. 1967. "Party Systems and the Political Process." In William Nisbet Chambers and Walter Dean Burnham, eds., *The American Party System: Stages of Political Development.* New York: Oxford University Press, pp. 277–307.

————. 1970. *Critical Elections and the Mainsprings of American Politics.* New York: Norton.

————. 1989. "The Reagan Heritage." In Gerald Pomper, ed., *The Elections of 1988.* Chatham, N.J.: Chatham House Publishers, pp. 1–32.

Burns, James MacGregor. 1963. *The Deadlock of Democracy.* Englewood Cliffs, N.J.: Prentice-Hall.

————. 1965. *Presidential Government: The Crucible of Leadership.* Boston: Houghton Mifflin.

Cain, Bruce, John Ferejohn, and Morris Fiorina. 1987. *The Personal Vote.* Cambridge, Mass.: Harvard University Press.

Calvert, Randall L., Mathew D. McCubbins, and Barry R. Weingast. 1989. "A Theory of Political Control and Agency Discretion." *American Journal of Political Science* 33:588–611.

Campbell, Angus, Philip E. Converse, Warren E. Miller, and Donald E. Stokes. 1960. *The American Voter.* New York: Wiley.

Carmines, Edward G., and James A. Stimson. 1980. "The Two Faces of Issue Voting." *American Political Science Review* 74:78–91.

Chambers, William Nisbet, and Walter Dean Burnham. 1967. *The American Party System: Stages of Political Development.* New York: Oxford University Press.

Chubb, John E. 1988. "Institutions, the Economy, and the Dynamics of State Elections." *American Political Science Review* 82:133–154.

Chubb, John E., and Paul E. Peterson. 1985. "Realignment and Institutionalization." In John E. Chubb and Paul Peterson, eds., *The New Direction in American Politics.* Washington, D.C.: Brookings Institution, pp. 1–30.

Chubb, John E., and Paul E. Peterson, eds. 1988. *Can the Government Govern?* Washington, D.C.: Brookings Institution.

Church, George J. 1981. "He'll Do It His Way." *Time* (June 15):10–12.

Clubb, Jerome M., William H. Flanigan, and Nancy H. Zingale. 1980. *Partisan Realignment: Voters, Parties, and Government in American History.* Beverly Hills, Calif.: Sage Publications.

————. 1990. *Partisan Realignment.* Boulder: Westview Press.

Cogan, John F. 1988. "The Evolution of Congressional Budget Decision Making and the Emergence of Federal Deficits." Domestic Studies Program, Working Papers in Political Science P–88–6, Hoover Institution, Stanford University, Stanford, Calif.

Colantoni, Claude S., Terrence J. Levesque, and Peter C. Ordeshook. 1975. "Campaign Resources Allocations Under the Electoral College." *American Political Science Review* 69:141–154.

Congressional Quarterly's Guide to U.S. Elections. 1975. Washington, D.C.: Congressional Quarterly Press.

Congressional Quarterly's Guide to Congress. 1982. 3d ed. Washington, D.C.: Congressional Quarterly Press.

Cook, Rhodes. 1989. "Is Competition in Elections Becoming Obsolete?" *Congressional Quarterly Weekly Report* 47:1060–1065.

Corwin, Edward S. 1978. *The Constitution and What It Means Today.* 14th ed. Princeton, N.J.: Princeton University Press.

Cover, Albert D., and David R. Mayhew. 1981. "Congressional Dynamics and the Decline of Competitive Congressional Elections." In Lawrence C. Dodd and Bruce I. Oppenheimer, eds., *Congress Reconsidered.* 2d ed. Washington, D.C.: Congressional Quarterly Press.

Cox, Gary. 1984. "An Unexpected Utility Model of Electoral Competition." *Quality and Quantity* 18:337–349.

————. 1987. "The Uncovered Set and the Core." *American Journal of Political Science* 31:408–422.

Cox, Gary W., and Mathew D. McCubbins. 1989. "Political Parties and the Appointment of Committees." (Paper delivered at the Conference on Congressional Structure and Elections, University of California, San Diego, February 11, 1989.)

————. 1991. *Parties and Committees in the House of Representatives.* Berkeley: University of California Press, forthcoming.

"Cut Out the Rough Stuff." 1987. *Time* (March 23):29.

Cutler, Lloyd N. 1980. "To Form a Government." *Foreign Affairs* 59:126–143.

———. 1989. "Now Is the Time for All Good Men." *William and Mary Law Review* 30:387–402.

Dahl, Robert A., and Charles E. Lindblom. 1953. *Politics, Economics, and Welfare.* New York: Harper and Row.

Davidson, Roger, and Walter Oleszek. 1977. *Congress Against Itself.* Bloomington: Indiana University Press.

"The Democrats: Caucus Fatigue." 1984. *Newsweek* (April 2):30.

Dodd, Lawrence C., and Sean Q. Kelly. 1990. "The Electoral Consequences of Presentational Style." (Paper delivered at the 1990 annual meeting of the American Political Science Association, San Francisco, August 30–September 1.)

Dodd, Lawrence C., and Bruce I. Oppenheimer. 1977. "The House in Transition." In Lawrence C. Dodd and Bruce I. Oppenheimer, eds., *Congress Reconsidered.* New York: Praeger, pp. 21–53.

Dowd, Maureen. 1990. "President Vetoes a Bill and Makes Threat on Second." *New York Times,* June 16.

Downs, Anthony. 1957. *An Economic Theory of Democracy.* New York: Harper and Row.

Drogin, Bob, and Thomas B. Rosenstiel. 1988. "Dukakis, Jackson Face Task of Forging Alliance in Party." *Los Angeles Times,* May 16.

Edwards, George C. 1980. *Presidential Influence in Congress.* San Francisco: W. H. Freeman.

Elving, Ronald D. 1990. "Hills Vows Not to Keep Congress in the Dark on Secret Talks." *Congressional Quarterly Weekly Report* 48:381.

Enelow, James, and Melvin Hinich. 1984. *The Spatial Theory of Voting: An Introduction.* New York: Cambridge University Press.

Erikson, Robert S. 1971. "The Partisan Impact of State Legislative Reapportionment." *Midwest Journal of Political Science* 15:57–71.

———. 1972. "Malapportionment, Gerrymandering, and Party Fortunes in Congressional Elections." *American Political Science Review* 66:1234–1245.

———. 1988. "The Puzzle of Midterm Losses." *Journal of Politics* 50:1012–1029.

———. 1989. "Why the Democrats Lose Presidential Elections." *PS.* 22:30–34.

Erikson, Robert S., John P. McIver, and Gerald C. Wright, Jr. 1987. "State Political Culture and Public Opinion." *American Political Science Review* 81:797–814.

Fenno, Richard, Jr. 1966. *The Power of the Purse.* Boston: Little, Brown.

Ferejohn, John A. 1977. "On the Decline of Competition in Congressional Elections." *American Political Science Review* 71:166–176.

Ferejohn, John A., and Randall L. Calvert. 1984. "Presidential Coattails in Historical Perspective." *American Journal of Political Science* 28:127–146.

Finer, Samuel, ed. 1975. *Adversary Politics and Electoral Reform.* London, Anthony Wigram.

Fiorina, Morris P. 1981. *Retrospective Voting in American National Elections.* New Haven, Ct.: Yale University Press.

———. 1988. "The Reagan Years: Turning to the Right or Groping Toward the Middle?" In Barry Cooper, Allan Kornberg, and William Mishler, eds., *The Resurgence of Conservatism in Anglo-American Democracies.* Durham, N.C.: Duke University Press, pp. 430–459.

———. 1989. *Congress: Keystone of the Washington Establishment.* 2d ed. New Haven, Ct.: Yale University Press.

———. 1990. "An Era of Divided Government." In Bruce Cain and Gillian Peele, eds., *Developments in American Politics.* London: Macmillan.

Fisher, Louis. 1975. *Presidential Spending Power.* Princeton, N.J.: Princeton University Press.

———. 1985. *Constitutional Conflicts Between Congress and the President.* Princeton, N.J.: Princeton University Press.

Fowler, Linda L., and Robert D. McClure. 1989. *Political Ambition.* New Haven, Ct.: Yale University Press.

Freeman, John Leiper. 1955. *The Political Process: Executive Bureau-Legislative Committee Relations.* Garden City, N.J.: Doubleday.

Fritz, Kurt von. 1964. *Aristotle's Constitution of Athens and Related Texts.* New York: Hafner Publishing Co.

"Fulbright Invites Truman to Resign." 1946. *New York Times,* November 7.

Gelman, Andrew, and Gary King. 1990. "Estimating Incumbency Advantage Without Bias." *American Journal of Political Science* 34:1142–1164.

Gerstenzang, James. 1990. "Bush Likely to Veto Bill on Gas, Biological Arms." *Los Angeles Times,* November 16.

Goldman, Peter. 1981a. "The Reagan Steamroller." *Newsweek* (May 18):40.

———. 1981b. "Tax Cuts: Reagan Digs In." *Newsweek* (June 15):26–27.

"GOP Attacks 'Debate,' Demands Equal Time." 1960. *Washington Post,* May 6.

Hamilton, Alexander, John Jay, and James Madison. 1961. *The Federalist Papers.* New York: NAL Penguin (Mentor edition).

Hardeman, D. B., and Donald C. Bacon. 1987. *Rayburn, A Biography.* Lanham, Md.: Madison Books.

Hartmann, Susan M. 1971. *Truman and the 80th Congress.* Columbia: University of Missouri Press.

Harvey, Andrew. 1990. *The Econometric Analysis of Time Series.* 2d ed. New York: Philip Allan.

Herrnson, Paul S. 1988. *Party Campaigning in the 1980s.* Cambridge, Mass.: Harvard University Press.

Hibbs, Douglas. 1987. *The American Political Economy: Macroeconomics and Electoral Politics.* Cambridge, Mass.: Harvard University Press.

Hofferbert, Richard I. 1966. "The Relation Between Public Policy and Some Structural and Environmental Variables in the American States." *American Political Science Review* 60:73–82.

Hoftstader, Richard. 1969. *The Idea of a Party System.* Berkeley: University of California Press.

Holmes, Steven A. 1990. "Sununu Proposes Rights Compromise." *New York Times,* July 11.

Hook, Janet. 1990a. "Budget Ordeal Poses Question: Why Can't Congress Be Led?" *Congressional Quarterly Weekly Report* 48:3471–3473.

_____. 1990b. "Avalanche of Veto Threat Divides Bush, Congress." *Congressional Quarterly Weekly Report* 48:2991–2993.

"Humphrey Denies League Against JFK in Debate by Two Senators." 1960. *Los Angeles Times,* May 5.

Hyneman, Charles. 1938. "Tenure and Turnover of Legislative Personnel." *Annals of the American Academy of Political and Social Science* 190:21–31.

Ingberman, Daniel E., and Dennis A. Yao. 1986. "Circumventing Formal Structure Through Commitment: Presidential Influence and Agenda Control." Discussion Paper No. 198, Center for the Study of Organizational Innovation, University of Maryland, College Park, Md.

Inman, Robert. 1978. "The Fiscal Performance of Local Governments: An Interpretive Review." In P. Mieszkowski and M. Straszheim, eds., *Current Issues in Urban Economics.* Baltimore, Md.: Johns Hopkins University Press, pp. 270–321.

Iyengar, Shanto, and Donald R. Kinder. 1987. *News That Matters: Television and American Opinion.* Chicago: University of Chicago Press.

Jacobson, Gary C. 1987. "The Marginals Never Vanished: Incumbency and Competition in Elections to the U.S. House of Representatives." *American Journal of Political Science* 31:126–141.

_____. 1989a. "Parties and PACs in Congressional Elections." In Lawrence C. Dodd and Bruce I. Oppenheimer, eds., *Congress Reconsidered.* 4th ed. Washington, D.C.: CQ Press, pp. 117–152.

_____. 1989b. "Strategic Politicians and the Dynamics of U.S. House Elections, 1946–1986." *American Political Science Review* 83:773–793.

_____. 1990a. *The Electoral Origins of Divided Government: Competition in U.S. House Elections, 1946–1988.* Boulder: Westview Press.

_____. 1990b. "Meager Patrimony: The Reagan Era and Republican Representation in Congress." In Larry Berman, ed., *Looking Back on the Reagan Presidency.* Baltimore, Md.: Johns Hopkins University Press, pp. 288–316.

_____. 1991a. "Divided Government, Strategic Politics, and the 1990 Congressional Elections." (Paper delivered at the annual meeting of the Midwest Political Science Association, Chicago, April 18–20.)

_____. 1991b. *The Politics of Congressional Elections.* 3d ed. New York: HarperCollins.

Jacobson, Gary C., and Samuel Kernell. 1983. *Strategy and Choice in Congressional Elections.* 2d ed. New Haven, Ct.: Yale University Press.

Jewell, Malcolm E. 1982. *Representation in State Legislatures.* Lexington: University Press of Kentucky.

Jewell, Malcolm E., and David Breaux. 1988. "The Effect of Incumbency on State Legislative Elections." *Legislative Studies Quarterly* 495–514.

Jewell, Malcolm E., and Samuel C. Patterson. 1986. *The Legislative Process in the United States.* New York: Random House.

Kalecki, Michal. 1943. "Political Aspects of Full Employment." *Political Quarterly* 4:322–331.

Kamarck, Elaine Ciulla. 1990. "Structure as Strategy: Presidential Nominating Politics in the Post-Reform Era." In L. Sandy Maisel, ed., *The Parties Respond:*

Changes in the American Party System. Boulder: Westview Press, pp. 160–186.

Keefe, William J. and Morris S. Ogul. 1985. *The American Legislative Process: Congress and the States.* 6th ed. Englewood Cliffs, N.J.: Prentice-Hall.

Kenney, Patrick J., and Tom W. Rice. 1987. "The Relationship Between Divisive Primaries and General Election Outcomes." *American Journal of Political Science* 31:31–44.

Kernell, Samuel. 1986. *Going Public.* Washington, D.C.: CQ Press.

Key, V. O., Jr. 1949. *Southern Politics in State and Nation.* New York: Knopf.

———. 1956. *American State Politics: An Introduction.* New York: Knopf.

———. 1961. *Public Opinion and American Democracy.* New York: Knopf.

———. 1966. *The Responsible Electorate.* Cambridge, Mass.: Harvard University Press.

Kiewiet, D. Roderick. 1983. *Macroeconomics and Micropolitics: The Electoral Effects of Economic Issues.* Chicago: University of Chicago Press.

Kiewiet, D. Roderick, and Mathew D. McCubbins. 1985a. "Congressional Appropriations and the Electoral Connection." *Journal of Politics* 47:59–82.

———. 1985b. "Appropriations Decisions as a Bilateral Bargaining Game Between President and Congress." *Legislative Studies Quarterly* 10:181–201.

———. 1988. "Presidential Influence on Congressional Appropriations Decisions." *American Journal of Political Science* 32:713–736.

———. 1991. *The Logic of Delegation: Congressional Parties and the Appropriations Process.* Chicago: University of Chicago Press.

Kiewiet, D. Roderick, and Douglas Rivers. 1985. "The Economic Basis of Reagan's Appeal." John E. Chubb and Paul E. Peterson, eds., *The New Direction in American Politics.* Washington, D.C.: Brookings Institution.

King, Gary. 1988. "Statistical Models for Political Science Events Count." *American Journal of Political Science* 32:838–863.

———. 1989. "Representation Through Legislative Redistricting: A Stochastic Model." *American Journal of Political Science* 33:787–824.

———. 1991. "Constituency Service and Incumbency Advantage." *British Journal of Political Science,* forthcoming.

King, Gary, and Andrew Gelman. 1991. "Systemic Consequences of Incumbency Advantage in U.S. House Elections." *American Journal of Political Science,* forthcoming.

King, James. 1989. "Interparty Competition in the American States: An Examination of Index Components." *Western Political Quarterly* 42:83–92.

Kirst, Michael W. 1969. *Government Without Passing Laws.* Chapel Hill: University of North Carolina Press.

Kousser, J. Morgan. 1974. *The Shaping of Southern Politics: Suffrage Restriction and the Establishment of the One-Party South, 1880–1910.* New Haven, Ct.: Yale University Press.

Kreps, David, and Robert Wilson. 1982a. "Reputation and Imperfect Information." *Journal of Economic Theory* 27:253–279.

———. 1982b. "Sequential Equilibria." *Econometrica* 50:863–894.

Lamar, Howard Roberts. 1956. *Dakota Territory, 1861–1899: A Study of Frontier Politics.* New Haven, Ct.: Yale University Press.

Laski, Harold J. 1940. *The American Presidency*. New York: Harper & Brothers.

Lauter, David. 1989. "Bush Seeks to Fight It Out for 'Line-Item Veto' Power." *New York Times,* October 30.

Lehigh, Scot. 1990. "Poll Shows Rollback Would Win Decisively." *Boston Globe,* September 3.

Lengle, James I. 1980. "Divisive Presidential Primaries and Party Electoral Prospects, 1932–1976." *American Politics Quarterly* 8:261–277.

Lijphart, Arend. 1968. *The Politics of Accommodation.* Berkeley: University of California Press.

Lindblom, Charles E. 1965. *The Intelligence of Democracy.* New York: Free Press.

Lipset, Seymour Martin. 1963. *Political Man.* Garden City, N.J.: Doubleday.

Lockard, Duane. 1966. "The State Legislator." In Alexander Heard, ed., *State Legislatures in American Politics.* Englewood Cliffs, N.J.: Prentice-Hall, pp. 98–125.

Lowi, Theodore. 1979. *The End of Liberalism.* 2d ed. New York: W. W. Norton.

MacKinnon, James, and Halbert White. 1985. "Some Heteroskedasticity Consistent Covariance Matrix Estimators with Improved Finite Sample Properties." *Journal of Econometrics* 29:305–325.

Madden, Michael. 1990. "Memory of Blocking Northeastern Move Will Not Fade Away." *Boston Globe,* November 4.

Martis, Kenneth C. 1989. *The Historical Atlas of Political Parties in the United States Congress, 1789–1989.* New York: Macmillan.

Mayhew, David R. 1974a. *Congress: The Electoral Connection.* New Haven, Ct.: Yale University Press.

———. 1974b. "Congressional Elections: The Case of the Vanishing Marginals." *Polity* 6:295–317.

———. 1986. *Placing Parties in American Politics.* Princeton, N.J.: Princeton University Press.

McCubbins, Mathew D. 1985. "The Legislative Design of Regulatory Structure." *American Journal of Political Science* 29:721–748.

———. 1990a. "Divided Party Control and Budget Deficits." (Paper delivered at the Conference on the Causes and Consequences of Divided Government, University of California, San Diego, La Jolla, Calif., June 30, 1990.)

———. 1990b. "Party Governance and U.S. Budget Deficits: Divided Government and Fiscal Stalemate." (Paper delivered at the Conference on Politics and Economics in the Eighties, National Bureau of Economic Research, Cambridge, Mass., May 14–15, 1990.)

———. 1991. "Party Politics, Divided Government, and Budget Deficits." In Samuel Kernell, ed., *Parallel Politics: The Politics of Economic Policy in Japan and the United States.* Washington, D.C.: Brookings Institution, pp. 83–118.

McCubbins, Mathew D., and Talbot Page. 1987. "A Theory of Congressional Delegation." In Mathew D. McCubbins and Terry Sullivan, eds., *Congress: Structure and Policy.* Cambridge: Cambridge University Press, pp. 409–425.

McCubbins, Mathew D., and Thomas Schwartz. 1984. "Congressional Oversight Overlooked: Police Patrols Versus Fire Alarms." *American Journal of Political Science* 28:167–179.

McCubbins, Mathew D., Roger G. Noll, and Barry R. Weingast. 1987. "Administrative Procedures as Instruments of Political Control." *Journal of Law, Economics and Organizations* 3:243–277.

———. 1989. "Structure and Process, Politics and Policy: Administrative Arrangements and the Political Control of Agencies." *Virginia Law Review* 75:431–482.

McKelvey, Richard. 1986. "Covering, Dominance, and Institution-Free Properties of Social Choice." *American Journal of Political Science* 30:283–314.

McKitrick, Eric L. 1967. "Party Politics and the Union and Confederate War Efforts." In William Nisbet Chambers and Walter Dean Burnham, eds., *The American Party System*. New York: Oxford University Press, pp. 117–151.

McPherson, Edward. Various Years. *A Handbook of Politics*. Washington, D.C.: Chapman.

Miller, Arthur H., Ann Hildreth, and Christopher Wlezien. 1988. "Social Group Dynamics of Political Evaluations." (Paper delivered at the annual meeting of the Midwest Political Science Association, Chicago, April 14–16.)

Miller, Nicholas. 1977. "Graph-Theoretical Approaches to the Theory of Voting." *American Journal of Political Science* 21:769–803.

———. 1980. "A New Solution Set for Tournaments and Majority Voting." *American Journal of Political Science* 24:68–96.

Miller, Warren E., and the National Election Studies. 1989. *American National Election Study, 1988: Pre- and Post-Election Survey* (computer file). 2d ICPSR ed. Conducted by the Center for Political Studies of the Institute for Social Research, University of Michigan, Ann Arbor, Mich., Inter-University Consortium for Political and Social Research (producer and distributor).

Milton, George F. 1965. *The Use of Presidential Power: 1789–1943*. New York: Octagon Books.

Morris, John B. 1946. "Truman Rejects Resignation Idea, Plans 'National Welfare' Policy." *New York Times,* November 8.

Muris, Timothy. 1989. "The Uses and Abuses of Budget Baselines." Domestic Studies Program, Working Papers in Political Science P–89–3, Hoover Institution, Stanford University, Stanford, Calif.

Neustadt, Richard E. 1980. *Presidential Power: The Politics of Leadership from FDR to Carter*. New York: Wiley, pp. 28–29.

Nie, Norman H., Sidney Verba, and John R. Petrocik. 1979. *The Changing American Voter*. Enlarged ed. Cambridge, Mass.: Harvard University Press.

Niemi, Richard G., and Laura R. Winsky. 1987. "Membership Turnover in U.S. State Legislatures: Trends and Effects of Districting." *Legislative Studies Quarterly* 12:115–124.

Niou, Emerson M.S., and Peter C. Ordeshook. 1985. "Universalism in Congress." *American Journal of Political Science* 29:246–258.

Nordhaus, William. 1975. "Political-Business Cycle." *Review of Economic Studies* 42:169–189.

Noyes, Alexander D. 1909. *Forty Years of American Finance*. New York: Putnam.

O'Halloran, Sharyn. 1990. "Politics, Process, and American Trade Policy: Congress and the Regulation of Foreign Commerce." (Ph.D. diss., University of California, San Diego.)

Oleszek, Walter J. 1989. *Congressional Procedures and the Policy Process*. 3d ed. Washington, D.C.: CQ Press.

—————. 1991. "The Context of Congressional Policy Making." Quoted in James A. Thurber, *Divided Democracy*. Washington, D.C.: CQ Press, p. 94.

Oral History Interview with James H. Rowe, Jr., 1969 and 1970. Transcript, September 30, 1969, and January 15, 1970, Appendix A. Truman Library, Independence, Mo.

Oral History of the Truman White House. 1980 (February 20). Truman Library, Independence, Mo.

Palfrey, Thomas. 1984. "Spatial Equilibrium with Entry." *Review of Economic Studies* 51:139–156.

Paullin, Charles O. 1932. *Atlas of the Historical Geography of the United States*. New York: Carnegie Institution of Washington.

Paxson, Frederic L. 1929. *Recent History of the United States, 1865–1929*. Boston: Houghton Mifflin.

Perry, O. H. 1887. "Proposed Tariff Legislation Since 1883." *Quarterly Journal of Economics* 2:69–79.

Peterson, Mark A. 1990. *Legislating Together*. Cambridge, Mass.: Harvard University Press.

Petrocik, John R. 1989. "An Expected Party Vote: New Data for an Old Concept." *American Journal of Political Science* 33:44–46.

—————. 1991. "The Theory of Issue Ownership: Issues, Agendas, and Electoral Coalitions," Under submission.

Pfiffner, James P. 1979. *The President, the Budget, and Congress*. Boulder: Westview Press.

—————. 1990. "Establishing the Bush Presidency." *Public Administration Review* 50:64–73.

Pindyck, Robert S., and Daniel L. Rubinfeld. 1981. *Econometric Models and Economic Forecasts*. 2d ed. New York: McGraw-Hill.

Polsby, Nelson W. 1983. *Consequences of Party Reform*. New York: Oxford University Press.

Polsby, Nelson W., and Aaron Wildavsky. 1988. *Presidential Elections*. 7th ed. New York: Free Press.

Pommerehne, Werner. 1978. "Institutional Approaches to Public Expenditure: Empirical Evidence from Swiss Municipalities." *Journal of Public Economics* 7:225–280.

Popkin, Samuel, J. W. Gorman, C. Phillips, and J. A. Smith. 1976. "Comment: What Have You Done for Me Lately? Toward an Investment Theory of Voting." *American Political Science Review* 70:779–805.

"President Faces Questions on Budget, Persian Gulf Policies." 1987. *Congressional Quarterly Weekly Report* 45:2626.

Raines, Howell. 1984. "Democrats' Forum Becomes a Vehicle to Criticize Hart." *New York Times,* March 12.

Ranney, Austin. 1965. "Parties in State Politics." In Herbert Jacob and Kenneth Vines, eds., *Politics in the American States: A Comparative Analysis.* Boston: Little, Brown, pp. 61–99.

Rasmusen, Eric. 1989. *Games and Information.* Cambridge: Cambridge University Press.

Regan, Donald T. 1988. *For the Record.* New York: Harcourt Brace Jovanovich.

Repass, David E. 1971. "Issue Salience and Party Choice." *American Political Science Review* 65:389–400.

"Republicans Neck and Neck with Democrats for First Time Since 1946." 1990. *San Diego Union,* January 21.

Riker, William H. 1955. "The Senate and American Federalism." *American Political Science Review* 49:452–469.

Rohde, David. 1991. "Parties and Leaders in the Post-Reform House." Unpublished manuscript, Michigan State University, East Lansing, Mich.

Rohde, David, and Kenneth A. Shepsle. 1973. "Democratic Committee Assignments in the House of Representatives: Strategic Aspects of a Social Choice Process." *American Political Science Review* 67:889–905.

Romer, Thomas, and Howard Rosenthal. 1979. "The Elusive Median Voter." *Journal of Public Economics* 12:143–170.

Rosenstone, Steven J., Roy L. Behr, and Edward H. Lazarus. 1984. *Third Parties in America.* Princeton, N.J.: Princeton University Press.

Rosenthal, Howard. 1990. "The Setter Model." In James M. Enelow and Melvin J. Hinich, eds., *Advances in the Spatial Theory of Voting.* New York: Cambridge University Press, pp. 199–234.

Rovner, Julie. 1988. "Turnover in Congress Hits an All-Time Low." *Congressional Quarterly Weekly Report* 46:3362–3365.

Runkel, David R., ed. 1989. *Campaign for President: The Managers Look at '88.* Dover, Mass.: Auburn.

Sabato, Larry J. 1988. *The Party's Just Begun: Shaping Political Parties for America's Future.* Glenview, Ill.: Scott, Foresman.

Salmore, Barbara G., and Stephen A. Salmore. 1989. *Candidates, Parties, and Campaigns.* 2d ed. Washington, D.C.: CQ Press.

Sartori, Giovanni. 1976. *Parties and Party Systems: A Framework for Analysis.* Cambridge, Mass.: Harvard University Press.

Savage, James D. 1988. *Balanced Budgets and American Politics.* Ithaca, N.Y.: Cornell University Press.

Schelling, Thomas. 1960. *The Strategy of Conflict.* Cambridge, Mass.: Harvard University Press.

Schick, Allen. 1984. "Legislation, Appropriations, and Budgets: The Development of Spending Decision-Making in Congress." *Congressional Research Service Report* 84–106 GPO.

Schlesinger, Arthur M., Jr. 1973. *The Imperial Presidency.* Boston: Houghton Mifflin.

Schlesinger, Joseph. 1965. "Political Party Organization." In James G. March, ed., *Handbook of Organization.* Chicago: Rand McNally, pp. 764–801.

Schlesinger, Joseph, and Mildred Schlesinger. 1990. "The Reaffirmation of a Multiparty System in France." *American Political Science Review* 84:1077–1102.

Shafer, Byron. 1983. *Quiet Revolution.* New York: Russell Sage.

———. 1988. *Bifurcated Politics.* Cambridge, Mass.: Harvard University Press.

———. 1989. "The Election of 1988 and the Structure of American Politics: Thoughts on Interpreting an Electoral Order." *Electoral Studies* 8:5–21.

Shepsle, Kenneth A. 1978. *The Giant Jigsaw Puzzle.* Chicago: University of Chicago Press.

———. 1979. "Institutional Arrangements and Equilibrium in Multidimensional Voting Models." *American Journal of Political Science* 23:27–60.

Shepsle, Kenneth A., and Barry R. Weingast. 1984. "Legislative Politics and Budget Outcomes." In Gregory B. Mills and John L. Palmer, eds., *Federal Budget Policy in the 1980s.* Washington, D.C.: The Urban Institute, pp. 343–367.

———. 1987. "The Institutional Foundations of Committee Power." *American Political Science Review* 81:85–104.

Shin, Kwang S., and John S. Jackson III. 1979. "Membership Turnover in U.S. State Legislatures: 1931–1976." *Legislative Studies Quarterly* 4:95–104.

Smith, Hedrick. 1989. *The Power Game.* New York: Ballantine Books.

Smith, Steven. 1989. *Call to Order: Floor Politics in the House and Senate.* Washington, D.C.: Brookings Institution.

Smith, Steven, and Christopher Deering. 1984. *Committees in Congress.* Washington, D.C.: CQ Press.

Sorauf, Frank, and Paul Allen Beck. 1988. *Party Politics in America.* Boston: Scott, Foresman.

Stanley, Harold W., and Richard Niemi. 1988. *Vital Statistics on American Politics.* Washington, D.C.: CQ Press.

Stanwood, Edward. 1903. *American Tariff Controversies in the Nineteenth Century.* 2 vols. Boston: Houghton Mifflin.

Stewart, Charles, III. 1989. *Budget Reform Politics: The Design of the Appropriations Process in the House of Representatives, 1865–1921.* New York: Cambridge University Press.

———. Forthcoming. "Responsiveness in the Upper Chamber: The Constitution and the Institutional Development of the U.S. Senate." In Peter Nardulli, ed., *The Constitution and the American Political Process.* Urbana: University of Illinois Press.

Stone, Walter J. 1984. "Prenomination Candidate Choice and General Election Behavior: Iowa Presidential Activists in 1980." *American Journal of Political Science* 28:361–378.

Studenski, Paul, and Herman Kroos. 1963. *Financial History of the United States.* 2d ed. New York: McGraw-Hill.

Sundquist, James L. 1981. *The Decline and Resurgence of Congress.* Washington, D.C.: Brookings Institution.

———. 1982. "Party Decay and the Capacity to Govern." In J. Fleishmann, ed., *The Future of American Political Parties.* Englewood Cliffs, N.J.: Prentice-Hall.

————. 1983. *Dynamics of the Party System.* 2d ed. Washington, D.C.: Brookings Institution.

————. 1986. *Constitutional Reform and Effective Government.* Washington, D.C.: Brookings Institution.

Taussig, F. W. 1885. *The History of the Present Tariff, 1860–1883.* New York: Putnam.

————. 1931a. *Some Aspects of the Tariff Question.* Cambridge, Mass.: Harvard University Press.

————. 1931b. *Tariff History of the United States.* New York: Putnam.

Tufte, Edward E. 1973. "The Relationship Between Seats and Votes in Two-Party Systems." *American Political Science Review* 67:540–554.

————. 1975. *The Political Control of the Economy.* Princeton, N.J.: Princeton University Press.

U.S. Congress, House. *Communication from the President of the United States, Transmitting Laws Relating to the Estimates of Appropriations, the Appropriations, and Reports of Receipts and Expenditures.* 67th Cong., 1st sess., 1921. H. Doc. 67–129.

U.S. Department of Commerce. *National Income and Products Accounts of the United States 1929–1974.* Statistical tables. Washington, D.C.: Government Printing Office.

————. *National Income and Product Accounts of the United States 1976–1979.* Special supplement. Washington, D.C.: Government Printing Office.

U.S. Department of Commerce, Bureau of Economic Analysis. Various years. *Survey of Current Business.* Washington, D.C.: Government Printing Office.

U.S. Department of Commerce, Census Bureau. 1975. *Historical Statistics of the United States, Colonial Times to 1970, Bicentennial Edition.* 2 vols. Washington, D.C.: Government Printing Office.

U.S. Department of the Treasury. Various years. *Statistical Abstract of the United States.* Washington, D.C.: Government Printing Office.

————. 1982. *Annual Report.* Washington, D.C.: Government Printing Office.

U.S. Executive Office of the President, Office of Management and Budget. Various years. *Budget of the United States Government.* Washington, D.C.: Government Printing Office.

U.S. Executive Office of the President, Office of Management and Budget. 1990. *Historical Tables, Budget of the United States Government, Fiscal Year 1990.* Washington, D.C.: Government Printing Office.

Wattenberg, Martin P. 1986. *The Decline of American Political Parties: 1952–1984.* Cambridge, Mass.: Harvard University Press.

————. 1990. "From a Partisan to a Candidate-Centered Electorate." In Anthony King, ed., *The New American Political System.* 2d ed. Washington, D.C.: American Enterprise Institute.

Wehr, Elizabeth. 1985. " '86 Budget Hung Up on Senate Floor." *Congressional Quarterly Weekly Report* 43:768–771.

Weingast, Barry R., and Mark Moran. 1983. "Bureaucratic Discretion or Congressional Control? Regulatory Policymaking by the Federal Trade Commission." *Journal of Political Economy* 91:675–700.

White, Halbert. 1980. "A Heteroskedasticity-Consistent Covariance Matrix and a Direct Test for Heteroskedasticity." *Econometrica* 48:817–838.

White, Leonard D. 1958. *The Republican Era.* New York: Free Press.

Wildavsky, Aaron. 1974. *The Politics of the Budgetary Process.* 2d ed. Boston: Little, Brown.

Wilmerding, Lucius, Jr. 1943. *The Spending Power.* New Haven, Ct.: Yale University Press.

Wilson, Woodrow. 1885. *Congressional Government: A Study in American Politics.* Boston: Houghton Mifflin.

Witcover, Jules, and Jack Germond. 1989. *Whose Broad Stripes and Bright Stars?: The Trivial Pursuit of the Presidency, 1988.* New York: Warner Books.

Wittman, Donald. 1973. "Parties as Utility Maximizers." *American Political Science Review* 67:490–498.

———. 1983. "Candidate Motivation: A Synthesis of Alternative Theories." *American Political Science Review* 77:142–157.

———. 1990. "Spatial Strategies When Candidates Have Policy Preferences." In James Enelow and Melvin Hinich, eds., *Advances in the Spatial Theory of Voting.* New York: Cambridge University Press, pp. 66–98.

Wood, Gordon S. 1969. *The Creation of the American Republic, 1776–1787.* Chapel Hill: University of North Carolina Press.

Zupan, Mark A. 1991. "An Economic Explanation for the Existence and Nature of Political Ticket Splitting." *Journal of Law and Economics,* forthcoming.

ABOUT THE BOOK AND EDITORS

Partisan conflict between the White House and Congress is now a dominant feature of national politics in the United States. What the Constitution sought to institute—a system of checks and balances—divided government has taken to extremes: institutional divisions so deep that national challenges like balancing the federal budget or effectively regulating the nation's savings and loans have become insurmountable.

In original essays written especially for this volume, eight of the leading scholars in American government address the causes and consequences of divided party control. Their essays, written with a student audience in mind, take up such timely questions as: Why do voters consistently elect Republican presidents and Democratic congresses? How does divided control shape national policy on crucial issues such as the declaration of war? How have presidents adapted their leadership strategies to the circumstance of divided government? And, how has Congress responded in the way it writes laws and oversees departmental performance?

These issues and a host of others are addressed in this compact yet comprehensive volume. The distinguished lineup of contributors promises to make this book "must" reading for both novice and serious students of elections, Congress, and the presidency.

Gary W. Cox is professor of political science at the University of California, San Diego. **Samuel Kernell** is professor of political science and coordinator of the American Political Institutions Project at the University of California, San Diego.

INDEX